The Black Madonna

in Latin America and Europe

THE BLACK MADONNA

IN LATIN AMERICA AND EUROPE

Tradition and Transformation

Małgorzata Oleszkiewicz-Peralba

University of New Mexico Press

Albuquerque

Printed in China by Four Colour Imports, Ltd.

13 12 11 10 09 08 07   1 2 3 4 5 6 7

LIBRARY OF CONGRESS CATALOGING-IN-PUBLICATION DATA

Oleszkiewicz-Peralba, Małgorzata, 1954–

The Black Madonna in Latin America and Europe :

tradition and transformation / Małgorzata Oleszkiewicz-Peralba.

p. cm.

Includes bibliographical references and index.

ISBN-13: 978-0-8263-4102-0 (cloth : alk. paper)

1. Black Virgins—Latin America. 2. Black Virgins—Europe.

3. Mary, Blessed Virgin, Saint—Cult. I. Title.

BT670.B55O44 2007

202'.114—dc22

2006024482

DESIGN AND COMPOSITION: *Mina Yamashita*

To my grandfather, who taught me about freedom,

To my father, who taught me about different cultures,

And to Josep, who taught me about love

Holy Virgin, thou who defend the Bright Częstochowa

And shine in Ostra Brama!

—Adam Mickiewicz

⁂

*Culture is a discourse, a language, and as such it has no beginning
or end and is always in transformation, since it is always looking
for the way to signify what it cannot manage to signify.*

—Antonio Benítez-Rojo

⁂

*[I]n the Brazilian case we have a complicated house, where
apparently singular and even mutually exclusive styles seem to
coexist in an intimate relationship. . . . I am afraid that what was
conventionally called the Baroque was not exhausted in the past,
but it constitutes a Brazilian art to the extent that its stylistics is
precisely this: One with the capacity to relate (or to intend to unite
with force, suggestivity and an incomparable desire) the high with
the low; the sky with the earth; the saint with the sinner; the interior
with the exterior; the weak with the powerful; the human with the
divine, and the past with the present.*

—Roberto DaMatta

CONTENTS

✧

List of Illustrations / xi

Acknowledgments / xix

Introduction / 1

CHAPTER ONE

From Neolithic Traditions to Contemporary Fairy Tales: Popular Religiosity, Folklore, and Symbolic Space in East-Central Europe / 11

CHAPTER TWO

The Virgin of Guadalupe and the Creation of National *Mestizo* Identity in Mexico / 49

CHAPTER THREE

Brazil and the Caribbean: Afro-Indo-European Syncretism / 81

Color Plates / 125

CHAPTER FOUR

Aztlán: The Subversion of the Virgin in the Mexican American Southwest / 141

Conclusion / 161

Notes / 169

Glossary / 183

Bibliography / 193

Index / 211

List of Illustrations

❧

Color Plates:

1. Our Lady of Częstochowa, Jasna Góra, Poland / 125

2. The Virgin of Guadalupe, Basilica of Guadalupe, Mexico City / 126

3. Procession for the Black Madonna of Częstochowa in Poronin, Poland / 127

4. Matachines–Danza Guadalupana de Pablo Olivarez, Sr., dancing in front of Our Lady of Guadalupe Church, San Antonio / 128

5. *The Virgin of the Immaculate Conception of El Escorial* by Bartolomé Esteban Murillo / 129

6. Our Lady of Guadalupe, Cáceres, Spain / 130

7. "Estandarte de Cortés con la Virgen de la Inmaculada Concepción." Banner with the Virgin of the Immaculate Conception wearing a crown with twelve stars used by Hernán Cortés during the Conquest of Mexico / 131

8. *Verdadero retrato de santa María Virgen de Guadalupe, patrona principal de la Nueva España jurada en México* (Real Portrait of Holy Mary Virgin of Guadalupe, Main Patron of New Spain Sworn in Mexico) by Josefus de Ribera i Argomanis, 1778 / 132

9. Multiple Iemanjá statutes at a Salvador, Bahia *botánica*, Brazil / 133

10. Iemanjá and Oxum represented as mermaids at the Casa de Iemanjá in Salvador, Bahia, Brazil / 134

11. Our Lady of Charity of El Cobre syncretized with Ochún, Havana, Cuba / 135

12. *Botánica* in Salvador, Bahia, Brazil / 136

13. Lowrider car with a mural of the Virgin of Guadalupe by Milton Chávez on the hood, Albuquerque / 137

14. Blending of two Mexican icons: The Virgin of Guadalupe and Frida Kahlo, Santa Fe, New Mexico / 138

15. *Portrait of the Artist as the Virgin of Guadalupe*, 1978, by Yolanda M. López / 139

Introduction

1. Black Madonna of Czestochowa Shrine and Grottos, Eureka, Missouri / 4

2. The Polish Black Madonna and Our Lady of Guadalupe, Czestochowa, Texas / 5

3. Church in Panna Maria, Texas, first Polish settlement in the United States (1854) / 5

4. Author in front of the Shrine-Grotto of Our Lady of Częstochowa, San Antonio / 5

5. Our Lady of Ostra Brama, Wilno (Vilnius), Lithuania / 7

6. Procession for the Virgin of El Carmen, Paucartambo, Peru / 7

7. Candomblé ceremony. The *orixás* wear sumptuous, Baroque-inspired attire. Itaparica Island, Bahia, Brazil / 8

8. Matachines holding a banner with Our Lady of Guadalupe in front of the Alamo, San Antonio / 8

Chapter One

9. Our Lady of Częstochowa dressed and crowned, Jasna Góra, Poland / 12

10. Baba Yaga and her hut / 13

11. Coatlicue, Aztec Mother Goddess / 13

12. *Citlali, La Xicana Super Hero* by deborah kuetzpalin vasquez / 13

13. *Vénus of Laussel*, 25,000–20,000 BC, France / 15

14. Mother Earth, Poland / 15

15. Greek goddess Diana / 15

16. Egyptian goddess Isis with Horus / 15

17. Milking Madonna, Italy / 16

18. Catalonian Virgin of Montserrat, Spain / 16

19. Rusałka, a Slavic folk figure, Polish popular art / 17

20. Monastery at Jasna Góra, Poland / 18

21. Image of the Black Madonna of Częstochowa at her sanctuary at Jasna Góra, Poland / 18

22. A wooden representation of Baba Yaga from Poland / 20

23. A nineteenth-century house crowned by two crossed birds from the Kurpie region of Poland / 21

24. Quetzalcoatl, Mesoamerican civilizing god, represented as a plumed serpent, Teotihuacan, Mexico / 21

25. Virgin of Regla, Chipiona, Spain / 22

26. Our Lady Aparecida, Brazil / 22

27. The Holy Trinity / 22

28. Baba or Żywa—goddess as the center of a flowering Tree of Life, Poland / 27

29. *Virgin Mary with a Distaff*, Master of Erfurt, fifteenth century, Germany / 31

30. Polish village of Mokrzesz / 33

31. Iron cross placed on a stone, village of Święta Anna, Poland / 33

32. Woman selling nosegays of herbs, sprouts of grain, and flowers in front of a Warsaw church / 38

33. *Panno Święta co Jasnej bronisz Częstochowy, 1939–1945* (Holy Virgin, Thou Who Defend the Bright Częstochowa) by J. Ostrywska, 1945 / 43

34. *Boże zbaw Polskę* (God Save Poland). Religious-patriotic image, ca. 1900 / 44

35. The Black Madonna with the Polish coat of arms / 44

36. and 37. Eighteenth-century pectorals with the Black Madonna of Częstochowa / 44

38. Stamp from the Solidarność (Solidarity) mail with Our Lady of Częstochowa, 1982? / 45

39. *Matko uwięzionych i internowanych módl się za nami* (Mother of the Interned and the Imprisoned, Pray for Us). Banner with the Black Madonna made out of a towel by Solidarity prisoners in Darłówek, 1982 / 45

40. Mexican American prisoners' *arte de paño,* or cloth art. Pillowcase with the Virgin of Guadalupe from the New Mexico State Prison / 45

41. *Stabat Mater* by Wanda Gałczyńska, 1982 / 45

42. Copy of the painting of Our Lady of Częstochowa Wearing a Hetman Coat, 1976–77 / 46

43. "Śmierć w powietrzu" (Death in the Air). Cover of the Polish magazine *Wprost*, 21 August 1994, with Our Lady of Częstochowa wearing a gas mask / 47

CHAPTER TWO

44. Ex-votos at the Black Madonna of Częstochowa Sanctuary at Jasna Góra, Poland / 51

45. Pilgrimage to the Virgin of Guadalupe Basilica at the Tepeyac Hill, Mexico City / 51

46. *La Virgen de los Mareantes* (Virgin of the Sailors), Spain / 55

47. Chalchutlicue, Aztec water and fertility goddess / 57

48. Contemporary depiction of the Virgin of Guadalupe with colors of the Mexican flag / 61

49. *China Poblana en la Ciudad Universitaria de Mexico* (Typical China Poblana Costume), 1950s / 63

50. Caduceus by Eligiusz Oleszkiewicz and Ania Aldrich / 66

51. Crowned serpent. Wooden sculpture, Druskininkai, Lithuania / 66

52. Voodoo altar crowned by serpents Damballah-Ayida Wedo, New Orleans / 66

53. Goddess Tanit, fourth–third century BC, from the Necropolis Puig des Molins in Eivissa (Ibiza, Spain) / 68

54. *Feast of Blessed Virgin Mary, Queen of Heaven* by Diego Velázquez / 68

55. The Virgin Mary. Wooden road chapel from the Kurpie region, Poland / 68

56. *San Miguel Arcángel con estandarte guadalupano* (Saint Michael Archangel with the Guadalupan Banner), eighteenth century, anonymous. Museum of the Basilica of Guadalupe, Mexico City / 69

57. Paper cutout representing the Tree of Life with mythical birds. Polish popular art / 73

58. Wooden sculpture representing the Tree of Life with flowers and birds. Polish popular art / 73

59. Native American decorative rug from Arizona representing the Tree of Life with flowers and birds / 73

60. Paper cutout representing the Tree of Life, identified with the goddess (baba). Polish popular art / 73

61. The Mother of God on a linden tree, Święta Lipka (Saint Linden), Poland / 74

62. Syncretic road cross with the symbolic representation of the sun, the moon, flowers, and a base with a carved female figure. Polish-Lithuanian village Puńsk / 75

63. Sacred *iroko* (*ceiba*) tree at the Gantois *terreiro* in Salvador, Bahia, Brazil / 77

64. Mexican clay tree with Adam, Eve, and the serpent / 78

CHAPTER THREE

65. Oxum represented as a mermaid at the entrance to the Casa Branca *terreiro* in Salvador, Bahia, Brazil / 84

66. Iemanjá in trance at a Candomblé ceremony. Ilê Asé Orisanlá J'Omin *terreiro*, Itaparica Island, Bahia, Brazil / 85

67. House of Oxum with golden and yellow offerings near a pond with fresh water. Ilê Asé Orisanlá J'Omin *terreiro*, Itaparica Island, Bahia, Brazil / 85

68. Oxalá in trance. Ilê Asé Orisanlá J'Omin *terreiro*, Itaparica Island, Bahia, Brazil / 85

69. Altar for Changó, Regla, Cuba / 85

70. Two Omolús in trance accompany an *ogão* on his three-year ceremony. Ilê Asé Orisanlá J'Omin *terreiro*, Itaparica Island, Bahia, Brazil / 86

71. Women from the Irmandade da Boa Morte (Sisterhood of the Good Death), a Catholic sisterhood at Cachoeira, Bahia, Brazil, wearing white Candomblé attire / 87

72. As Águas de Oxalá (the Waters of Oxalá) ritual, Asé Ilha Vera Cruz, Bahia, Brazil / 87

73. Entrance to the Casa Branca *terreiro*, Salvador, Bahia, Brazil / 90

74. Gantois *terreiro*, Salvador, Bahia, Brazil / 90

75. *Contas*, or sacred necklaces, of the Brazilian *orixás* / 91

76. Initiation ceremony (*confirmação*) of two *ékédes* led by the *iyalorixá* in trance. Ilê Asé Orisanlá J'Omin *terreiro*, Itaparica Island, Bahia, Brazil / 92

77. Confirmed *ékédes* take seats at both sides of the *iyalorixá* throne in the *barracão*. Ilê Asé Orisanlá J'Omin *terreiro*, Itaparica Island, Bahia, Brazil / 92

78. A goat sacrificed by the *axôgún* is prepared at the Ilê Asé Orisanlá J'Omin *terreiro*, Itaparica Island, Bahia, Brazil / 93

79. Offerings of sacred dishes at an *orixá* house. Ilê Asé Orisanlá J'Omin *terreiro*, Itaparica Island, Bahia, Brazil / 93

80. A sacrificed goat's skin is used to elaborate an *atabaque*, or ritual drum. Ilê Asé Orisanlá J'Omin *terreiro*, Itaparica Island, Bahia, Brazil / 94

81. Drums adorned for the *orixá* Ogum ceremony are being played at the Ilê Asé Orisanlá J'Omin *terreiro*, Itaparica Island, Bahia, Brazil / 94

82. Alda d'Alcántara Arruda, *iyalorixá* of the Ilê Asé Orisanlá J'Omin *terreiro*, dressed in her everyday white clothes. Itaparica Island, Bahia, Brazil / 96

83. and 84. Women handling food and cooking at the Ilê Asé Orisanlá J'Omin *terreiro*, Itaparica Island, Bahia, Brazil / 98

85. Members of the *família-de-santo* of the Ilê Asé Orisanlá J'Omin *terreiro* with author. Itaparica Island, Bahia, Brazil / 98

86. *Bóveda espiritual,* or Spiritist altar, Havana / 101

87. Regla de Palo altar in a Havana house / 101

88. and 89. Cuban *canastilleros*, with attributes of the *orichas* placed on different shelves. Regla and Havana / 102

90. Sanctuary of the Virgin of Regla, Cuba / 103

91. Virgin of Regla, Cuba / 104

92. Ezili Dantò, or Mater Salvatoris, identified with the Polish Black Madonna of Czestochowa, Port-au-Prince, Haiti / 104

93. Women dancing at a Voodoo ceremony, with Ezili Dantò represented as the

Black Madonna of Częstochowa in the background, Port-au-Prince, Haiti / 104

94. Nossa Senhora da Conceição da Praia (Our Lady of Immaculate Conception of the Beach), patron of Bahia. Salvador, Bahia, Brazil / 105

95. Nossa Senhora da Conceição da Praia Church in Salvador, Bahia, Brazil / 105

96. Church of Sant' Anna (Saint Anne), Salvador, Bahia, Brazil / 106

97. Casa de Iemanjá (House of Iemanjá), a gathering place for Salvador, Bahia fishermen / 106

98. Iemanjá with offerings inside Casa de Iemanjá, Salvador, Bahia, Brazil / 107

99. Offerings inside Casa de Iemanjá, Salvador, Bahia, Brazil / 107

100. New Orleans Voodoo altar with the goddess Ezili Dantò as the Polish Black Madonna of Częstochowa / 110

101. Entrance to the Ilê Asé Orisanlá J'Omin *terreiro*, Itaparica Island, Bahia, Brazil / 112

102. *Barracão*, or ritual space, at the Ilê Asé Orisanlá J'Omin *terreiro*, Itaparica Island, Bahia, Brazil / 112

103. Entrance to the *barracão* adorned by palm branches at the Ilê Asé Orisanlá J'Omin *terreiro*, Itaparica Island, Bahia, Brazil / 113

104. A crucifix over the *iyalorixá* throne in the *barracão* at the Ilê Asé Orisanlá J'Omin *terreiro*, Itaparica Island, Bahia, Brazil / 113

105. A crucifix on the *eguns*', or ancestors', house at the Ilê Asé Orisanlá J'Omin *terreiro*, Itaparica Island, Bahia, Brazil / 114

106. Offerings hanging from the trees for the *orixá* Ossain and at the *aldeias de caboclos* (villages of the Indian spirits). Ilê Asé Orisanlá J'Omin *terreiro*, Itaparica Island, Bahia, Brazil / 114

107. Itaparica Island, across All Saints Bay from the city of Salvador, Bahia, Brazil / 115

108. The house of Oxalá, identified with Jesus Christ, adorned by the symbol of the dove. Ilê Asé Orisanlá J'Omin *terreiro*, Itaparica Island, Bahia, Brazil / 116

109. Everyday white outfits at a Candomblé ceremony, Ilê Asé Orisanlá J'Omin *terreiro*, Itaparica Island, Bahia, Brazil / 118

110. Syncretic altar with Catholic, Indian, and African elements at the Ilê Asé Orisanlá J'Omin *terreiro*, Itaparica Island, Bahia, Brazil / 118

111. Santería offerings for *oricha* Elegguá, San Antonio / 122

112. El Santo Niño de Atocha, syncretized with Elegguá / 122

113. Fidel Castro with white doves during his inaugural speech, Havana, 1959 / 122

CHAPTER FOUR

114. *The Legacy of César Chávez*, 1997, mural by Emigdio Vasquez / 142

115. *Tradicion Cultura*, San Antonio's West Side Mexican American mural / 143

116. Mural with Pachucos at a parking lot in the San Francisco Mission District / 143

117. Velvet painting featuring the ill-fated lovers Mixtli or Ixta (Ixtacihuátl) and Popo or Popoca (Popocatépetl) / 145

118. Tattoo with the Virgin of Guadalupe from La Española, New Mexico / 145

119. Pilgrim to Chimayó, New Mexico, with a tattoo featuring the Virgin of Guadalupe / 145

120. Mural with pre-Columbian motifs on a house in the San Francisco Mission District / 146

121. and 122. Shopping bags and other objects with the image of Guadalupe and Frida Kahlo at the Mexican Mercado (Market), San Antonio / 147

123. *End Barrio Warfare*, 1998. Mural led by Augustine Villa, Lisa Mendiola, and Sonny Mendiola, San Antonio / 148

124. *Nicho/Mural para la Virgen de Guadalupe*, 2001. Mural led by Mary Agnes Rodriguez and Janie Tabares Orneles, San Antonio / 149

125. *Our lady of Guadalupe Veladora*, 2003. Sculptural mosaic by Jesse Treviño, San Antonio / 149

126. *The Last Supper of the Chicano Heroes*, detail of the mural *Mythology and History of Maiz*, 1986–89, by José Antonio Burciaga, Stanford University, California / 149

127. Graffiti combined with mural art in the barrio, San Antonio / 151

128. T-shirts with the Virgin of Guadalupe, San Antonio / 151

129. T-shirt with the Virgin of Guadalupe and a lowrider car, San Francisco Mission District / 152

130. The Virgin of Guadalupe at a coffee shop in Las Cruces, New Mexico / 152

131. *Guadalupe Defending Xicano Rights*, 1976, by Ester Hernandez / 153

132. *The Walking Guadalupe*, 1978, by Yolanda M. López / 153

133. *Margaret F. Stewart: Our Lady of Guadalupe*, 1978, by Yolanda M. López / 154

134. *Victoria F. Franco: Our Lady of Guadalupe*, 1978, by Yolanda M. López / 154

135. *La Sirena* (The Siren), from the Mexican Lotería (Lottery) game / 155

136. *Water Lady* by Michael Isaac Cardenas / 157

137. *Soy el Corazón* by Ramón Vásquez y Sanchez / 157

CONCLUSION

138. *Botánica* in Salvador, Bahia, Brazil / 163

139. Devotional objects for sale near the Basilica of Our Lady of Guadalupe in Mexico City / 165

140. Devotional store in the vicinity of the Black Madonna of Częstochowa Sanctuary at Jasna Góra, Poland / 166

Acknowledgments

❧

This book would not have been possible without the trust and support of the people who opened their doors to me during my fieldwork in Brazil and Cuba and all those who provided interviews in Poland and the United States throughout my ten years of fieldwork from 1995 TO 2005. I give special thanks to the *iyalorixá* of the Ilê Asé Orisanlá J'Omin *terreiro*, mãe Alda d'Alcántara Arruda, and all the members of this *família-de-santo* spiritual community from Bahia, Brazil, for their openness, help, and confidence that my work will serve a good purpose.

Very special thanks to Sam Pochucha and Linda Moran, who painstakingly commented on, revised, and edited my manuscript at different stages of writing, and to my father, Eligiusz Oleszkiewicz, who enthusiastically helped me to gather and translate Russian, Polish, and Lithuanian materials.

Thanks to my students from the Popular Religions of Latin America classes at the University of Texas at San Antonio, who supported and inspired me with their passionate comments and research, especially to Gilberta Turner, who generously provided devotional materials from Spain.

I am grateful to my colleague Dr. Jill Heydt-Stevenson for helping me articulate my first ideas about the Black Madonna in the mid-1990s, to Drs. Alan West-Durán, Louis Mendoza, and Chris Wickham, for reading and conscientiously commenting on the whole or part of my manuscript, and to Dr. Mansour El-Kikhia for providing valuable advice on publishing.

I owe thanks also to all the individuals and institutions around the world who supported me by providing materials and granting me permissions to reproduce their work, especially to Jacqueline Orsini Dunnington of Santa Fe, New Mexico, Father Eustachy Rakoczy of Jasna Góra, Poland, Stefan Świetliczko of Warsaw, Poland, and Ania Aldrich of Barrytown, New York, as well as to Dr. Barbara Ogrodowska and others at the Ethnographic Museums of Warsaw and of Cracow, Poland.

I am indebted to my husband, Josep Maria Peralba, for his patience and constant support during the writing and review process, and to my friends and family from

San Antonio, New York, and Warsaw for their enthusiasm and interest in seeing my project come to light.

Thanks to David Holtby, Sonia Dickey, and Maya Allen-Gallegos of the University of New Mexico Press for their continuous interest and support in making my book a reality.

The research and writing of this book between 1996 and 2006 has been possible thanks to financial support from the University of Texas at San Antonio in the form of faculty research awards, faculty research grants, and a faculty development leave, as well as contributions from the College of Liberal and Fine Arts dean's office and the Department of Modern Languages and Literatures. I appreciate the technical support from the Instructional Design and Development Office and from the College of Liberal and Fine Arts Multimedia Services. I also thank the International Research and Exchanges Board (IREX) and the Polish Ministry of Education under the aegis of the Kosciuszko Foundation for providing research travel grants in 1998 and 1999.

All translations in this book, unless otherwise noted, are mine.

Introduction

Intersections are rich in energy; they mark the place where the ways

of different people cross, where space opens out in different directions.

—Maria-José, Mother of the Gods

This book is both academic and personal. It recounts ways in which popular Catholicism, Amerindian traditions, and African *òrìṣà* worship have been woven together through their syncretic contact in the New World. It also mirrors my personal cross-cultural encounters with the different worlds I describe. Special emphasis is placed on the comparative analysis of the Black Madonna/Great Mother Goddess figure, as manifested since the Neolithic Age in east-central European, Iberian, African, and Amerindian cultures, and particularly on syncretic interconnections of these cultures in Latin America. A final inquiry into contemporary hybrid manifestations of cultural and religious icons in postmodern global space closes the discussion of this book, opening the way for further explorations.

Themes and Organization

Each chapter focuses on a different geographical/cultural area: east-central Europe, Mexico, Brazil and the Caribbean, and the southwestern United States. The main themes of this book are (1) the transformation of sacred symbols as a visual and conceptual manifestation of the hybridization of cultures, termed syncretism; (2) the Black Madonna as an example of such transformation during the Christianization process; (3) the Madonna and her adoration as a symbol of matriarchal beliefs, religious practices, and feelings of national identity; and (4) appropriation and use of the Madonna in various unexpected forms as an example of cultural transformation and hybridity in postmodern times.

Chapter 1, "From Neolithic Traditions to Contemporary Fairy Tales: Popular Religiosity, Folklore, and Symbolic Space in East-Central Europe," traces the history of transformations and superimpositions of female holy figures and other symbols from the pre-Slavic matriarchal worship of the goddess Mokosz, the Mother Moist Earth, and the Holy Earth since the "Old Europe" era of 7,000—3,500 BC, to the Mother of God/Black Madonna figure introduced with the tenth-century Christianization.[1] The most famous manifestation of this blending of cultures in Poland is the fervent worship of the black Our Lady of Częstochowa, which persists to this day (see plate 1). She has played multiple roles during Polish social and political history, primarily as a fighter for justice and independence, and defender of the weak and the dispossessed. Recent examples of her appropriation in support of social causes saw her pressed into service in the struggle against communist rule during the Solidarity movement of the 1980s and the environmentalist concerns of the 1990s.

Chapter 2, "The Virgin of Guadalupe and the Creation of National *Mestizo* Identity in Mexico," focuses on the Virgin of Guadalupe as an Indian-Creole syncretic blending of Aztec and pre-Aztec goddesses and Spanish Virgin Mary icons (see plate 2). The Virgin of Guadalupe, an object of fervent worship analogous to the Polish Madonna of Częstochowa, was constructed during Spanish colonization and Christianization of New Spain and has served multiple functions throughout Mexican history, from the physical struggles for independence from Spain in the nineteenth century and the Mexican Revolution in the twentieth century to the emotional struggles for identity and unity as a people and nation since the sixteenth century. In addition, in chapter 2 I discuss other Mexican identity icons, such as La Malinche and La China Poblana. I also explain the transformation and superimposition of ancient religious symbols, such as the cross and the tree, including relatively new examples, which occurred during the Conquest and colonization of America.

Chapter 3, "Brazil and the Caribbean: Afro-Indo-European Syncretism," examines intense syncretic developments in the blending of African, European, and Amerindian cultures of the highly African-influenced areas of northeastern Brazil and the Caribbean. This process results in surprising borrowings and exchanges of cultural elements within each country. I demonstrate similarities and differences between these lusophone, hispanophone, and francophone societies. I focus on the manifestations of African female deities, such as Iemanjá, and their encounters with Christian manifestations of the holy feminine, such as the Virgin of the Immaculate Conception and Our Lady Aparecida in Brazil; Ochún and her identification with the Virgin of Charity of El Cobre in Cuba; and Mater Salvatoris, represented by the Polish Black Madonna of Częstochowa/Ezili Dantò in Haiti. I discuss the woman-focused organization of the Brazilian terreiros (religious communities) and life in the impoverished sectors of northeastern Brazil. Finally, I make evident the stunning parallels between these living cultures and the Neolithic matriarchal society described in chapter 1.

Chapter 4, "Aztlán: The Subversion of the Virgin in the Mexican American Southwest," discusses the radical transformation of images and functions of the Virgin of Guadalupe in the United States. From the second half of the twentieth century, the icon of Guadalupe has been appropriated by various secular groups and causes, such as the United Farmworkers Union, the Chicana lesbians, and the peace movement. They often transform Guadalupe's image, going against the Catholic tradition and institutionalized sociopolitical values. Chapter 4 weaves together important themes from the three previous ones, assessing contemporary uses and transformations of the Black Madonna/holy female figure and her role in present and future hybrid contexts.

Background and Research Methods

Much of this book's research is based on my own fieldwork and on-site data gathering, such as participant observation and note taking, interviews, and photographic and video documentation. It also includes extensive archival and library research and feedback from conference presentations. My fluency in the Indo-European languages necessary to conduct the research and fieldwork—Polish, Russian, Spanish, Portuguese, French, and English, as well as a reading knowledge of Latin, Italian, and Catalan—and basic notions of the Amerindian Nahuatl, Quechua, and the Afro-Latin American Yoruba were essential in completing this study.

During my childhood, the figure of the Black Madonna, the famous medieval icon of the Mother of God—Queen of Poland—situated in her sanctuary of Częstochowa, was a pervasive presence. She was and still is the object of multiple processions and peregrinations in all regions of Poland. Her images seemed to be everywhere and were manifested in different ways, as the Częstochowa rendition is only one of hundreds of sacred icons of the dark Madonna in Poland. When Poles emigrated to distant lands, they took the Madonna with them and often established new sanctuaries, such as the Black Madonna of Czestochowa Shrine and Grottos in Eureka, Missouri; in Doylestown, Pennsylvania; and in Czestochowa, Texas. Significantly, the town of Panna Maria (Virgin Mary), near San Antonio, Texas, dedicated to the Black Madonna of Częstochowa, was the first Polish settlement in the United States (1854). A grotto dedicated to Our Lady of Częstochowa was built in San Antonio in 1966 to commemorate the Polish millennium of Christianity (966–1966).

Visit the:

**Black Madonna
of
Czestochowa
Shrine & Grottos**

**A Franciscan Shrine dedicated to
Poland's Black Madonna
Our Lady of Czestochowa Queen of
Peace and Mercy**

Fig. 1. Black Madonna of Czestochowa Shrine
and Grottos, Eureka, Missouri. The
Madonna appears as a woman much
younger and of lighter complexion than in
the Polish original. (Author's collection.)

When I moved to North America in 1977, I kept noticing signs of the familiar Madonna as well as her new manifestations. But it was during the years of my PhD studies at New York University in the early eighties that my close Nuyorican friend and colleague, Pilar Blanco Ruiz, first pointed out to me the striking similarity in the roles of the Polish Black Madonna and the Virgin of Guadalupe. This idea stayed with me into the nineties, when I first started to research this phenomenon in Latin America. I was intrigued by the Afro-Brazilian goddess Iemanjá figure, and in 1996 I traveled to Salvador, Bahia to conduct fieldwork on the Candomblé religion. I spent three intense months attending terreiros sacred ceremonies and activities, interviewing their members and scholars, and documenting them with video and audio. Trips to Puerto Rico and Cuba in 1998 and 1999, respectively, expanded and deepened my view of syncretic Afro-Caribbean religiosity. I interviewed *santeros* and visited sanctuaries, museums, and *botánicas*. I also conducted research trips to Poland in 1997, 1998, 1999, 2000, 2001, and 2002; to Lithuania in 1997; to Russia in 2001; and to Spain in 1998, 2001, 2002, 2003, and 2004. My journeys to the sanctuary of the Virgin of Guadalupe in Mexico City, as well as to various communities in the states of Oaxaca and Chiapas in 1992, 1993, and 1994, gave me insight into syncretic religious practices

Fig. 2. In Czestochowa, Texas, the Polish Black Madonna is accompanied by Our Lady of Guadalupe. (Photo by author.)

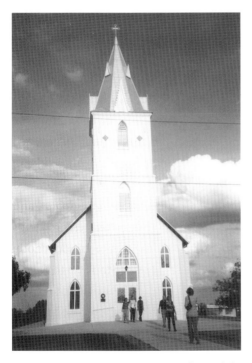

Fig. 3. Church in Panna Maria, Texas, first Polish settlement in the United States (1854). (Photo by author.)

Fig. 4. Author in front of the Shrine-Grotto of Our Lady of Częstochowa, San Antonio, 2003. (Photo by Josep Maria Peralba, author's collection.)

in Mexico. I also conducted field research on Mexican American and Caribbean American religious and artistic manifestations in San Francisco in 2000 and 2002, in Santa Fe in 2001, and in San Antonio from 1998 to 2006.

I was born in Poland less than a decade after World War II, which saw the destruction of 90 percent of my hometown Warzawa (Warsaw). To this day I remember vestiges of the prewar city with its distinct flavor, as well as the ruins, and the stories accompanying them. I also recall the Slavic folktales read to me at bedtime and the legends studied in school. Those tales reemerged as I was researching the fervent worship of the Black Madonna for this book. My family's experience was typical of postwar Poland. My father was born in Wilno, now Vilnius, capital of Lithuania. Wilno was an important Polish cultural center, supporting four languages and cultures before World War II. Poles, Lithuanians, Russians, and Jews shared this corner of northeastern Europe. They had their own Dark Madonna, Our Lady of Ostra Brama, whose picture crowns the city gate. Even today, people kneel on the street in front of her.[2] My father was subjected to the postwar events that led to the diaspora of eastern Poland, whereby its inhabitants were forced to relocate to the western region if they wanted to remain in the Polish nation after Lithuania became incorporated into the Soviet Union in 1940 and was occupied by the Nazis in 1941. The family settled in Gdańsk in 1946, and three years later my father moved to Warsaw to study at Warsaw's School of Economics. Wherever he went, he took the image of the Dark Madonna with him. His own life experience of relocation and exposure to different cultures led him to become a multilingual translator, an international trade expert, and a world traveler. His example instilled in me the love for different cultures, languages, and lands. In Warsaw he met my mother, who came from a family whose female line had been there for five generations.

As a child I lived with my family in a quarter of Warsaw where I could regularly observe colorful processions honoring the Catholic saints, among which the dark Mother of God was the most venerated. I regularly witnessed the same phenomenon during vacations in small towns and villages in other regions of Poland. There, the display of icons, adornments, and chants during the ritual parades was even more profuse (see plate 3).

During my elementary school years, when my family lived in Montevideo, Uruguay, I was surprised at the lack of such exuberant public manifestations of the Catholic faith. Yet, this was compensated for by Brazilian-style carnival parades and the sounds of the drums played at night by the street *candomberos*.[3] These South American memories were stimulated thirty years later during a lecture on Afro-Uruguayan music I attended at the New York City Museum of Natural History.

Fig. 5. Our Lady of Ostra Brama, Wilno (Vilnius), Lithuania.

Fig. 6. Procession for the Virgin of El Carmen, Paucartambo, Peru, 1987. (Photo by author.)

When I lived in Peru between 1987 and 1990 in order to conduct fieldwork on Andean popular theater for my PhD dissertation, my recollections of exuberant displays of popular Catholicism in Poland were reawakened. Moreover, the ritual fervor exhibited in the Andean processions surpassed that of my childhood memories. They were massive and exuberant, full of Baroque excess (*derroche*), and seemingly unending. The feasts devoted to the Virgin La Candelaria, which I observed in Puno, and to the Virgin of El Carmen in Paucartambo were two-week-long uninterrupted carnivals. Moreover, they were performed by Indians and mestizos with non-Christian elements intermingled. Clearly, these feasts were manifestations of the superimposed faith and ritual tradition of pre-Reformation Iberian popular Catholicism, with all its exaggeration and drama, and ritualistic American indigenous worship. African elements were also evident.

During my trips to Mexico City, Oaxaca, and Chiapas in 1992, 1993, and 1994, I noticed a similar type of effusive, hybrid popular devotion in Mexico. The first Spanish viceroyalties in America, New Spain (Mexico and Central America), and Peru preserved most of the popular medieval Catholic traditions, which were later syncretized with Amerindian beliefs.

What I witnessed during my three-month research trip to Salvador, Bahia, Brazil, in 1996 was without precedent in my experience and my research. The degree of

Fig. 7. Candomblé ceremony. The *orixás* wear sumptuous, Baroque-inspired attire. Second from left to right: Iemanjá, Nanã, and Oxossi. Ilê Asé Orisanlá J'Omin *terreiro*, Itaparica Island, Bahia, Brazil, 1996. (Photo by author.)

Fig. 8. Matachines holding a banner with Our Lady of Guadalupe in front of the Alamo, San Antonio, 12 December 1998. (Photo by author.)

syncretism and refinement of the ritualistic system of the Candomblé religion, my topic of research, was striking. Candomblé, a fully coherent ancient African religious system, was alive and well in modern-day South America, practiced in the guise of Catholic saints and Baroque attire.

When I moved from New York to San Antonio, Texas, in 1995, I again witnessed something remarkable. The disappearing traditions of Spanish medieval Catholicism with such manifestations as the Pastores and the Posadas were vibrant here. Special focus was given to the worship of the Virgin of Guadalupe and her feast on 12 December in the form of Matachines dances (see plate 4), performed by modern-day mestizos of Mexican origin dressed as Aztec Indians and called Los soldados de la Virgen (the Virgin's Soldiers).[4] Cross-cultural dressing and other hybrid practices, where multilayered identities are negotiated, are idiosyncratic of postcolonial societies, such as those of Latin America and the Caribbean I describe in the following chapters.

SUMMARY

My book examines the phenomenon of the Black Madonna, a fluid syncretic blend of the Virgin Mary and ancient Mother Goddesses from Eurasian, Native American, and African cultures who is worshipped and adored by millions of people around the world. In Mexico, Greater Mexico,[5] Poland, and Brazil, the Black Madonna, manifested in the figures of the Virgin of Guadalupe, Matka Boska Częstochowska, and Nossa Senhora Aparecida/Iemanjá, has been a symbol of identity and resistance against oppression and the subject of curious iconographic transformations. These often conflict with the official control of church and state. I examine this figure from a comparative, cross-cultural, and dynamic perspective in four cultural areas, going beyond the Spanish-speaking world. Until now, no comparative analysis of the Black Madonna in east-central Europe, Brazil, Mexico, and Aztlán has been published, in English or in any other language. By encompassing and comparing Spanish American/Indian, Afro-Brazilian and Afro-Caribbean, east-central European, and Mexican American traditions, this book fills a void in scholarship on the Dark Madonna figure. It addresses fundamental questions of culture, such as interaction at the borderlands and parallel developments in distant locations. It examines these topics in the light of the theories of transculturation and syncretism, concluding with an analysis of contemporary uses of the Black Madonna and her role in a time of global culture and hybridization.

Mother of God our black earth

With free bread bless the peasant.

—Nikolai Kluiev, Russian peasant poet

❧

O, nubble of my earth,

O, holy relic!

Some incomprehensible force links us together!

You feel in my hand,

As my blood circulates.

The blood that pulsates in me

Is but Your blood.

For these vital juices

You generously give

Become blood of mine

And give me life.

—Paulina Hołyszowa, Polish peasant poet

CHAPTER ONE

From Neolithic Traditions
to Contemporary Fairy Tales

Popular Religiosity, Folklore, and Symbolic Space

in East-Central Europe

❧

A careful examination of today's most venerated icons and beliefs, encompassing the full range of pop stars, cartoon characters, and mass media images, reveals the presence of a specific icon—a compassionate, feminine figure portrayed as the Virgin Mary, Mother of God. Most often, she is represented as a young virgin (see plate 5) or a mature mother (see plate 1), but we can also detect her presence in her less accepted "underground" representations of the witch or the old hag, known as Baba Yaga (Baba Jaga), Coatlicue, or Nanā (see fig. 7).[1] At other times, as in the paintings of contemporary Chicana artists Isis Rodriguez and Ester Hernandez, she is depicted as a cartoon character or, as in the works of deborah kuetzpalin vasquez, she is disguised as *Citlali, La Xicana Super Hero*. In her parallel ancient and modern incarnations, her image is not as important as the functions she performs—she is the protector, the consoler, the defender, the fighter for freedom and justice, and the great equalizer. Before her, gender, race, class, and ethnic origin are not debilitating distinctions but a foundation of strength. And it seems that this uniting and equalizing function on a social and national level has been one of the main bastions of her popularity. It provides a common denominator for such ethnically, historically, and geographically distant countries as Poland, Mexico, and Brazil. Nevertheless, this balancing function alone cannot fully explain the enduring popularity of this figure for millennia. In this chapter, I explore the Paleo- and Neolithic origins of this cult along with its history and scope in central and eastern Europe. Major emphasis is placed on regions of Poland and Russia, while making relevant references to selected Afro- and Indo-Latin American cultures. Like many world regions, these have been the sites of impressive migrations and ethnic mixing since the most remote of times. In the

Fig. 9. Our Lady of Częstochowa dressed and crowned, Jasna Góra, Poland. Mary is shown here as a
mature mother.

Fig. 10. Baba Yaga and her hut by Ania Aldrich. (Author's collection. Reproduced with permission of the artist.)

Fig. 11. Coatlicue, Aztec Mother Goddess associated with death. (Photo by author.)

Fig. 12. *Citlali, La Xicana Super Hero* by deborah kuetzpalin vasquez. Note card. (Author's collection. Reproduced with permission of the artist.)

last five hundred years, the dynamic character of cultural fusion has been especially evident on the American continent, where a vigorous process of colonization was initiated in the sixteenth century.

THE GREAT MOTHER/BLACK MADONNA AND HER JOURNEY
FROM PREHISTORIC TIMES TO THE PRESENT

The concept of an all-encompassing Great Mother Goddess, life giver and creator, has been known from the earliest of times, as evidenced by numerous archeological findings of female figurines dating back to the Paleolithic period. An example is the *Vénus of Laussel* (25,000–20,000 BC), found in southern France, a figurine of a pregnant woman with one hand on her belly and the other holding a horn with thirteen incisions (Gimbutas, *Language of the Goddess* 142). These correspond to the thirteen lunar months contained in a solar year and to the thirteen twenty-day months of gestation, as in the Mayan lunar calendar. The concept of the Mother Goddess survived millennia, adopting different forms and names, and today is still vibrant and in constant flux. The beginning of the aretalogy of Maronea describes the origin of the black goddess Isis in the following words: "Earth, they say, is the mother of all, from her who was first (to be) you were born (as her) daughter" (Zabkar 142). The Great Mother Goddess has been identified with the fertile Mother Earth, who nourishes and sustains all. This is manifested in such figures as the Russian Mother Moist Earth, who is fertile and black. In other cultures, the veneration of the female principle took the form of a powerful goddess, such as the Sumerian Inanna, "Queen of Heaven and Earth," responsible for all growth. The Egyptian goddess Isis, like Inanna, was "the Lady of Heaven, Earth, and the Netherworld" (Zabkar 51, hymn 4), but she also was the "God's Mother" and "God's Wife" (Zabkar 42, hymn 3). Greek Diana/Roman Venus was a Virgin Mother Goddess of fertility, her black body covered with breasts. Isis appears as a direct predecessor to the Virgin Mary figure. Like the latter, Isis is represented as a black figure seated on a throne with her divine child Horus on her lap. Moreover, like the Christian Milking Madonna or Our Lady of Milk, she is often portrayed as suckling Horus or as part of a triune holy family, composed of her brother-husband Osiris, her son Horus, and herself.[2] In addition, she is the "ruler of every land," the "mistress of rivers and winds and sea"; she "showed the paths of the stars" and "regulated the course of the sun and the moon" (Zabkar 140–41). Similarly, Mary in numerous renditions is portrayed as black, sitting on a throne with her divine child on her lap. Good examples are the Catalonian Virgin of Montserrat and the Extremaduran Virgin of Guadalupe (see plate 6). Like Isis, Mary sometimes is portrayed as part of a holy trinity composed of her husband, her son,

Fig. 13. [left] *Vénus of Laussel*, 25,000–20,000 BC, Musée d'Aquitaine, Bordeaux, France. (Copyright © Musée d'Aquitaine, Bordeaux. Photo by L. Gauthier. Reproduced with permission.)

Fig. 14. [right] Mother Earth, Poland, 2002. (Photo by author.)

Fig. 15. [left] Greek goddess Diana. (Photo by Wallace Birnbaum. Reproduced with permission.)

Fig. 16. [right] Egyptian goddess Isis with Horus. (Photo by author.)

Fig. 17. Milking Madonna, Italy, Middle Ages. (Photo by author.)

Fig. 18. Catalonian Virgin of Montserrat, Spain. (Photo by author.)

and herself, as in the Francisco Zurbarán's seventeenth-century painting, *The Holy Family*,[3] and she is venerated as the ruler of Heaven and Earth, war and seamanship (Zakbar 140–41).[4]

The Christian Mary inherited the tradition of her powerful female predecessors, although she was gradually stripped of some of her powers, such as her dominion over life and death, her wisdom, and her sexuality. Nevertheless, like other goddesses, she too may be considered part of a trinity, currently manifested in the Slavic folk figures Rusałka, Mother Moist Earth (see fig.14), and Baba Yaga (see fig.10). The first embodies the fertile young virgin; the second, the nourishing mother; and the third, the crone or old wise woman connected to death. In the Indo-Latin American culture of Mexico and the Afro-Latin American of Brazil, this concept is manifested by the trinities Xochiquetzal–Tonantzin–Toci and Oxum–Iemanjá–Nanã (see fig. 7), respectively.

Syncretism is an attribute of all evolving societies and a natural consequence of dynamic cultural contact. It occurs during millennia of evolution of cultures, even those considered stable and bound to one particular area. Christianity is a good example of the syncretic processes, as it has absorbed a gamut of preexistent beliefs and practices, incorporating them into its symbols and rituals. The Virgin Mary, Mother of God,

Fig. 19. Rusałka, a Slavic folk figure. Polish popular art. (Author's collection and photo.)

Fig. 20. [left] Monastery at Jasna Góra, Poland, where the image of the Black Madonna of Częstochowa
is located, 1997. (Photo by author.)

Fig. 21. [right] Image of the Black Madonna of Częstochowa at her sanctuary at Jasna Góra, Poland,
1997. (Photo by author.)

is a clear example of syncretism. During this process different cultures enter into
contact with each other, because of either geographical proximity or superimposition
by force. In either circumstance, rather than being totally eliminated, one culture
becomes blended with the other. I describe this issue in more detail in chapter 3, but
each chapter of this book is structured around a discussion of religious syncretic
phenomena in a particular geographical/cultural area of the world, especially as they
relate to the Virgin Mary/Mother of God figure.

The Polish Black Madonna of Częstochowa (see plate 1) is a particular manifestation of syncretism. She is a Byzantine painting of a Black Madonna holding
a child, of the type called *Hodegetria*, or "Indicator of the Way," dating from the
sixth–ninth century. The fervent worship of this icon started when she was brought
to the Pauline monastery at Jasna Góra, next to the town of Częstochowa, Poland,
in 1384, but even preceding the arrival of this painting this image was considered
miraculous. The fame of the Black Madonna spread even further when the icon
"performed" various miracles, such as saving Poland from the 1655 Swedish invasion,
called *Potop* (Deluge).

East-central Europe, although not subjected to major efforts of colonization,
did not escape the external influences superimposed by numerous migrations and
invasions. The first known invasions affecting the culture and population of Old
Europe were carried out by Indo-European tribes coming from the east. They occurred
between the fifth and the third millenniums BC and imported a warrior culture to

this area. In spite of subsequent modifications, vestiges of the Old European way of life, such as the strong position of women, still survive in several "corners" of Europe today.[5] Such traditions are preserved in myths, legends, tales, popular beliefs, customs, and rituals. These are most clearly visible among remote, rural populations where Indo-European and, later, Christian civilizations were more resistant to change.

Christian beliefs were superimposed on Indo-Europeans who inhabited eastern and central Europe at the onset of the tenth century. Each new stratum of culture introduced to the existing system was gradually integrated into the old set of beliefs and rituals, resulting in syncretic cultures and religions. This process explains the persistence and "recycling" of concepts over vast stretches of time and is exemplified by the Finno-Slavic goddess Mokosh, who reappears in the figure of the Mother Moist Earth, which in turn reappears as Mary, the Mother of God, during the Christian era. As stated, these evolutions occurred over such immense time periods that today we cannot prove that the original figure of the Great Mother Goddess Mokosh was totally eliminated and then replaced with the Virgin Mary. Rather, the previous effigies have been reassimilated and adapted to the new ones. Although specific attributes may be discarded, there is a tendency toward retention of ancient archetypal figures in the collective subconscious and their reemergence in a disguised form. This is the story of the Slavic witch Baba Yaga, or *wiedźma*[6] (see fig. 10), who embodies the chthonic, fertility, and transformative aspects of the all-encompassing goddess of life, death, and regeneration. These aspects have been eradicated from the persona of the Virgin Mary so that she incorporates only accepted virtues such as virginity and motherhood.[7] Considered dangerous by patriarchal society, the uncontrollable aspects of wisdom, sexuality, dominion over death, and transformation are viewed as incompatible with this figure. Mary's officially sanctioned qualities are submission, humility, purity, suffering, and renunciation. For centuries, these qualities have been endorsed as a model for women in the Western world, depriving them of the full range of their power. Even old age, in its capacity to free women from the control of men, has been demonized. Old women are either witches, Yagas, or *baby*.[8] All present-day female icons are young. None of them exercise actual power over their own destiny or sexuality, but rather they exist as instruments for procreation or for male sexual pleasure. Ironically, amid the confusion, the ancient archetype of a powerful woman is reemerging. This "new" prototype is prominent in contemporary contexts where the Madonna is freed from her passivity and presented as a jogger (see plate 15), a karate fighter (see fig. 131), or a warrior for justice and independence at the personal, social, and national levels.[9] In these works of art the Madonna becomes the embodiment of feminine strength and power. A most striking phenomenon is that the great majority

Fig. 22. A wooden representation of
Baba Yaga from Poland. (Author's
collection and photo.)

of the ancient Mother of God/Virgin icons venerated in Europe, Latin America, or other continents are depicted with dark skin tones.

In order to find the origins of today's omnipresent worship of the Black Madonna in such seemingly distant cultures as the Slavic, the Indo-American, and the Afro-Latin American, we need to closely examine their development. I will discuss the influences on the Slavic and Baltic peoples inhabiting mainly eastern and central Europe as well as parts of the north and the southeast of that continent. This area is located either within or on the outskirts of the "Old European" civilization. Numerous archeological findings suggest that a well-organized, sedentary civilization thrived there for millennia, until it was conquered by Indo-European horsemen coming from the eastern steppes around 3,000 BC.[10] Old Europe had a peaceful, matrifocal, and matrilineal culture, venerating the all-powerful goddess of all creation, death, and regeneration. Archeological evidence indicates that it was permeated by symbols related to the life-creating female body. "The world was regarded as the body of the goddess, constantly creating new life from itself" (Gimbutas, *Living Goddesses* 112). Images of the mother or of mother-daughter were found in abundance, while the father image was conspicuously absent.[11] Old women seem to have been especially revered. As in any matrilineal society, mothers and daughters maintained the same residence and ownership of property. The goddess was represented by a priestess and was portrayed as crowned or enthroned. The regenerative symbols related to the Neolithic goddess figure were eggs, horns, phalli, snake coils, plants, butterflies, bucrania, trees of life, triangles, concentric circles, rising columns, and eyes. Other significant symbols were V's, chevrons, spirals, meanders, parallel lines, and trilines. Many of those signs are related to the figures of the bird and the snake, which are linked to heavenly, earthly, and subterranean worlds and regeneration.[12] But the

Fig. 23. A nineteenth-century house crowned by two crossed birds from the Kurpie region of Poland, 2002. (Photo by author.)

Fig. 24. Quetzalcoatl, Mesoamerican civilizing god, represented as a plumed serpent, Teotihuacan, Mexico, 1992. (Photo by author.)

central and most pervasive life-giving and regenerative symbol from prehistory to modern times is the triangle, representing the sacred pubic triangle of the goddess.[13] This symbol can already be observed in the lower Paleolithic, ca. 300,000 BC, as well as in today's triangular images of the Virgin Mary (for example, the Spanish Guadalupe (see plate 6), the Virgin of Regla, or the Brazilian Aparecida and the Holy Trinity). It appears frequently in Neolithic art as a triangular stone representing the goddess. In ceramics from Sardinia and the Ukraine dating from the fourth millennium BC, we can observe triangular goddess figures with sprouts, branches, suns, and heads

Fig. 25. Virgin of Regla, Chipiona, Spain. (Author's collection.)

Fig. 26. Our Lady Aparecida, Brazil. Religious card. (Author's collection.)

Fig. 27. The Holy Trinity, *Misal Diario*, Spain, 1954. (Gilberta Turner's collection. Reproduced with permission.)

radiating as the sun—the same sprouts and sun that later reappear as a halo on the images of the Christian Mother of God.

By the end of the Neolithic period, between 4,500 and 2,000 BC, Indo-European warriors invaded Europe, the Near East, and South Asia, substantially altering society, religion, and lifestyle. Old Europe became warfare oriented, class stratified, and patriarchal. Women and the all-encompassing female deities were stripped of their power and superseded by their male counterparts. For example, in the Roman Empire women began to be known as their father's daughters or their husband's wives. In classical times, Old European goddesses were eroticized and militarized, becoming brides, wives, and daughters of the Indo-European gods. This contrasted with the earlier matrilocal household where women raised their own children, owned property, and practiced matrilineal succession. Nonetheless, enclaves still exist where women have retained parts of their traditional power. These are found in the Greek, Aegean, and Mediterranean region as well as other peripheral areas of northern and western Europe inhabited by such peoples as the Basques and the Balts.

But how did the situation unfold in the Balto-Slavic area of eastern and central Europe, on the periphery of today's so-called Western civilization? Was the marginality of this area a factor in the preservation of its ancient customs and beliefs? In order to answer this question, we need to examine the area's traditional folktales and rituals.

FOLKLORE AND RITUAL

Perhaps the best-known figure appearing in Polish and Russian folktales is BabaYaga/Jędza/Wiedźma/Czarownica, an old witch with magical powers, especially those of transformation. She dwells in a dense forest, spinning and cooking in a hut that rests on bird's feet (see fig. 10). The hut itself has spinning abilities. Her thread is made of bones and entrails of the dead, and her hut is surrounded by a fence of human skulls and bones. The house, constructed of human body parts, is guarded by a lock formed of a mouth with sharp teeth and a pair of hands. Baba Yaga travels in a mortar, pushing herself along with a pestle and erasing her tracks with a birch broom. The mortar and the pestle are simultaneously instruments of destruction and nurture, serving both to grind grain and prepare flax for spinning cloth. They also symbolize human sexual organs. Riding the pestle (in Russian) or the broom (in Polish folklore) (see fig. 22), Yaga rules over the masculine generative organ. Baba Yaga cooks and eats human flesh, her cannibalistic tendencies recalling memories of human sacrifice. She bestows both birth and death. In her double function of genetrix and cannibal, she helps the hero to reach his bride (Hubbs 38–39, 47; Afanasiev, "Vasilisa prekrasnaia" 161). According to Erich Neumann, "baking, like weaving, is one of the primeval mysteries of the Feminine. The woman is a giver and transformer of nourishment" (234). In order to achieve whatever she considers necessary for the continuance of life on earth, Baba Yaga not only bakes and weaves, she may transform into a bird, a reptile, or a fish. Like Mother Earth, she feeds and devours life.

Although Baba Yaga—the old hag—has been demonized, in folktales she also retains positive qualities. In fact, she is "good" and "bad," young and old, concurrently. She devours children, but she helps couples to reunite; she appears as a horrifying, bird of prey-like old woman, but she is also the beautiful and wise princess or the young maiden. She may be represented as twofold or triune, as when she appears as the three sisters. The number two symbolizes the beginning, creation, the balance of opposites, as well as the feminine principle and the Great Mother, among others (Kopaliński 76). According to Erich Neumann, "the correlation of the starry firmament with the Feminine determines the whole early view of the world [and it is the] primordial darkness which bears the light as moon, stars, and sun, and almost everywhere these luminaries are looked upon as the offspring of the Nocturnal Mother" (224, 212). Similarly, Gardner affirms that the Black Madonna "is black because Wisdom (Sophia) is black, having existed in the Chaos before the Creation" (105). She is also a triune goddess of birth, death, and regeneration, embodied in the Aztec trinity Xochiquetzal–Tonantzin–Toci,[14] or young virgin–mature mother–old wise woman. A similar trinity of goddesses existed in the Old European (Neolithic) society, embodied today by the Slavic folk figures of Rusałka–Mother Moist Earth–BabaYaga, as well as in the Yoruba-Brazilian goddesses Oxum–Iemanjá–Nanã, worshipped in Candomblé and Umbanda, and the Yoruba-Cuban goddesses Ochún–Yemayá–Naná, worshiped in Regla de Ocha or Santería. "The reason for their appearance in threes or nines, or more seldom in twelves, is to be sought in the threefold articulation underlying all created things . . . [and] it refers most particularly to the three temporal stages of all growth (beginning-middle-end, birth-life-death, past-present-future)" (Neumann 228).

In the quintessential Russian folktale "Vasilisa prekrasnaia" (Vasilisa the Fair) (Afanasiev, "Vasilisa prekrasnaia" 159–65), all of the above elements are present. There is the triune old woman represented by the bad stepmother, the dual Baba Yaga, and the good old woman. In the good old woman's house, the beautiful orphan girl Vasilisa performs all the tasks of a life creatrix, represented by spinning flax, weaving cloth, and sewing shirts. The czar, impressed by her beauty and skills, falls in love and marries her. The old woman and the doll who guided the girl are not forgotten but invited to live in the palace. Vasilisa achieves her incredibly good fortune by employing all of her abilities, including her intuition (represented by the doll), and her wisdom (represented by the old woman). Only after a series of hardships and difficult tasks does the maiden learn all the lessons that qualify her as a mature and wise woman.[15] Although the royal wedding serves as an ending to the story, its promise of procreation will originate a new cycle of birth, growth, death, and regeneration, typifying Vasilisa as the triune goddess of all creation—young, mature, and old—who spins all life out of herself. The mysterious white, red, and black riders that appear in the tale correspond to the three sacred colors of the goddess as Virgin, Mother, and Crone respectively (Walker, *Woman's Dictionary of Symbols* 89).[16]

In the Polish tale "O królewnie zaklętej w żabę" (About a Princess Bewitched into a Frog) (Gliński 38–47), Baba Yaga helps a young prince win the competition for the kingdom.[17] He acquires a frog-bride,[18] who in reality is an enchanted princess—the daughter of the queen-sorceress Światowida. The king-father gives the kingdom to the youngest son because his bride possesses abilities unmatched by the brides selected by the two older sons. The criteria of the competition set by the king-father are not based on the abilities of his three sons but rather on those of their brides. This may be seen as a remnant of matriarchal times when society was governed by priestesses representing the Mother Goddess of all creation. The fact that the frog princess is the daughter of Światowida underscores this hypothesis.[19]

Hidden, symbolic meanings permeate Slavic folklore. Ancient ways of life were consciously and subconsciously preserved in rituals and customs. By analyzing them, we can reconstruct the principles and beliefs governing the pre-Indo-European social structure. One such ritual, known in several European countries and preserved in Poland even today, is Topienie Marzanny (Drowning of Marzanna),[20] and the subsequent Gaik Zielony (Little Green Grove). On the fourth Sunday of Lent, a female straw figure dressed in a maiden's attire was carried away from the village and drowned or burned. Then, a Maik, Gaik, or Nowe Lato (New Summer), represented by a large, adorned branch, was carried into the village. This ritual is believed to symbolize the destruction of winter and the revival of nature. Sometimes a male figure, Marzaniok, was also carried by young boys. The latter tradition is related to the Ukrainian Kostrobonko—a dying and reviving spring god (Ogrodowska 148–53). According to Orgelbrand (625), during the feast of Zielone Świątki on the sixth Sunday after Easter, usually in May, the oldest *baba* (woman) of a village was carried away to a tavern on a cart covered with fresh green branches called *Maj*. This feast, celebrating abundance and fertility, was accompanied by the use of such symbolic elements as green branches, water, eggs, and fire as well as sacrifices (Ogrodowska 240, 243). In this ritual, we can observe the supplanting of the old with the new, signifying the regeneration of vital forces of nature.

One of the most important ritual dates in European cultures was the summer solstice, preserved in Poland to this day as Sobótka, Kupalnocka, or Noc Świętojańska. It is celebrated on the night between the 23 and 24 June, a date dedicated to Saint John (Święty Jan), but its connection to this Christian saint is very weak. It has more to do with Kupało, a pagan god celebrated previously on this date. The summer solstice was a feast of fertility, abundance, and ritual cleansing with water and fire. It celebrated sexual union with a series of magical practices, including dancing *korowody*, or round dances performed by women around campfires, in which young maidens wrapped themselves in the magical herb *bylica* (*Arthemisia*). In another practice, unmarried women disrobed, loosened their hair, gathered *nasięrzal* (adder's tongue) from the meadows and, before midnight, repeated magical incantations believed to make them attractive to young men. It was also customary to jump across campfires and sing special songs. These celebrations sanctioned sexual freedom and even ritual orgies. Predictably, most of the above practices were forbidden by the church as early as the fourteenth and fifteenth centuries (Ogrodowska 260–66). The contemporary ritual of Wianki (Wreaths) is a remnant of such celebrations and is still as popular today in the cosmopolitan cities of Warsaw and Cracow as it is in small villages. It is customary that on 23 June, unmarried women weave wreaths out of field flowers, light a candle on them, and place them in the river. The movements of the wreaths in the water foretell the woman's future regarding love and marriage. The wreath, a symbol of virginity, is later substituted by a headpiece at the marriage ceremony, a ritual that includes cutting the woman's hair.

Another Polish tale, "Czarownica znad Bełdan" (The Witch from Bełdany) (Oleksik 163–68), portrays the witch as a woman who is trying to untangle her very long hair from the bulrushes growing along the shore of the Bełdany lake. During the three days that she is engaged in that task, the fishermen are afraid to fish in the lake. They say that the witch is "washing her hair." This *czarownica* also has a young "double" or "daughter" to whom she gives a miraculous necklace.[21] The owner of this necklace is imbued with eternal beauty and youth while wearing it. But there is one condition—if the young woman falls in love with a man, both of them will be doomed. Despite the forewarning, the village girl falls in love and ends up drowning herself in the lake.

The linkage of both women to the lake, to long hair, and to each other takes us on an exploration of another Slavic folk figure—the Rusałka (see fig. 19).[22] The Rusałka, which most often appears as one of a group, is believed to be a young maiden with long, flowing hair, running freely in the proximity of lakes and trees. The combination of lake and tree symbolizes the center of the world where extraordinary power is generated. The lake is also a female and fertility symbol as well as a frontier between single/married life and life/death (Bartmiński 355, 174). The Rusałka represents the untamed life-giving and life-taking forces of woman and nature.[23] She enhances reproduction, as her behavior is reenacted in women's orgiastic fertility rites, but she is also believed to be dangerous because of her connection to the underworld and water realm of the dead. Like the siren, she may lure men into the deep waters of no return. Yet, there is a strong connection between the Rusałka and Baba Yaga. They are both dichotomous figures—givers of life and perpetrators of destruction—connected to weaving and to spinning and able to control the forces of nature. They are believed to spin out rain, bring warmth, and make the land fruitful (Zguta 229). They also have powers of transformation. In fact, they are two aspects of the same triune goddess of all creation, corresponding to the three faces of the waxing, full, and waning moon and represented by the archetypes of the young maiden, the mother/lover, and the old wise woman.

MOTHER EARTH AND MOTHER OF GOD

The mother archetype is embodied by the powerful Mother Moist Earth or the Holy Earth among the eastern and the western Slavs, respectively. She is the mother of all

Fig. 28. Baba or Żywa—goddess as the center of a flowering Tree of Life, Poland. Paper cutout. (Author's collection.)

and should be venerated and relied upon in adversity as well as in happiness. This figure is probably derived from such all-encompassing Great Mother figures as the Finno-Slavic goddess Mokosh and the Slavic Złota Baba (Golden Woman), sometimes represented with a child in her arms.[24] She has also been called goddess Zhiva (Żywa) or Zhivie (Żywie) in Poland. Other names assigned to her were Zalęta, Języ Baba, Baba Jaga, and Baba-Jędza (which correspond to the Russian Baba Yaga). There are many places in central Europe that take their name from this ancient goddess: Babia Góra, Babi Jar, Babiec, Babie Łono, or Babenberg (Perkowska 22; Orgelbrand 625). Many of these places are mountains, high places perceived as holy dwellings of the gods (Bartmiński 86). According to Marija Gimbutas (*Living Goddesses* 209), "the earth mother was worshipped on mountain summits crowned with large stones." Stones were also believed to be the bones of Mother Earth (Kopaliński 139). The figure of a Golden Baba may still be seen today on ritual embroidered towels in Russia and the Ukraine and on cutouts used to adorn peasant houses in Poland. This is also the western Slavic goddess Zhiva (*żywa*—"alive") represented as the center of a flowering Tree of Life. Related effigies, called *kamienne baby* (stone babas), were represented as either a male or an old female and were widespread throughout the central Asian and Black Sea-area steppes (Doroszewski 280; Orgelbrand 624). According to Hubbs, the huge stone female figures are of Scythian and Finno-Ugric origin and date from the first millennium AD (8, 20).[25] Currently, the figure of the Baba is reemerging. Between 28 June and 3 August 2003, Warsaw's art gallery Galeria Laboratorium held an exposition of works by the young artist Alicja Łukasiak, entitled *Baba*. It featured overweight and incomplete woman's body-shaped sculptures made out of dough of wheat, rye, and yeast.[26]

During transitions from one set of beliefs to another, two or more religions often coexist (as in the Russian *dvoievierie*, where official Christianity was paralleled by pre-Christian peasant practices). We may also observe the creation of transition figures and phenomena, such as the Russian, Ukrainian, Bulgarian, and Macedonian cult of the saint Paraskeva Piatnitsa, who was "on the margin between official sanction and denunciation" (Hubbs 121). In contrast to Mary, "the Most Pure" mother-maiden ruling from the sky, Paraskeva was called "the Dirty One" and was represented as an elderly woman connected to earth fertility, a spinner of flax and wool whose great head was identified with a spindle. She was one of the very few Russian female saints, certainly a pagan deity accommodated to the demands of the church. In fact, according to some Russian scholars, the figure of Paraskeva stemmed from the ancient cult of Mokosh, goddess of marriage and spinning. Piatnitsa, whose name means "Friday," was associated with the heathen cult of Fridays and with trade. Other female deities whose sacred day was Friday were the western Slavic Zhiva, the Roman Venus, and the Scandinavian Freya. The pagan cult of Fridays, when orgiastic rites reinforcing female fertility were performed, was officially banned by the Patriarch of Constantinople in 1589 (Hubbs 20, 117–18; Lazariev 24). Earliest traditions that linked women to Mother Earth also valued them as the important life-giving and nourishing entities. The cycle of life depended on their fertility. This concept was promoted by orgiastic rites performed near lakes by women. The tenacity of such practices was underscored by the difficulty the church had in eradicating them. As a material witness, we have the fifteenth-century sermon to the Poles making reference to the "feminine fertility nature of these orgiastic rites . . . [performed by] girls and women playing and dancing . . . we hear that they do not allow the male relatives—only female in the family—to take part . . . and much evil takes place."[27] The freedom and power of contemporary Slavic women most likely spring from this ancient tradition of powerful females dating back to the matriarchal societal structures of the Scythians, Sarmatians, and proto-Slavs.[28]

On embroidered ritual napkins, such as the ones offered to Paraskeva, woman is often represented as a spinner. This image reflects the divinity who "spins all living things out of her body" (Hubbs 25). In fact, the actions of spinning, weaving, sewing, and dancing symbolize the stimulation of fertility. Ritual dances are often performed near lakes and ponds and, like the round dance *khorovod* (Russ.)/*korowód* (Pol.), symbolize the "womb which 'spins out' life" (Hubbs 249). The proximity to water and moisture further enhances the sexual connotations of the above actions. The goddess Mokosh and Saint Paraskeva were often portrayed spinning next to a well of water, and flax spinning wheels, wool thread, and fabrics were thrown into these wells as offerings. The picture of Saint Paraskeva, often paired with the picture of Mother of God Mary on the reverse side, was placed next to water wells (Ivanov and Toporov, "K rekonstrukcii Mokoshi" 192–93). The concept of the female as spinner of life is reflected in the portrayal of Slavic folk figures such as Rusałki, Baba Yaga, and the Christian Mother of God as spinners.[29] In ancient Greece human fate was directed by the goddess Moera. Later, she was substituted by three Moerae or Parcae, identified with the three stages of human life. The three deities were represented "spinning a thread of gold, silver, or wool. . . . Clotho, the youngest, put the wool round the spindle, Lachesis spun it, and Atropos, the eldest, cut it off when a man had to die" (Murray 227–28). Similarly to the Slavic witch Baba Yaga, Aztec and pre-Aztec goddesses, such as Tlazolteotl–Ixcuina, represent the Great Mother and genetrix of all living things. "The Great Mother not only spins human life but also the fate of the world, its darkness as well as its light . . . all the Great Mothers—Neith, Netet, and Isis; Eileithyia or Athene; Urth, Holda, Percht, or Ixchel; and even the witch in the fairy tales—are spinners of destiny" (Neumann 229, 228). Several Aztec and pre-Aztec goddesses, such as Tlazolteotl–Ixcuina (Goddess of Filth–Lady Cotton), Teteo-innan or Toci (Mother of the Gods or Our Grandmother), Temazcalteci (Grandmother of the Bathhouse), Huixtocihuatl (Goddess of Salt), are represented with headbands and ear adornments of unspun cotton, spindles wound with cotton, and/or hanging strands of cotton (Sullivan 8–21; Durán plate 24). The goddess Ciuacoatl (Snake Woman) "carried a turquoise-colored weaving stick" (Sahagún, *Florentine Codex* 1:4), and the Mociuaquetzque, or women who died in childbirth, thus ascending to the status of goddesses, "took, they sought the spindle, the weaving stick, the reed basket; they sought all the equipment of women" (6:163). The ceiba (*yaxche*), or sacred Mayan cotton tree, which produces silky cotton thread, symbolizes the eternal spinning of life, and the flowers symbolize human hearts:

> I come to weave
> Smiling flowers
> Into the Flowering Tree. . . .
> You have come back from there,
> You are interweaving them.
> Let's enjoy. (Garibay 1:29)

The Virgin Mary, who is represented in medieval paintings spinning thread, is a heiress to this aspect of the feminine as spinner of fate.[30] Another spinning figure is immortalized in the popular Catalonian song "La Balanguera" (The Spinner), since 1996 declared the official anthem of the island of Mallorca. The central figure of the song—the female spinner—identified with the motherland, spins the thread of the past, present, and future in an eternal cycle of birth, death, and regeneration:

> The mysterious Balanguera,
> as a spider of subtle art,
> empties, empties the distaff,[31]
> she takes the thread of our lives.

> As a Parca she ponders,
> weaving the cloth for tomorrow.
> The Balanguera spins, spins,
> the Balanguera shall spin.

> . . .

Fig. 29. *Virgin Mary with a Distaff*, Master of Erfurt, fifteenth century, oil on canvas. (Gemaeldegalerie, Staatliche Museen, Berlin, Germany. Photo by Joerg P. Anders. Reproduced with permission of Bildarchiv Preussischer Kulturbesitz/Art Resource, NY.)

From traditions and hopes,
she weaves the banner for the youth.
as one who makes a bride's veil,
with golden and silver hair.

Of the childhood that spins up,
of the old age that goes away.
The Balanguera spins, spins,
the Balanguera shall spin. (Alcover 3–5)

This spinning action is related to a rhythmic, circular dance from which "La Balanguera" takes its name.[32]

The superimposition of Christian over pagan belief systems often took the physical form of Christian temples and sanctuaries built on the sites of pagan worship.[33] A good example is the current sanctuary of Święty Krzyż in southern Poland, erected on the ruins of a pagan temple to the triple deity Świst, Poświst, and

Pogoda[34] or Pogoda, Gwizd-Pogwizd, and Łada.[35] This pagan triune was later re-placed by the theology of the Holy Trinity. The sanctuary of Święty Krzyż (Holy Cross) was built on top of the mountain Łysiec or Łysa Góra (Bold Mountain), a holy mountain surrounded by a stone wall that most likely served to delimit the ritual space. In the world's oldest beliefs, a mountain was considered a holy place inhabited by gods, and structures pertinent to the cult were placed upon it (Bartmiński 86). In the Polish and Russian languages, the earth, the mountains, and the rivers are significantly feminine in gender and may be called *Mateczka Ziemia* (Polish for "little mother earth"), *Matushka Zemlia* (Russian) and *Mateczka Woda* (Polish for "little mother water"), *Matushka Volga, Don*, and so on. (Russian) (Perkowska 168; Hubbs xiii–xiv). In the eighteenth-century church standing today on top of the Łysiec mountain, an enormous painting representing the Holy Trinity dominates the space. Curiously, nearby villages are called Bieliny, Makoszyn, and Złota Woda, alluding to the ancient holy white (*biały*) and gold (*złoty*) colors. We cannot help but speculate about the previously discussed goddesses Złota Baba (Golden Woman) and Mokosh (spelled "Mokosz" in Polish), whose names closely resemble the names of these villages. According to a widespread legend, "Łysiec," or "Bold Mountain,"[36] is the place of witches' Sabbaths.[37] This presumed darkness is countered by the nearby Jasna Góra, or "Bright" (meaning holy) Mountain, where the sanctuary of the most venerated Polish icon, ironically the Black Madonna of Częstochowa, is located. In the thirty kilometers that separate the "dark" from the "bright" mountain, we find a proliferation of villages and towns whose names seem to echo the name of the great goddess: Mokrzesz, Pniaki Mokrzeskie, Wola Mokrzeska, Małogoszcz, and Magdasz. In a recent visit to research this area, two intriguing elements surfaced. One was the realization that, unlike any other Polish region I know, the traditional iron road crosses were placed upon enormous stones, as in the village of Saint Anna (Święta Anna—corresponding to the archetype of the old woman or mother of Mary).[38] The second was the common practice among villagers of placing the image of the Black Madonna in niches built into the houses. This area is well known for its caves, natural formations traditionally understood as parts of the earth's womb.[39] This accumulation of data strongly suggests that long before Christianity arrived, this area was the site of ancient sanctuaries over which Catholic monasteries and crosses were constructed following the baptism of Poland in AD 966.

Mother Earth embodies the fertility, nourishment, and abundance aspects of the triune goddess of birth, death, and regeneration. The earth gives life to everything but also takes in dead plants, animals, and humans, only to be reborn with new life each spring. The earth is perceived as a living being who "talks, breathes, sleeps, moans,

Fig. 30. Polish village of Mokrzesz, 2002. (Photo by author.)

Fig. 31. Iron cross placed on a stone, village of Święta Anna, Poland, 2002. (Photo by author.)

smiles" (Bartmiński 55). In Polish peasant poetry, she is specifically identified with a woman, a mother who gives birth and feeds her children:

> People took me up
> the earth nourished me
> how may I not love her
> she was a mother to me.[40]

Also, she will receive her children at death:

> And when death makes your tired head to lay
> this mother-earth will never reject you
> but she will gladly take you into her motherly womb.[41]

The earth represents the utmost ethical values of truth and justice and is invoked as a witness in disputes. She may punish the guilty by devouring them (approximates *zapaść się pod ziemię*) (Bartmiński 27, 30). Not only does she accept and treat all humanity equally, regardless of social status—"The earth like a mother hugged them in her innards, the same a nobleman, a peasant, and an artisan"[42]—but she is also the utmost judge and oath-taker, to whom sins are confessed. "When conflicts over land occurred, the judge who was appointed the 'voice' of Mother Earth was required to eat some soil before pronouncing his verdict" (Hubbs 57). The Polish expressions of self-condemnation "Let the earth swallow me up" (*Niech mnie ziemia pochłonie*) or "Let the earth sink under me" (*Niech się ziemia pode mną zapadnie*) are remnants of old earth oaths (Bartmiński 30). Furthermore, at contemporary funerals it is still customary to say *Niech mu/jej ziemia lekką będzie* (Let the earth be light to him/her, meaning Let the earth accept him/her).

Even today, Mother Earth is widely venerated in Slavic countries. Pope John Paul II knelt to kiss her whenever he visited the Polish land. Emigrants took with them treasured pieces of their native earth: "On 2 November 1830, Chopin left Warsaw. . . . They used to tell and write, that upon leaving they handed him over an urn with his native earth, which seems to have been put into his grave."[43] The earth was also used in magical rites for love, protection, and healing, and touching her gave power and enabled magical transformation (Bartmiński 23, 43). Even at present, in the Christian Orthodox church, believers touch the ground each time they make the sign of the cross. The black and moist earth, equated with protection and nourishment, is the holiest and most venerated:

> And then kneeled down [the peasant] on her [the earth's] black bosom
> full of sun and of moisture
> and started to whisper a low supplication . . .
> give us earth—dear mother
> the black tasty bread.[44]

In Russian culture, the most venerated figure was called Mother Moist Earth, and black earth was considered the most fertile.

The earth, as giver and taker of all life, is the Great Mother. In Greek mythology, the mountains, the sea, and the sky outcropped from the Mother Earth, Gaia, who was personalized as Demeter. The cult of Mother Earth as the origin of all creation goes back to matriarchal times and manifests itself in such goddesses as Prythiwi, Isis, Ishtar, Cybele, Ceres, Aphrodite, Venus, and Freya. In fact, Adam, the first man, according to Judeo-Christian tradition, was formed out of clay, and his name is derived from *adamah*—earth (Heb.). In Europe, the cult of the earth as the Mother Goddess continued in the form of a popular Marian devotion (Bartmiński 17–18; Durant 60).

It was expressed as the veneration of the God Birth-Giver, Boguroditsa, in Russia, and of the Mother of God, Matka Boska, in Poland.

The cult of the Mother Goddess took various forms: the black Isis, whose spouse was her own brother, Osiris; Ishtar, who sacrificed her lover Tammuz; or the mother-daughter duo of Demeter and Koré. In all Asia Minor, she was considered to be the mistress of her son (Cybele and Attis). A number of reliefs found near Ephesus portray the Mother Goddess as a central erect figure flanked by lions. Her son-lover, destined to die young, stands by her side (Quispel 12). The veneration of Mary emerges in the fourth century AD after failed missionary attempts to eliminate the widespread cult of Mother Earth. In AD 431, at the Council of Ephesus, Mary was officially proclaimed Theotocos, or Mother of God, and her temple was constructed next to the temple of Diana/Artemis (see fig. 15), the Greek black virgin goddess of fertility and regeneration (*The Madonna*). When the Greeks came to Ephesus in the twelfth century BC, this goddess was already worshipped there, and in the thirteenth century BC, she had her own temple (Quispel 11–12). Thus, "Ephesus which was once a center of the mother goddess [in the fifth century AD], became a center of the cult of the Mother of God" (13). "Greek Orthodoxy had accommodated the Hellenistic mysteries of Demeter and Koré at Eleusis to the liturgy of the Mass, stressing the birth, death, and rebirth of Christ as the Dying and Reviving God" (Hubbs 100). Thus, the Orthodox Church stresses motherhood and not virginity, unlike the Roman Catholic Church. This is also true for Catholic Poland, indicating that its cultural roots are closer to its eastern Slavic neighbors than to western ones who are not Slavs and do not share a common tradition.[45] A good illustration of the perception of Mary in the Orthodox Church is the Novogrodian painting *In Thee Rejoiceth* (*O Tebie raduietsia*). According to Lazarev: "the image of the Virgin [Bogomater' or God Birth-Giver] is rendered here in its cosmic significance, as the 'joy of every living thing'" (43). In fact, the God Birth-Giver is depicted here as central to the universe, sitting on a throne in front of a white, circular, world-encompassing temple, surrounded by angels, saints, and all living things.[46] The "Poem about a Beautiful Queen" is a valid indicator of the way Mary is perceived in Russian literature:

> Beautiful Queen God Birth-Giver!
> Hear the prayers of your servants,
> Receive our hot tears,
> The heavenly kingdom gates do not close,
> From eternal agony save us!
> Because you are the earth, the earth mother moist from tears! (Nikitin 108)

In this poem, as in the painting, it is clear that Mary performs the dual role of all-powerful mistress of the universe and Mother Moist Earth.

Similarly, the Babylonian goddess Ishtar, as well as the Sumerian goddess Inanna, corresponding to Greek Astarte, Semitic Ashtoreth, and Egyptian Isis, represented the creative principle in everything. She was the goddess of love, motherhood, war, and the creatrix and governess of the universe. She was titled the Virgin Mother, Queen of Heaven and Earth, and Lady of Hosts, Lady of Battles. She was regarded as guardian of the oppressed and bringer of justice. Her power made "the dead come to life, and the sick rise and walk" (Durant 235–36; Briffault 88–89). In the Book of Revelation, "the Virgin was identified with Isis, the Egyptian Queen of Heaven (*regina coeli*), who is being pursued by the monster Seth, and who gives birth to a divine child called Horus (i.e., the young sun)" (Quispel 77). The paradoxical Gnostic text *The Thunder, Perfect Mind* implies the "absolute transcendence of the [feminine] revealer, whose greatness is incomprehensible":

> For I am the first and the last.
> I am the honored and the scorned one.
> I am the whore and the holy one.
> I am the wife and the virgin.
> . . .
> I am the barren one
> and many are her [*sic*] sons.
> . . .
> I am the silence that is incomprehensible
> . . .
> I am the utterance of my name.
> . . .
> For I am the one who alone exists,
> and I have no one who will judge me.
> (*Nag Hammadi Library* 271–77)

Both Polish literature and folklore point to the tremendous meaning the Mother of God figure holds for the nation and its inhabitants. She is considered and called the Queen of Heaven and Earth, the Mother of All Creation, and the Queen of Poland. In Marian songs she is named Mistress of the Sky, of the Beginning and of the End and Eternal Lady, and is placed above the moon, the sun, and the stars: "More beautiful than the moon, purer than the stars, brighter than the sun" (Perkowska 27).

In Polish popular religiosity and apocryphal writings, where the *sacrum* and the *profanum* are parts of the same reality, the Mother of God is a protectress and a creator or a cocreator of the world. This is apparent in such Marian songs as "Pieśń do Najświętszej Maryi Panny" (Song to the Holiest Virgin Mary), which states: "Before God created this earth/I was already conceived," or "Zawitaj Córko Ojca Przedwiecznego" (Come Daughter of the Eternal Father):

> Before the heavens were formed,
> And the seas drowned into their shores,
> When God's wisdom was pondering the hills,
> You were there![47]

Mary is the mother of the world and of humanity, the regulator of human and natural life. The rural ritual calendar is organized according to moments related to earth's fertility, and Catholic Marian holidays have double names, one of which stands for functions of the earth ascribed to Mary.[48] This is a vestige of the phenomenon called dvoievierie, or "two faiths," in Russia and reinforces the conceptual cohabitation of pagan and Christian beliefs. The Polish Marian calendar reflects the agricultural cycle. It starts with the Dedication of the Virgin Mary on 21 November and is followed by the Cleansing of the Virgin—the Mother of God Gromniczna, or of the Candles, on 2 February; the Annunciation of the Virgin—the Mother of God Roztworna, or of the Opening, on 25 March; the Visitation of the Virgin—the Mother of God Jagodna, or of the Berries, on 2 July; the Ascension of the Virgin—the Mother of God Zielna, or of the Herbs, on 15 August; the Birth of the Virgin—the Mother of God Siewna, or of the Sowing, on 8 September; and the Virgin of Protection—the Russian Pokrov on 1 October. Each of these church Marian holidays has its corresponding name related to the functions of the earth with which Mary is identified. Thus, for example, Roztworna—"of the Opening"— refers to the fact that by the beginning of spring the earth is starting to open to receive the seeds of new life, just as a woman "opens" in the sexual act. The Mother of God of the Berries, in the very middle of the agricultural work cycle, indicates that it is already safe to gather and eat ripe berries. This observance probably originated in the pagan custom of offerings to the deities (Ogrodowska 273). The Mother of God of the Herbs is the most important holiday in both the agricultural and the Catholic Marian calendar, and it is related to the feast of the harvest. At this time women carry nosegays of crops, including sprouts of grain, vegetables and fruits, flax, poppies, and medicinal herbs and flowers to be blessed in the churches.

Fig. 32. Woman selling nosegays of herbs, sprouts of grain, and flowers in front of a Warsaw church. Feast of the Mother of God of the Herbs, 15 August 1998. (Photo by author.)

These are later removed and placed in the fields, barns, and houses next to the "holy picture" for protection of people and animals. They are believed to have magical and medicinal powers and are used to heal human and animal disease. The fifteenth of August is also the feast of abundance and fertility when couples traditionally get married.[49] The Mother of God of the Sowing initiates the beginning of fall agricultural labor, while the day of Protection of the Virgin on 1 October ends the farming calendar. Several of these holidays indicate crucial points in the natural cycle, and their dates are considered to be especially favorable for magical practices and unusual events to occur. For example, for the Mother of God of the Opening, when the earth is waking up at the beginning of spring, it is believed that "serpents go up the trees and listen to ringing, and the one that hears it gets its head attached to its body, and if it has seven heads it becomes a dragon" (Eisele and Renik 42–43). Again, it is significant that in the official Marian holidays the Western name of "Maiden" or "Virgin" is used, while in the traditional understanding of these celebrations only the name "Mother of God" appears.[50]

PATRIOTIC MARY

Mary as Mother Earth is also linked to the notion of one's own mother, family, motherland, and the state. Thus, she is called Matka Polka and Matka Polska, indicating that she is Mother Pole and Mother Poland.[51] In her name, and under her protection, numerous private and public battles for independence from foreign and internal oppression took place. Perhaps the poem "Strażniczko granic" (Guardian of Borders) best expresses this idea:

> Dressed in the glory and metal brilliance of white eagles
> you entered all Polish history, Knight full of grace.
> Mary! Keeper of Borders.
> Vigilant Queen of the outskirts and of the camps.
> Let not the enemy wound the Motherland, let the scars heal.
> Come, come to us with relief, wounded Lady!
>
> The Battle for God keeps burning on the faithful Polish land.
> Lady in a Queen's crown with your victorious feet
> tread down pride . . . Command us!
> Brave Mother, calm, safe harbor!
>
> We will go to your call fed by God's words.
> And always ready to serve our Queen![52]

The wounded image of Our Lady of Częstochowa, which may be seen as symbolic of the abused feminine, parallels the injuries inflicted on the Polish people and motherland. This idea is also voiced in the poem "Hymn do Czarnej Madonny" (Hymn to the Black Madonna) by Roman Brandstaetter:

> Pray,
> Madonna of Israel,
> Old Christian,
> Of the cypresses,
> Of Lucas,
> Virgin of Jasna Góra,
> Black,
> With your face full of scars
> Like the Polish land. (Rakoczy 157)

The wounds, presumably inflicted by infidel plunderers who desecrated the famous painting in 1430, appear as three saber lines on her left cheek. They are also a symbolic reflection of the wounds of Christ.

In the poem "Guardian of Borders," Mary, placed above God, is identified with the Polish land. She is the only queen and representative of the people. Where there are wars, injustices, and suffering, she is present as the hetman (military commander) and the bravest warrior who defends the country's borders. Conversely, she is also the "calm harbor," a refuge where her children can feel safe and sheltered, the children afflicted by hundreds of years of foreign invasions and partitions, Russian deportations, and German extermination camps.

In physical wars or in social battles, the Marian figure is a source of courage and the sole mainstay. This sentiment is expressed by Lech Wałęsa, a former shipyard worker and leader of the Solidarność movement who later became president of Poland. In a letter placed at the beginning of the 1995 book *Jasnogórska Hetmanka*, dedicated to the Mother of God as hetman of the Polish nation, he states:

> At a time when Poles' place on earth was not indicated by any border posts, by any national colors, nor White Eagles, the image of Our Lady of Jasna Góra infallibly indicated where we were. Through the centuries it accompanied the nation in good and bad fortune, in times of peace and in war struggles, which fate did not spare Poles. It adorned knights' armor, uhlans' saber blades, battle banners, and partisans' scapulars.
>
> As a testimony to this truth, the Hetman's Cloak, whose monograph is this book, came into being. Woven from mementos dearest to the soldier's heart, it constitutes a symbolic gift from the defendants of the Fatherland— to their dearest Hetman through the centuries—the God Birth-Giver of Częstochowa. It constitutes the expression of the deepest homage to the One who was with us always. To the One, who was with us in the shipyard and later in the armless struggle of "Solidarność." (Rakoczy 7)

As president of Poland, Lech Wałęsa signed this letter, "With a son's devotion," on 3 May 1995, a national holiday commemorating the anniversary of the first Polish constitution of 1791.

A similarly devotional attitude toward the Mother of God may be observed in both Cardinal Stefan Wyszyński and Pope John Paul II. In 1956, when the Primate of Poland was interned by the communist government, he originated the "National Vows of Jasna Góra" (Jasnogórskie Śluby Narodu), and in 1966, on the millennium of Polish Christianity, he initiated the "Act of Yielding Prisoners to Mary's Love" (Akt Oddania w Niewolę Miłości Maryi), by which the Mother of God officially became chief guardian of the Polish nation in the second millennium of Christendom. While still a bishop, Pope John Paul II coined the Latin motto *Totus Tuus* (All Yours), indicating his special devotion to Mary. In 1978, it became part of his papal coat of arms as a slogan guiding his life and his papacy (Podgórzec 25). Moreover, in 1979 he entrusted the Universal Church to the Mother of God and offered all people and nations of the world to her as captives of her motherly love (Smykowska 52).

The tradition of surrender and trust in the protection of the all-powerful God Birth-Giver dates from the beginning of Christianity. The oldest known prayer to her, "Under Your Protection," comes from third-century Egypt. Its currently known Greek version reads:

> To Your mercy
> we recur, God Birth-Giver,
> do not despise our requests in need,
> but save us from danger,
> The only pure one, the only Blessed one. (Paprocki 15)

The oldest Polish written text is the medieval hymn "Bogurodzica Dziewica" (God Birth-Giver Virgin), devoted to Mary. The only known copies of this document date from the fifteenth century. To this day, the worship of Mary is one of the most important features of Polish devotion, manifested in the veneration of thousands of her images. In the beginning of the twentieth century, over eleven hundred miraculous images of Mary were registered in the Polish land, and, in the 1980s, around four hundred such representations existed within the country's territory. The most famous of all such images is the icon of the Black Mother of God of Częstochowa (see plate 1). It is an icon of the Hodegetria type, most probably brought to Jasna Góra in Poland from Constantinople via Russia. The first written record, in the fifteenth-century work *Liber Beneficiorum* by the Polish historian Jan Długosz, refers to 1382 as the year that the God Birth-Giver was brought to the newly established Pauline monastery at Jasna Góra. From the beginning, it became a place of international pilgrimage, but it achieved unprecedented renown when this miraculous icon "saved" Poland from the Swedish invasion in 1655. The advancement of the Swedish troops, the so-called Swedish Deluge of Poland, was detained at the Jasna Góra monastery, and the country was saved from the invasion of Protestant Swedes. As their troops were much larger and stronger than the meager Pauline monks' defense at Jasna Góra, this was considered a miracle. In

1656, King Jan Kazimierz officially proclaimed the Mother of God of Częstochowa as Queen of Poland. When in 1717 Pope Clement XI crowned her by official decree, she also acquired the title of Queen of the World (Podgórzec 25–26).

This aspect of the Virgin as a powerful commander in chief and a defender of justice can already be found in the antecedents of the Old Testament, where she was called "Fortress of Heavenly Jerusalem," "Well-Formed Battle Array," and "Brave and Invincible Woman."[53] Later on, Mary was given the names of "Brave Hetman," "Wall of God's Kingdom," and "Invincible Bulwark of the Church." The cult of the Victorious God Birth-Giver (Gr. Nikopoi) was born during the Byzantine Empire's struggles against foreign troops. It is believed that her intervention saved Constantinople from invaders in AD 626. Later, this belief was reinforced by the Byzantine victory over the Arabs in 717. Similar triumphs were attributed to Mary during crucial battles of Russia, such as the defense of Novgorod in 1170, of Smolensk in 1238, of Borodino in 1380, of Moscow in 1395, and against Napoleon in 1812. In western Europe, an important milestone was the victory over the Turks at Lepanto in 1571 and the Polish victory over them in Vienna in 1683 (Rakoczy 21–22). All of these victorious battles waged against infidels such as Tartars or Turks were attributed to the miraculous patronage of the Mother of God, whose image was emblazoned on standards and banners carried into battle by Christian troops. This reinforced a tradition of Mary as a brave fighter and generous protectress of her devotees.

In Poland, the image of the God Birth-Giver as a Victorious Madonna was already present during the decisive 1410 Grunwald battle against the Teutonic Order.[54] Nevertheless, the beginning of a military cult of the Mother of God of Częstochowa may be traced to 1514 when King Zygmunt Stary deposited his victorious battle trophies at the Black Madonna altar in Jasna Góra. Later, victorious defense battles at Jasna Góra in 1655, 1771, and 1809 consolidated the link between religious and patriotic elements in Polish social consciousness.[55] The image of the Mother of God of Częstochowa, located at the Jasna Góra monastery, became a palladium of Poland, providing a symbol of national identity through numerous partitions, invasions, and wars. In recent history, the extremely devastating experience of Hitler's invasion of Poland in 1939 and the subsequent German occupation until 1945 brought about the almost total destruction of the capital city of Warsaw, among other cities, and the extermination of millions of people. During the occupation, the German governor of Poland, Hans Frank, wrote in his 1940 diary: "The Church is a central rallying point for Polish minds, which radiates in silence and therefore functions as a perpetual light. When all lights for Poland became extinct, then always there still was the Saint from Częstochowa and the Church. One should never forget about that" (Rakoczy 172).

Fig. 33. *Panno Święta co Jasnej bronisz Częstochowy, 1939–1945* (Holy Virgin, Thou Who Defend the Bright Częstochowa, 1939–1945) by J. Ostrywska, 1945. (Photo by Zbyszko and Maciej Siemaszko. Father Eustachy Rakoczy's collection. Reproduced with permission.)

The image of the Madonna as a powerful leader and protectress was already present in medieval Slavic representations of the Mother of God, such as the eleventh-century "Inviolable Wall" of the Saint Sophia cathedral in Kiev (Averinciev 340). From the Middle Ages, she protected and gave courage to fighters for just causes. Her image has been reproduced on banners, sabers, pectorals, breastplates, medallions, patriotic rings and wedding bands, watches and pins during innumerable struggles for the Polish land and for social justice. A contemporary example is the Solidarność (Solidarity) movement that started in the Gdańsk shipyards in 1980 and led to the collapse of the communist regime in 1989. During the Solidarity struggle, the Black Madonna image was worn on lapels, standards, and guidons and used as a stamp for Solidarity correspondence. Political prisoners elaborated her image on towels, in the same way that Chicano/a and Mexican prisoners in the United States and Mexico paint the Virgin of Guadalupe in their *arte de paño*. During martial law in Poland in 1982, Wanda Gałczyńska created a painting of the Black Madonna as a wounded *Stabat Mater* with a crying face and a halo of arrows. In 1977, a special "Hetman Coat" full of military insignia and medals from 1914 to 1945 was created for Our Lady of Częstochowa by Polish military veterans. In 1992, for the bicentennial celebration of the creation of the *Virtutti Militari* medal, a postal stamp with the Madonna wearing

Fig. 34. *Boże zbaw Polskę* (God Save Poland). Religious-patriotic image with dates of the 1831 and 1863 uprisings against foreign partitions of Poland, ca. 1900. (Photo by author.)

Fig. 35. The Black Madonna with the Polish coat of arms, the white crowned eagle, is a frequent motif in Polish religious-patriotic imagery. (Photo by author.)

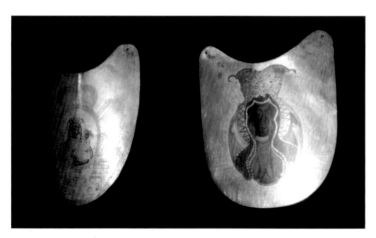

Figs. 36 and 37. Eighteenth-century pectorals with the Black Madonna of Częstochowa. (Photos by author.)

Fig. 38. Stamp from the Solidarność (Solidarity) mail with Our Lady of Częstochowa, 1982? (Photo by Zbyszko and Maciej Siemaszko. Father Eustachy Rakoczy's collection. Reproduced with permission.)

Fig. 39. *Matko uwięzionych i internowanych módl się za nami* (Mother of the Interned and the Imprisoned, Pray for Us). Banner with the Black Madonna made out of a towel by Solidarity prisoners in Darłówek, 1982. (Photo by Zbyszko and Maciej Siemaszko. Zygmunt Goławski's collection. Reproduced with permission.)

Fig. 40. Mexican American prisoners' *arte de paño*, or cloth art. Pillowcase with the Virgin of Guadalupe from the New Mexico State Prison. (Photo by Charles Mann. Reproduced with permission.)

Fig. 41. *Stabat Mater* by Wanda Gałczyńska, 1982. (Photo by Zbyszko and Maciej Siemaszko. Jasna Góra collection. Reproduced with permission.)

Fig. 42. Copy of the painting of Our Lady of Częstochowa Wearing a Hetman Coat, 1976–77. Copy of painting by Edward Sejfryd, project of coat by Eustachy Rakoczy, execution by Leon Machowski. (Photo by Zbyszko and Maciej Siemaszko. Jasna Góra collection. Reproduced with permission.)

Fig. 43. "Śmierć w powietrzu" (Death in the Air). Cover of the Polish magazine *Wprost*, 21 August 1994, with Our Lady of Częstochowa wearing a gas mask in protest against air pollution. (Author's collection. Reproduced with permission of the Publishing and Advertising Agency *Wprost.*)

the Hetman Coat was issued, thus bringing her image to people all over the world (Rakoczy 58). Currently, the image of the Black Madonna appears in environmental social struggles such as the one for clean air.[56]

Summary

The veneration of the Mother of God as an all-encompassing deity who dominates the earth and the universe is a worldwide phenomenon. As Mother Earth, Tonantzin, or Iemanjá, she is a triune goddess who spins life and death from within herself. She is a just goddess and offers protection to all without partiality. This tradition, generated in the ancient worship of the omnipotent mother of all creation, death, and regeneration, was later manifested in figures such as the Mother Moist Earth, the goddess Isis, and the Dark Madonna. Today in Poland, the Black Madonna, successor of Mokosh and the Holy Earth, is still the most venerated figure. Her functions go beyond religion, as she has also been a symbol of national identity and justice that has accompanied Poles throughout their history of struggles for freedom and independence. Her worship is still very vital and is being reinvigorated by adopting new functions in response to the demands of changing contemporary contexts.

[T]here used to come men and women, youths and maidens to these feasts; the concourse of people was great in these days, and everyone said let us go to the feast of Tonantzin; and when the church of Our Lady of Guadalupe was erected there they also call her Tonantzin. . . . and they come now to visit this Tonantzin from very far away, as far away as before, and this devotion is also suspect, because everywhere there are many churches of Our Lady, and they don't go there, but they come from distant lands to this Tonantzin, as formerly.

—Fray Bernardino de Sahagún

⚜

In the last extreme, in the most desperate cases, the cult of the Mexican Virgin is the only bond that unites them.

—Ignacio Altamirano

Chapter Two

The Virgin of Guadalupe and

the Creation of National *Mestizo* Identity

in Mexico

❧❦☙

The venerated figure of the dark female assumed various forms in different historical times and geographical areas. In chapter 1, I discussed the development of the phenomenon of the Black Madonna and its manifestation in central Europe, particularly in my native country, Poland. In this chapter I examine the case of the Mexican Virgin of Guadalupe as an example of syncretic blending of Spanish and Indian cultures, including her appropriation by the Creoles, and her significance for the creation of Mexican national consciousness. In addition, I study such complementary Mexican identity icons as La Malinche and La China Poblana, and I analyze pertinent universal symbols, their ancestral meaning, and their transformation in the Old and in the New World.

The Polish Black Madonna and
the Mexican Virgin of Guadalupe

While it is undeniable that Poland is one among many countries in the Eastern Hemisphere that hold an image of a Dark Madonna dear to their heart, an equally potent, parallel cult is found across the Atlantic in Mexico. What are the reasons for this surprising cross-cultural phenomenon? A quick comparison of the geographical and racial components sets these two countries worlds apart. Yet, in spite of their many differences, they are both fervent worshippers of a Dark Madonna, the Mother of God of Częstochowa (see plate 1), and the Virgin of Guadalupe (see plate 2), respectively. Moreover, both icons embody a specific national identity character whose impact is unparalleled in any other country.

Poland and Mexico would appear to have very little in common. Poland is a central European nation with a relatively uniform, Polish-speaking population of primarily Slavic origin. Conversely, Mexico is located at the southern end of

North America and contains a multilingual, multiracial population composed of descendants of Spaniards, other Europeans, Indians, mestizos, blacks, mulattos, and a small component of Asians. Besides the official Spanish, sixty-two indigenous languages are spoken ("The Indigenous Languages of Mexico"). With the baptism of Poland in AD 966, a date also corresponding to the beginnings of Poland's statehood tradition, Catholicism established an early influence. Mexico did not experience that influence until the beginning of the Spanish Conquest, 1519–21, and many centuries passed before independent statehood was attained in 1821. Climate is also a point of contrast. While Poland experiences a harsh climate most of the year, Mexico's ranges from tropical to moderate.

In spite of these disparities, an examination of both countries from a popular and national religiosity point of view uncovers surprising analogies. The Mother of God of Częstochowa for Poles and the Virgin of Guadalupe for Mexicans are each the utmost national and religious identity symbol. Moreover, the status of the dark Mary as the saint most often invoked for personal aid and protection is affirmed by her pervasive presence in home altars and innumerable churches, chapels, and shrines. She is the principal recipient of adoration, manifested in paintings, ex-votos, songs, poems, books, processions, and pilgrimages. Significantly, she is displayed on medallions and portraits worn close to the body. A special place is always reserved for her. Her church or basilica is the site of continual individual and group visits, besides being the object of major peregrinations that bring millions of people from all over the country and from abroad. They arrive on foot, walking the countryside for weeks, or on buses, cars, and planes, in order to share private and collective time with this embodiment of female protection, nourishment, consolation, and strength. The Dark Madonna is the understanding and forgiving mother of all creation that will grant her worshippers most of their requested favors. Her faithful perceive her as a repository of strength and courage, invoked in battles for freedom and social justice. Only she understands her children's needs and knows about their every hardship. As Eric R. Wolf comments, the Virgin of Guadalupe symbol represents "mother; food, hope, health, life; supernatural salvation and salvation from oppression. . . . [She] links together family, politics and religion; colonial past and independent present; Indian and Mexican" (38). In all of life's struggles, she is the one to be most often invoked directly, rather than her son Jesus or God the Father. Officially, she is the intercessor between mortal beings and a divine god, but in practice she is, in fact, a goddess, the ancient, all-powerful Great Mother of birth, death, and regeneration.

A historical approach reveals additional parallels between Mexico and Poland. In both countries, Catholicism was superimposed over preexistent native beliefs:

Fig. 44. Ex-votos at the Black Madonna of Częstochowa Sanctuary in Jasna Góra, Poland, 1997. (Photo by author.)

Fig. 45. Pilgrimage to the Virgin of Guadalupe Basilica at the Tepeyac Hill, Mexico City. (Photo by Jacqueline Orsini Dunnington. Reproduced with permission.)

in Poland over the Slavic religion and vestiges of the pre-Indo-European Goddess religion, and in Mexico over Indian, Mesoamerican religions. Documentation by various sources dating back to the sixteenth century confirms that, before Cortés's Conquest of Mexico-Tenochtitlan in 1519–21, Mesoamerican peoples worshipped the Mother Goddess Tonantzin–Ciuacoatl (Our Mother–Wife of the Serpent or Snake Woman) in her many forms, performing a yearly pilgrimage to her shrine on the Tepeyac hill. One of the aspects of this goddess was Teteo innan–Toci (Mother of the Gods or Our Grandmother), also named Tlalli yiollo (Heart of the Earth) and Grandmother of the Baths (Sahagún, *Florentine Codex* 1: 4.), an earth mother with powers of transformation:

> The yellow flower blossoms
> She's our mother
> . . .
> The goddess on the barrel cactus
> Is our mother
> The obsidian butterfly
> . . .
> She our mother
> She goddess of the earth
> . . .
> A deer's what she's become
> There on the desert plain[1]

GUADALUPE: BLENDING OF INDIAN AND EUROPEAN CULTURES

Tonantzin was revered in the same location where the Virgin of Guadalupe's 1531 apparitions later took place and where the Virgin's Basilica stands today. The sixteenth-century Franciscan Fray Bernardino de Sahagún, referring to the state of things at the onset of the Conquest, affirmed: "[O]n Tepeyacac. . . . they had a temple consecrated to the mother of the gods, called Tonantzin, which means 'our mother' . . . and people came from afar . . . and they brought many offerings" (*Historia general* [1956] 3: 352). Sahagún's testimony was further confirmed by Fray Juan de Torquemada, who wrote that Tonan or Tonantzin "was the divinity for whom [the Indians] felt the greatest devotion . . . innumerable crowds came from a hundred leagues around to celebrate the feast days of this goddess." In the same way, the Jesuit Clavijero validated that "Tonantzin had a temple on a hill one league north of Mexico City, and her feasts were attended by an immense concourse of people and many sacrifices."[2] During the conversion process of the Indian population, the ancient sacred place of Tepeyac was imbued with new powers by substituting the preexistent Aztec goddess with a Christian holy figure. This common practice was promoted by the church. At the first Council of Lima of 1552 it was ordered "that all the cult idols and edifices found in the villages where Christian Indians reside be burned and destroyed, and if the site is suitable, a church or at least a cross should be planted there."[3] Although this mandate was carried out, the goddess Tonantzin–Ciuacoatl did not disappear. More correctly, she was synthesized into the Virgin of Guadalupe. This new hybrid figure proved to be an ideal focal point of common faith for the eclectic population of New Spain. The process, however, did not occur without surprises.[4]

According to the Virgin of Guadalupe legend, Mary appeared to the humble Indian Juan Diego Cuauhtlatonzin on the Tepeyac hill in 1531, expressing her will that a temple be built for her there.[5] It took four apparitions, a miraculous healing, roses out of season, and the imprint of Mary's image on Juan Diego's rustic *tilma* (cloak) to finally convince Archbishop Zumárraga that the apparitions were true. Interestingly, sixteenth-century sources, such as Sahagún's *Historia general*, document the great devotion to the goddess Tonantzin–Ciuacoatl centered on the Tepeyac hill,[6] but there is no written record of the apparitions or of the Virgin of Guadalupe until the mid-seventeenth century.[7] In fact, what can be found prior to 1648 are omissions or attacks regarding the Tepeyac cult (Maza 39–40). For example, on 8 September 1556, Fray Francisco de Bustamante delivered a sermon in Mexico City, denouncing the excessive cult attached to a painting made by the Indian Marcos and placed in the Guadalupe shrine, because he saw this cult as idolatrous: "It seemed to him that the devotion that this city has placed on a certain hermitage or house of Our Lady, that they titled Guadalupe, (was) in great harm of the natives, because they made them believe that that image which an Indian [Marcos] painted was performing miracles . . . and that now to tell them [the Indians] that an image painted by an Indian was performing miracles, that this would be a great confusion and would undo the good that was sowed, because other devotions, like Our Lady of Loreto and others, had great grounds and that *this one would be erected so much without foundation*, he was astonished."[8] Even now, a great controversy surrounds the issue of the apparitions of the Virgin of Guadalupe to the newly baptized Indian Juan Diego. In countless studies related to different aspects of the apparitions and the famous image itself, such as those analyzing the paint, the fabric, the reflections in the Virgin's eyes, and so on, *aparicionistas* and *antiaparicionistas* try to prove their point.[9] What we know for sure is that apparitions are impossible to prove, especially six centuries later. Whether they were real or constructed, we will concentrate on the consequences the alleged apparitions brought to the colonial church, to the national cause, and to the people of Mexico.

Following a precedent established by other Spanish and Portuguese conquistadores, Hernán Cortés came to Tenochtitlan (today's Mexico City) in 1519, under the protecting banners of the Apostle Santiago (Saint James) and the Virgin Mary. In Spanish minds, the Conquest of America was the continuation of the *Reconquista* or Reconquest of Spain opposing eight centuries (AD 711–1492) of domination by the Moors. The year 1492—a date that marks the "discovery" of America—held multiple significance. It was the year of the final defeat of the Moors in Granada and of the expulsion of the Jews from Spain. Another important event of 1492 was the publication of the first Spanish (Castilian) grammar book and the first printed grammar of a vernacular language, *The Art of the Castillian Language*, by Antonio de Nebrija. These actions reflect the zeal to reinforce the political unity of Spaniards by "cleansing" their faith and by systematizing the official language of the newly united Spain. The popular dramatized dances of *Moros y cristianos*, representations of battles between Moors and Spaniards, continued in the New World as *Danza de la conquista, Danza de la pluma*, and *Tragedia de la muerte de Atahuallpa*, with one alteration—the Moors were replaced by the new infidels, the Indians.[10] The Virgin Mary, traditionally connected to the seas,[11] was long the protectress of the sailors (Nuestra Señora de los Navegantes) and of the Conquest. Cristóbal Colón (Columbus) named his flagship caravel Santa María in her honor. Hernán Cortés, like many other conquerors of the New World, came from the poor Spanish region of Extremadura.[12] He was a devotee of the Virgin of Guadalupe of Villuercas (see plate 6), whose famous sanctuary was located near his place of origin, Medellín. Villuercas, founded in 1340 by King Alfonso XI, was the most favored Spanish sanctuary from the fourteenth century until the times of the Conquest. It contained the famous black, triangular, fifty-nine-centimeter-high statue of the Virgin with the Christ on her lap, found by a local shepherd in 1322 (Lafaye 217, 295).

What demands our attention, though, is a different representation of the Virgin Mary carried on a banner accompanying Cortés in his Conquest of Mexico (see plate 7). This image portrays a gentle, olive-skinned Mary with folded hands, her head slightly tilted to the left, with hair parted in the middle. A red robe drapes her body, and a crown with twelve stars rests on her mantle-covered head. This rendering of the Virgin Mary bears a striking resemblance to the famous representation of the Mexican Virgin of Guadalupe.[13] The Italian historian Lorenzo Boturini (1702–75) described Cortés's banner thus: "A beautiful image of the Virgin Mary was painted on it. She was wearing a gold crown and was surrounded by twelve gold stars. She

Fig. 46. *La Virgen de los Mareantes* (Virgin of the Sailors), Spain. (Photo by author.)

has her hands together in prayer, asking her son to protect and give strength to the Spaniards so they might conquer the heathens and christianize them" (qtd. in Tlapoyawa). According to Kurly Tlapoyawa, the Indian Markos Zipactli's (Marcos Cipac de Aquino's) painting, which was placed at the Tepeyac temple, was based on Cortés's banner. This image is also very similar to a 1509 central Italian representation of the Madonna del Soccorso by Lattanzio da Foligno and by Francesco Melanzio.[14] The expression of her face, the pattern of her robe and mantle, and the halo surrounding her body and crown are almost identical to those of the Mexican Virgin of Guadalupe. The difference is that on the Madonna del Soccorso paintings Mary is represented defending her child from the devil with a whip or a club. Moreover, Francisco de San José, in his *Historia*, affirms that the Mexican Guadalupe is a copy of a relief sculpture of Mary placed in the choir opposite the Spanish Guadalupe statue in her Villuercas sanctuary.[15] On the other hand, Lafaye (233) as well as Maza (14) and O'Gorman (9–10) believe that the original effigy placed by the Spaniards at Tepeyac was that of the Spanish Guadalupe, La Extremeña, which only years later was replaced by the Mexican Virgin. Lafaye supposes that the change of images corresponds to the change of the dates of the Guadalupe celebration in

Mexico from 8 or 10 December[16] to 12 December: "we know for certain . . . that the substitution of the image took place after 1575 and the change of the feast day calendar after 1600" (233). Fray Bustamante's sermon discussed previously further supports this view.

Whether appearing in person or on canvas, Guadalupe is clearly a syncretic figure, possessing both Catholic and Indian elements. Her original name comes from the Arabic *wadi* (riverbed) and Latin *lupus* (wolf) (Zahoor). There have been speculations arguing that the Mexican Guadalupe's name comes from the Nahuatl *Cuauhtlapcupeuh* (or *Tecuauhtlacuepeuh*)—She Who Comes from the Region of Light as an Eagle of Fire (Nebel 124), or *Coatlayopeuh*—the Eagle Who Steps on the Serpent (Palacios 270). Curiously, Juan Diego's name was Cuauhtlatonzin (or Cauhtlatoahtzin). *Cuahtl* means "eagle," *Tlahtoani* is "the one who speaks," and *Tzin* means "respectful." This would suggest that Juan Diego was the Eagle Who Speaks, someone of a very high rank in the Order of Eagle Knights, ("Where Does the Name Guadalupe Come From?"), but some scholars doubt the very existence of Juan Diego. Since the Nahuatl language does not include the sounds of "d" and "g," the use of Guadalupe's name with the above meaning may indicate a native adaptation of the Arab-Spanish word.

As to other particularities of the Mexican Virgin of Guadalupe, her attire is of primary importance. Guadalupe's mantle is not blue, a characteristic of the European Virgins, but turquoise or blue-green,[17] which in Aztec mythology symbolizes water, fire, prosperity, and abundance. Turquoise is also the sacred color of the earth and moon Mother Goddess Tlazolteotl (Goddess of Filth), the water and fertility goddess Chalchutlicue (The One with a Skirt of Green Stones), and the fire and war god of the south, Huitzilopochtli. This god was believed to be "immaculately" conceived with a feather by his mother, the goddess Coatlicue (Lady of the Serpent Skirt). Blue is also the color of the south and of fire, and "in Mexican theological language 'turquoise' means 'fire.'" On the other hand, the Virgin's robe is red, signifying the east (rising sun), youth, pleasure, and rebirth (Soustelle 33–85). Thus, the Aztec symbology of the main colors worn by Mary—red and blue-green—corresponds to her Christian duality as young virgin and mature mother. It is indeed remarkable that the skin tone of the faces of both Guadalupe and the angel are brown, as in the image of Cortés's banner and the faces of the Indians themselves.

Additional correlations surface in prophetic literature between Guadalupe, the woman of the Apocalypse, and the Virgin of the Immaculate Conception (see plate 5).[18] According to the Book of Revelation, "there appeared a great wonder in heaven; a woman clothed with the sun, and a moon under her feet, and upon her head a crown

Fig. 47. Chalchutlicue, Aztec water and fertility goddess. (Photo by author.)

with twelve stars" (12:1, qtd. in Quispell 76). In her Mexican representations prior to the nineteenth century, Guadalupe also wore the crown with twelve stars, present on the image of Cortés's banner. Later, the crown was eliminated. Obviously, the distinctive elements of the Apocalyptic woman were reproduced quite precisely in the Virgin of Guadalupe image, who also wears a starry mantle, a crown of twelve stars, is surrounded by the rays of the sun, and stands on the moon. These cosmic elements—the sun, the moon, and the stars—played an important part in the Aztec religion as well. In fact, Tonacaciuatl, the goddess of the upper skies and the Lady of Our Nutrition, was also called Citlalicue—the One with a Starry Skirt (Soustelle 102). Other goddesses such as Xochiquetzal (Flowery Quetzal Feather), Tlazolteotl–Cihuapilli (Goddess of Filth–Fair Lady), Temazcalteci (Grandmother of the Bathhouse), Mayahuel (Powerful Flow, Lady Maguey), and Tlazolteotl–Ixcuina (Goddess of Filth–Lady Cotton) were represented with crescent-shaped adornments as part of their attire.[19] Moreover, the passage from Revelation "And when the dragon saw that he was cast unto the earth, he persecuted the woman. . . . And to the woman were given two wings of a great eagle, that she might fly to the wilderness, into her place, where she is nourished" (qtd. in

Quispel 162) coincides with the Aztec foundational legend. The legend describes how the Aztecs were instructed to look for the sign of an eagle devouring a serpent while perched on a *nopal* cactus. The sign functioned as a divine indication of a permanent homeland, Tenochtitlan, for the nomadic people coming from the northern region of Aztlán. The eagle motif occurs frequently in Aztec mythology. For example, the goddess Ciuacoatl, or Wife of the Serpent (also identified with Tonantzin), appears in her warrior aspect adorned with eagle feathers:

> The eagle
> The eagle Quilaztli
> With blood of serpents
> Is her face circled
> With feathers adorned
> Eagle-plumed she comes
> . . .
> Our mother
> War woman
> Our mother
> War woman
> Deer of Colhuacan
> In plumage arrayed[20]

The association of the Virgin of Guadalupe with the eagle and the cactus may be seen in New Spain's iconography as early as 1648,[21] and it intensifies during the nationalist surge of the mid-eighteenth century.

THE NATURALIZATION OF GUADALUPE

The first historical references to the Mexican Virgin of Guadalupe cult appeared in the form of essays by Miguel Sánchez in 1648 and Lazo de la Vega in 1649. According to Lafaye, "they had a special meaning . . . for they were the first step toward recognition of Guadalupe as a Mexican national symbol." The Creole *bachiller* Sánchez created a prophetic vision of the Spanish Conquest, stating "that God executed his admirable design in this Mexican land, conquered for such glorious ends, gained in order that a most divine image might appear here." As the title of the first chapter of his book, "Prophetic Original of the Holy Image Piously Foreseen by Evangelist Saint John, in Chapter Twelve of Revelation," makes explicit, Sánchez draws a parallel between the appearance of Guadalupe at Tepeyac and Saint John's vision of the Woman of the Apocalypse at Patmos (Lafaye 248–51). Eighteenth-century paintings, such as Gregorio José de Lara's *Visión de san Juan en Patmos Tenochtitlan* and the anonymous *Imagen de la Virgen de Guadalupe con san Miguel y san Gabriel y la visión de san Juan en Patmos Tenochtitlan*,[22] illustrate Saint John's vision of a winged Guadalupe and of a Guadalupe accompanied by the Aztec eagle at the Tepeyac hill. By providing a parallel not only between the Woman of the Apocalypse and Guadalupe but also between Patmos and Tenochtitlan, local painters portrayed Mexico as a chosen land. This idea was also reflected in poetry. In 1690, Felipe Santoyo wrote:

> Let the World be admired;
> the Sky, the Birds, the Angels and Men
> suspend the echoes,
> repress the voices:
> because in New Spain
> about another John it is being heard
> a new Apocalypse,
> although the revelations are different! (qtd. in Maza 113)

It is evident that "the identification of Mexican reality with the Holy Land and the prophetic books," as well as statements such as "I have written [this book] for my *patria*, for my friends and comrades, for the citizens of this New World" and "the honor of Mexico City . . . the glory of all the faithful who live in this New World" (qtd. in Lafaye 250–51), make Miguel Sánchez a Creole patriot whose writings had important consequences for the emancipation of Mexico. Developments in the iconography reflecting Mexican history make it apparent that the Virgin of Guadalupe has gained increasing agency in the social and political realms.

There certainly was a need for a powerful protective entity among the populace of New Spain. From the late seventeenth century to the mid-eighteenth century, thousands fell victim to yearly calamities such as floods, earthquakes, and epidemics. There was also an urgency for the appearance of a native symbolic figure, one that could reconcile and fraternize the diverse racial, cultural, and class components of Mexico, serve the purpose of identification, and instill national pride. The historical perspective explains why Guadalupe becomes a presence sine qua non during colonial times—there is no important image or event from which she may be omitted. The nineteenth-century Mexican historian Ignacio Manuel Altamirano made reference to the 1870 Guadalupe celebrations when he wrote that the worship of Guadalupe united "all races . . . all classes . . . all castes . . . all the opinions of our politics. . . . The cult of the Mexican Virgin is the only bond that unites them" (qtd. in Gruzinski 209).[23]

This increase in devotion to Guadalupe responded to a need by Creoles to find a feature of their own that would clearly distinguish them from the Spaniards: "[T]here will be then the Creoles, who in the seventeenth century will give a definitive position in history to *guadalupanismo*" (Maza 40). As a consequence, the first Spanish sanctuary was built at Tepeyac in 1609. As early as 1629 the image of Guadalupe was carried in solemn procession from Tepeyac to Mexico City by pilgrims who implored her to deliver the population from the menace of floods. Having achieved this goal, Guadalupe was proclaimed the city's "principal protectress against inundations," and she "achieved supremacy over the other protective effigies of the city" (Lafaye 254). By the end of the seventeenth century, a legend was added to the image of Guadalupe, thus making her emblem complete. The legend, *Non fecit talliter omni nationi* ([God] Has Not Done the Like for Any Other Nation), was taken by Father Florencia from Psalm 147. It became attached to the sacred image (Lafaye 258), further reinforcing its national character. But it wasn't until the mid-eighteenth century that Guadalupe became the center of collective fervor. In 1737 the effigy was proclaimed the official patroness of Mexico City, and, in 1746, of all of New Spain. In 1754, Pope Benedict XIV confirmed this oath of allegiance, and Guadalupe's holiday was established in the Catholic calendar (Gruzinski 209).

Guadalupe also played an important role in the Mexican War of Independence from Spain (1810–21). She was then carried on banners of the insurgents, lead by Father Miguel Hidalgo y Costilla and later by Father José María Morelos, confronting the Spanish royalists who carried the Peninsular Virgen de los Remedios. The first president of independent Mexico changed his name from Manuel Félix Fernández to Guadalupe Victoria in homage to the patriotic Virgin. Other Mexican political and social struggles, such as the War of Reformation (Guerra de la reforma, 1854–57), the Mexican Revolution (1910–18), and the Cristeros Rebellion (1927–29), were also performed under the banners of Guadalupe (Herrera-Sobek 41–43) . The process of exaltation of the Virgin of Guadalupe and of Juan Diego continues. On 30 July 2002, Pope John Paul II canonized the Mexican Indian, declaring him an official saint of the Catholic Church. This was done in spite of the fact that even some Mexican Catholic priests, such as father Manuel Olimón Nolasco, doubt the actual existence of Juan Diego (Olimón Nolasco). In turn, on 1 December 2000, after being sworn in as the new Mexican president, Vicente Fox directed his first steps to the Virgin of Guadalupe Basilica at the Tepeyac hill, where he asked the Virgin for grace and protection during his presidency. This constituted an unprecedented case in Mexican

Fig. 48. Contemporary depiction of the Virgin of Guadalupe with colors of the Mexican flag: red, green, and white. (Author's collection.)

politics ("Fox empezó la jornada en la Basílica"), as a strong division between church and state has been officially enforced since the Mexican Revolution. Once again, the Virgin of Guadalupe claimed victory over official customs and rules.

From the onset, the patriotic significance of the Virgin of Guadalupe was exhibited in iconography and other artistic expressions. As her image achieved increasing national and political significance, it was placed above the Aztec coat of arms—the eagle devouring a serpent on a nopal (prickly pear)—and Mexico City–Tenochtitlan. Sometimes the image was framed by allegorical figures representing America and Europe, as in the eighteenth-century painting *Nuestra Señora de Guadalupe de México, Patrona de la Nueva España* (Our Lady of Guadalupe, Patron of New Spain) (see Cuadriello, *Artes de México* 52). In Josefus de Ribera i Argomanis's 1778 painting *Verdadero retrato de santa María Virgen de Guadalupe, patrona principal de la Nueva España jurada en México* (Real Portrait of Holy Mary Virgin of Guadalupe, Main Patron of New Spain Sworn in Mexico), her image was framed by a non-Christianized Indian representing America, and Juan Diego—a European-influenced one (see plate 8).[24] In contemporary art, we see the progressive Mexicanization of Guadalupe reflected in the use of the colors of the Mexican flag—red, green, and white—as well as in the darkening and the Indianization of her features.[25] Similar depictions of Our Lady of Częstochowa, accompanied by the national coat of arms (the white eagle) and banners, are common symbols throughout Polish history of its struggles for independence from foreign aggressors, for freedom, and for social justice (see figs. 33, 34, and 35).

MALINTZIN AND CHINA POBLANA:
OTHER FEMALE SYMBOLS OF MEXICAN CULTURAL IDENTITY

The creation, metamorphosis, and persistence of the Guadalupe icon are related to other representations of Mexican cultural identity that appear throughout history. Such figures are those of Malinalli/Malintzin/La Malinche/Doña Marina and of China Poblana. Similar to the symbol of Guadalupe, they are ambiguous, multivalent, and have experienced numerous re-creations. At times, they function in connection with Guadalupe, being complemented by her image either as counterparts or as subjects of the same progressive chain. From her incurrence into Mexican history in 1519, as her different names indicate, Malinalli/Malintzin/La Malinche/Doña Marina has been a multilevel figure. Although a princess, Malinalli was offered to Cortés as a slave by her own people. Since the beginning, she played a crucial role in the Conquest, serving as a translator, advisor, and consort to Cortés. As shown in the images of *Lienzo de Tlaxcala*, the Indians saw her as a central figure.[26] Early on, her image is accompanied by that of the Virgin, as in the scene depicting Malintzin's baptism. Later, she was called "La Malinche," labeled as a traitor, and this name became the base for a neologism, *malinchismo*, or an excessive love for the foreign. Her ambiguity springs from the fact that she served the Spaniards, but she was also the mother of the first mestizo and, by extension, the symbolic mother of all Mexicans and Latin Americans. The mother figure in Mexican culture has been traditionally revered, a contemporary manifestation being the sumptuous celebration of Mother's Day. But what is the implication if a mother—perceived as a saintly figure—is also seen as a traitor? This issue engenders ambiguity and confusion and has been the constant dilemma for many Mexicans, consciously or subconsciously. This paradox has been addressed by intellectuals, including Octavio Paz and Tzvetan Todorov. According to the former, La Malinche is one of many Mexican representations of maternity that include La Llorona,[27] "the long suffering Mexican mother," and the Virgin of Guadalupe. But while Malinche is *la chingada*, the violated mother, her counterpart Guadalupe is the virgin mother (Paz 68, 70, 77).[28]

Another multilayered figure, constructed into an icon of Mexican national identity, is the China Poblana (see plate 4 and fig. 49).[29] Strangely enough, the prototype of this

Fig. 49. *China Poblana en la Ciudad Universitaria de Mexico* (Typical China Poblana Costume). Postcard, 1950s. (Susan Toomey Frost's collection. Reproduced with permission.)

image was Catarina de San Juan, an Asian slave brought from seventeenth-century India to serve a wealthy Mexican family. She devoted her life to the poor and needy, and through a fusion with the figure of the *china*—a rather independent mestiza— became a national archetype of a Virtuous Mexican Woman. This archetype of a "beautiful, faithful, devoted, and virtuous woman" was officially adopted in 1941. Dressed in white, green, and red (the colors of the Mexican flag), the China Poblana was portrayed dancing the *jarabe tapatío*, a popular Mexican dance, or on Cerveza Corona ads (Gillespie 6, 9). She was even linked to the Virgin of Guadalupe, as in the 1899 patriotic poem "Guadalupe" by Amado Nervo:

> With her escort of ranch hands,
> ten robust partisans, and on her spirited mount
> that the reins can not hold back
> Guadalupe the *chinaca*[30] goes in search of Pantaleón.[31]
> . . .
> Guadalupe hurries on, returning from Mass
> where, on special holy days,
> there are always country maidens
> with their flowers and candles at the local church;
> . . .
> she heads toward the camp where all is lively
> there is clamor and there is liquor;
> because yesterday was a good day,
> as an invader's convoy fell in the hills.
>
> What a beautiful morning! So much greenery, so many roses!
> And how pretty, far away
> rose and green, stands out
> with her convoy, the *chinaca* who goes to see Pantaleón![32]

In this poem, Guadalupe–China Poblana appears as a patriotic fighter and a pious woman dressed in national Mexican colors. "In conjunction with the independence of the china poblana, the piety and chastity of the Virgin . . . provided a powerful example for female Mexicans" (Gillespie 9). It is interesting how in this case European and Asian ethnic characteristics were manipulated and combined with other desirable traits to lead to the construction of a Mexican national symbol. Similar exchanges can be perceived in the dynamics of representation of Brazilian and Polish icons. Such effigies consolidated an identity in multiethnic nations such as Mexico and Brazil and solidified resistance in the face of internal and foreign aggressions, as in the case of Poland.

The Serpent and the Bird: Multilayered Symbolism

An interesting correlation occurs between the ancient, the Christian, and the Aztec symbols recurring in Mexican imagery. Because New Spain was a hybrid, syncretic society, the images found in colonial iconography tend to have layers of meanings. For example, the skin-shedding serpent was an ancient symbol of immortality and the Great Goddess, and "the usual mythological association of the serpent is not, as in the Bible, with corruption, but with physical and spiritual health, as in the Greek caduceus" (Campbell, *Mythic Image* 286). The powerful symbol of the caduceus, or an intertwined, two-headed snake, is still used in our society to identify the medical profession.[33] The images of the serpent and of the dragon, as expressed in folktales, persist in collective memory and are still venerated by societies as diverse as the Chinese and the Lithuanians. The Lithuanian custom of keeping a serpent in the house was not uncommon.[34] Dragons and snakes were revered and represented with crowns, as in Slavic and Baltic legends and fairy tales.[35] The national emblem of Germany, Russia, and Albania is a two-headed eagle, or Bird of Fire, resembling the image of two intertwined serpents (Bayley 2:291). For Mesoamericans, such as the Aztecs, the feathered serpent Quetzalcoatl was the primary civilizing god (see fig. 24). Christianity propagated the demonization of the powerful serpent as a symbol identified with the devil. In Catholic iconography and writings, the serpent represents the evil that caused the fall of Eve and the subsequent loss of paradise, and the dragon always appears as a horrifying creature with one or seven heads (as in Revelation). In holy imagery, both creatures are conquered and usually placed at the feet of a Christian saint, such as the Archangel Michael or the Virgin Mary. Nevertheless, "the present form of the Biblical story is obviously a much-revised version of the original tales of the Great Mother and her serpent. Babylonian icons showed the Goddess attended by her snake, offering man the food of immortality" (Walker, *Woman's Encyclopedia* 906). "Today . . . the devotees of Voodoo [in Haiti] worship Damballah-wèdo, the serpent-god, one of the divinities of the Dahomey mythology. . . . Although it is not normal practice now to represent Damballah-wèdo by living serpents, it must have been otherwise in the [eighteenth and the nineteenth centuries]" (Métraux 38). It seems that in antiquity "there was a belief in two antagonistic Dragons, the one crooked, crawling, and slimy, the emblem of everything that was obstructive, loathsome, and disgusting; the other, winged,

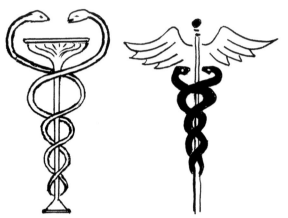

Fig. 50. Caduceus by Eligiusz Oleszkiewicz (left) and Ania Aldrich (right). (Author's collection. Reproduced with permission of the artists.)

Fig. 51. Crowned serpents are a frequent image in Lithuanian legends. Wooden sculpture, Druskininkai, Lithuania, 1997. (Photo by author.)

Fig. 52. Voodoo altar crowned by serpents Damballah-Ayida Wedo, New Orleans, 2002. (Photo by author.)

radiant, and beneficent, 'The reconciler, the deliverer,' the 'Angel of the Dawn,' the 'Spirit of All Knowledge'" (Bayley 2: 286).

Another symbol of the Paleolithic and the Neolithic goddess was the bird. According to Barbara Walker, "doves represented the Great Goddess in Asia Minor, under several of her names such as Aphrodite and Astarte . . . [and were] a primary symbol of female sexuality. . . . [There also was an] ancient belief that the essence of every soul is female" (*Woman's Dictionary* 399–400). This concept, assimilated by Christianity, represented souls flying to heaven as doves and incorporated this bird as part of the Christian Holy Trinity, along with Jesus the Son and God the Father (see fig. 27). But already pagan "Slavs considered that the Soul after Death flew from the mouth in the form of a dove" (Bayley 2: 301), and the name of the Roman goddess Venus Columba, or Dove, was incorporated into Christianity as Saint Columba.[36] The statue of the Carthaginian goddess Tanit from the fourth–third-century BC found at the Necropolis Puig des Molins in Eivissa (Ibiza, Spain) represents a crowned female figure seated on a throne while holding a dove at her navel.[37] In various localities of today's Spain, such as Madrid and Málaga, La Virgen de la Paloma (Virgin of the Dove) is among the most popular devotions, and great processions, which include the release of doves, are dedicated to her ("Semana Santa"). In Miguel de Cervantes's *Los trabajos de Persiles y Sigismunda*, the Virgin Mary is addressed as "the dove that for eternity [was] / called from the sky" (Cervantes bk. 3, ch. 5, fol. 139r: 73–74). "All Jewish Christians used to regard the Holy Spirit as both a lady and a mother, especially the Mother of Jesus. . . . Jesus said himself: 'My mother the Holy Spirit.'" It "is God the Holy Spirit in the role of the Lady and a Mother." The Holy Spirit was also seen as the church and as the lady clothed with the sun who appears in Revelation (Quispel 77, 15). The identification of Mary with the Holy Spirit–dove restores her ancient place as central to an original trinity of goddesses. In some paintings, Mary is portrayed as one with the Holy Spirit–dove, which either springs out of her body, as in the eighteenth-century Mexican print *Et hi tres unum sunt*,[38] or is placed above her, as in the seventeenth-century *Feast of Blessed Virgin Mary, Queen of Heaven* by Diego Velázquez. In both Polish and Mexican popular art she also takes the place of a central deity, standing between Jesus the Son and God the Father.[39]

There exists in New Spain's iconography yet another case of superimposed symbology where pre-Christian and Catholic layers of meaning are crowned with Aztec symbols, culminating in Mexican patriotic representations. A good example is the eighteenth-century New Spain's anonymous painting, *San Miguel Arcángel con estandarte guadalupano* (Saint Michael Archangel with the Guadalupan Banner), in which the Archangel, his foot upon a seven-headed dragon, is ready to give the final

Fig. 53. Goddess Tanit, fourth–third century BC from the Necropolis Puig des Molins in Eivissa (Ibiza, Spain). (Author's collection and photo.)

Fig. 54. *Feast of Blessed Virgin Mary, Queen of Heaven* by Diego Velázquez. (El Prado Museum, Madrid, Spain. Reproduced with permission.)

Fig. 55. In Polish popular art the Virgin Mary often takes the place of a central deity between Jesus the Son and God the Father. Wooden road chapel from the Kurpie region, Poland, 2002. (Photo by author.)

Fig. 56. *San Miguel Arcángel con estandarte guadalupano* (Saint Michael Archangel with the
Guadalupan Banner). Eighteenth century, anonymous. (Museum of the Basilica of Guadalupe,
Mexico City. Reproduced with permission.)

blow with his spade. Depicted as the victor in a red mantle and eagle's wings, he wears a blue robe imprinted with the sun, moon, and stars. In his left hand he carries the banner of Guadalupe. The resemblance of Michael's array to that of Guadalupe's is easily discerned. Moreover, this representation echoes the previously discussed image of the winged Guadalupe with a seven-headed dragon at her feet from *Visión de san Juan en Patmos Tenochtitlan.* Again, the stratification of symbols comes to light. The power of the primordial dragon is conquered by the Virgin, as the serpent is conquered by the eagle in the Aztec emblem. The winged Mary represents the Holy Spirit and Christianity, but she is also the triumphant eagle from the Aztec foundational legend, and Teteo innan, Mother of the Gods, whose skirt was made out of eagle feathers.[40] Traditional Christian iconography, whose roots are found in chapter 12 of Revelation, gained a nationalistic reinforcement through being infused with Mexican symbology.

The Power of Images

Here we need to make a note regarding the value of images for the Aztecs and for Spanish colonial society in general. As Serge Gruzinski remarks in *La guerra de las imágenes* (The War of the Images), the society of New Spain lived "saturated with images" (84). This was due to the extraordinary weight placed on the visual and sensual aspects of religion by Counter-Reformation Catholicism as well as to widespread illiteracy. As Protestants were stripping their churches of any sensual representations of the Virgin Mary, Jesus, and the saints, Spain and Portugal were filling theirs with Baroque paintings and sculptures. Many of these works of art were elaborated with vivid, contrasting colors and gold to create optical illusions of animation. The holy figures—larger than life statues—were not confined to the churches but paraded in the streets in frequent processions and visits to other parishes. They had natural hair, elaborate silk, costly gold- and pearl-encrusted robes, and were given the most beautiful, albeit exaggerated, expressions. This religious fervor, coupled with the Baroque tendency to excess (derroche), was taken to the extreme in the colonies. Such a phenomenon was due to the evangelizing zeal of the colonizers, for whom the image was sometimes the only means of transmission of ideas and beliefs. Thus the visual representation acquired tremendous significance and its possibilities were employed to the maximum.

A frequent means of expression that utilized images as well as words was the evangelizing theater. In their native tongues, Indian actors dramatically interpreted stories from the Bible, lives of saints, and miracles, such as the apparitions of the Virgin of Guadalupe. As it can be imagined, artistic performance was a powerful tool of indoctrination. The general tendency to theatricality in the earliest Spanish viceroyalties, such as New Spain, New Castile, and the Portuguese territory of Brazil, was especially notable.[41] The visual approach was crucial in newly colonized, multilingual societies, where knowledge of the official language was uncommon. This tendency persists until today in some Latin American countries with low literacy rates. For example, mural art became an important means of instructing the masses after the Mexican Revolution (1910–18). Famous artists such as Diego Rivera, David Alfaro Siqueiros, and Clemente Orozco painted a great number of murals on buildings and in other public spaces. They focused on historical, social, and allegorical imagery in order to educate the Mexican population. A similar phenomenon was observed after the Sandinista Revolution in Nicaragua. The Mexican muralist tradition persists until today in the southwestern United States as well as in other cities densely populated by Mexican Americans and other Latinos.[42]

The pre-Columbian Native American worldview was no less important than the motivations of the European conquistadores. The Mexican Indians worshipped their particular representations of divinities, the *ixiptla* (called "idols" by the Spaniards), which, according to Gruzinski, "captured and manifested the cosmic essence of things" (Gruzinski 96). The ixiptla was a multilayered concept that could include the image of a god, the priest who represented that god, and the victim to be sacrificed, transformed into a god. These meanings could be juxtaposed during rituals. The ixiptla, unlike the Catholic image, which was intended to be a point of reference to the divine, "was a receptacle of a power, a recognizable, epiphanycal presence, an actualization of a force imbued in an object. . . . It was not an appearance or a visual illusion, which remitted somewhere else, to a 'beyond.'" The Christian image, on the other hand, pointed to something outside of itself; it was only a semblance of the divinity (Gruzinski 96). When Catholic crosses and images of saints were placed in Indian holy places among their ixiptla, they acquired a power greater than the one given them by the Christians. This may in part explain the success of the effigy of the Virgin of Guadalupe, for whom the Mexicans—Indians, mestizos, Creoles, blacks, and mulattos—developed such a great devotion. The veneration of the Aztec lineage idols (*tlapialli*), connected to domestic chapels, or *santocalli,* was an intensely personal worship. As a consequence, the Nahua were characterized by an intimate affection for their domestic saints, calling them "my Lady of Guadalupe" or "my Lady of the Immaculate Conception" (Gruzinski 185–86). The conjunction of the anthropomorphic representation of the divinity by the Iberians and the Indian understanding of the ixiptla as carriers of the cosmic essence of things empowered the Catholic images by imbuing them with spiritual energy. This may be the key to the enormous popularity of holy figures, to whom inhabitants of the Latin New World were greatly attached.

THE CROSS AND THE TREE OF LIFE

A similar process of syncretism is manifested in the Indian understanding of the symbols of the cross and the Tree of Life. In the Old World tradition, the tree originally symbolized the axis of the world, uniting the heavens with the underworld, and was regarded as a dwelling place of the gods. A corresponding model was the Scandinavian tree Yggdrasil. This Cosmic Tree or World Tree was a symbol of life force, fertility, and regeneration and was often portrayed with mythical animals, the stars, moon, and sun, and souls of the dead as birds. Similar trees also appear in Native American art. Sometimes the tree was depicted with birds attacking a serpent. Its fruit or leaves (stars) symbolized destiny, and it was the origin of the Tree of Knowledge and the Tree of Life (Kopaliński 71–72). The god Othin hung on this tree for nine days. The Tree of Life was usually accompanied by a serpent at its foot and by an eagle at the top (Campbell, *Mythic Image* 192). Métraux (58) comments on Descourtilz's 1809 testimony from Haiti; he observed a "snake worshipped in front of a huge *mapou* [ceiba] tree in which it was living."[43] The adorned Christmas tree, which was introduced in the seventeenth century, springs from this ancient, sacred, jewel-bearing tree of immortal light, wisdom, and knowledge (Whittick 337). In Polish popular art, such as paper cutouts, frescoes, and wooden sculptures, the most pervasive motif is that of a Tree of Life with birds and flowers on its branches and a Baba (Goddess) in its center, flanked by animals (see fig. 28).

In these ancient designs, widespread even today, we can clearly perceive the Tree Goddess as the Lady of All Creation. Sometimes, the Virgin Mary, successor of the goddess, also appears as part of a tree. For example, one of the very miraculous images in Poland is considered that of the dark Mother of God of Święta Lipka or Saint Linden, who appeared on and is represented as part of a linden tree. In addition, many of the past and present Virgin Mary's apparitions around the world seem to have taken place on a tree. Dances performed around adorned trees (Gaik, Maik, Nowe latko) constituted a magical ritual to stimulate the forces of nature in the spring (Kopaliński 73). As Barbara Walker explains, the World Tree or Tree of Life "was assigned a female gender and was regarded as an all-nourishing, all-giving mother. Apparently, the blood shed on it in solemn sacrifice was intended to help maintain the life force of the tree, on which all other life depended" (*Woman's Dictionary* 472). The cross, an alter ego of the Tree of Life, existed in many world cultures with multiple forms and functions. It represented a world axis, the four directions, sun and fire,

Fig. 57. Paper cutout representing the Tree of Life with mythical birds. Polish popular art. (Author's collection.)

Fig. 58. Wooden sculpture representing the Tree of Life with flowers and birds. Polish popular art. (Author's collection and photo.)

Fig. 59. Native American decorative rug from Arizona representing the Tree of Life with flowers and birds, 2004. (Photo by author.)

Fig. 60. Paper cutout representing the Tree of Life, identified with the goddess (*baba*). The tree's trunk stands for the goddess's skirt and the branches for her arms. Polish popular art. (Author's collection.)

OBJAWIENIE MATKI BOŻEJ ŚWIĘTOLIPSKIEJ

Fig. 61. According to legend, the Mother of God appeared on a linden tree in the Polish town called Święta Lipka, or Saint Linden. Postcard. (Author's collection.)

Fig. 62. A road cross with the symbolic representation of the sun, the moon, and flowers stands on a disproportionately large base made out of a carved tree trunk, in which a seated female figure is represented. A variety of such syncretic crosses can be found in Lithuania and eastern Poland. Polish-Lithuanian village Puńsk, 2000. (Photo by author.)

the conjunction of opposites, and sexual union (Kopaliński 174). To this day, many Lithuanian road crosses have more resemblance to a tree with a baba-like trunk, the sun, and the moon than to a contemporary Christian cross. It is also one of the oldest diagrams for male genitals among the Arabs. The cross penetrating the labyrinth was one of the most ancient Western symbols for sexual union, dating back to the Neolithic (Walker, *Woman's Encyclopedia* 189, 190). Christ was represented on a cross for the first time in AD 608 (Bayley 2: 267), and the cross was not regarded as a symbol of Christianity until the ninth century AD (Whittick 224).

In many world myths, the Tree of Life appears associated with the creation of the universe, of humans, nourishment, and civilization. The supreme gods of the pre-Aztec culture of Teotihuacan formed an agricultural trinity consisting of the Goddess of the Cave, dispenser of fertility, life, and death; Tlaloc, the god of lightening, thunder, and rainwater; and the Plumed Serpent Quetzalcoatl, associated with vegetative renewal. The principal deity of this triad was the Goddess of the Cave, whose body, as a cosmic axis, "dominates the reproductive forces of the netherworld and the fertile forces of heavens." She "emerges in grandiose fashion from the humid cave of the underworld and rises up like a cosmic tree of the celestial region. Her fertilizing power makes plants sprout on the earth's surface" (Florescano, *Myth of Quetzalcoatl* 9, 132). The idea of the rebirth of warriors in the form of the Tree of Life and birds is expressed in Nahuatl (Aztec) poetry. The flowers represent human hearts, and nectar stands for sacrificial blood ("Narration Text for 'The Tree of Life'"):

THE FLOWERING TREE
Among jewels, among gold
The Flowering Tree is spreading. . . .
Sip the nectar, quetzal bird . . . !
You have become the Flowering Tree:
You open your branches and you bend.
You have offered yourself to the Giver of Life. (Garibay 2: 2)

THE SACRED BIRDS
Here where the Flowering Tree stands,
Here where its precious shoots sprout,
Come golden and black birds,
Come brown and black birds,
And the marvelous quetzal. (Garibay 2: 7)

At the time of the Spanish Conquest, the cross was already being used in Mexico as a Tree of Life (Bayley 2:267). The Mayan sacred Tree of Life or World Tree is represented by the yaxche or ceiba (silk-cotton tree). "The Mayan kings dressed themselves as the tree of life . . . [as they] were the embodiment of the ceiba as the central axis . . . of the world. . . . The entire universe was linked by a green ceiba tree that stood at the center of the world, its branches extending into the heavens and its roots into the underworld ("Ceiba"). In a *pataki* (myth or narrative) form Cuban Santería, the sacred ceiba tree is described in a similar fashion, having "her roots firmly planted in the earth and her branches reaching out to the skies" (Castellanos 39). At Brazilian terreiros sacred *iroko* or ceiba trees are venerated. Today in Mexico, the syncretized tradition of the Tree of Life continues. At Mayan ceremonies ceiba flowers are used to adorn crosses; to the Maya, "the cross was a living being having [the] anatomy of a human being" ("Ceiba"). Popular artists, such as the Castillo family from Izúcar de Matamoros, Puebla, elaborate detailed trees with different topics (Women, the Day of the Dead, and so on), and their art is transmitted from generation to generation. According to the patriarch of the family, Alfonso Castillo Orta, the Tree of Life tradition goes back to the ancient Olmec culture. In indigenous communities, a wooden version of

Fig. 63. Sacred *iroko* (*ceiba*) tree at the Gantois *terreiro* in Salvador, Bahia, Brazil, 1996. (Photo by author.)

the tree was presented to newlyweds as a means of encouraging their accountability to fulfill certain plans and promises for the next seven years. If the promises were kept, after seven years the wooden tree was burned and replaced with a clay one that served as a kind of testament (*Ecos desde un vientre de barro*). In recent years, the most popular trees are the ones that connect the New World (Indian) and the Old World (Christian and pre-Christian) traditions and are represented as the Biblical Tree with birds, stars/flowers, leaves, fruit, Adam and Eve, and the serpent.

Fig. 64. Mexican clay tree with Adam, Eve, and the serpent. (Author's collection and photo.)

Summary

Similar to the Mexican Trees of Life, Guadalupe also carries complex layers of meaning. As an icon born on the soil of the Americas that bears characteristics of two main cultural and ethnic groups inhabiting Mexico, the Indian and the European, she is transformed into an important national and patriotic symbol. Her syncretic nature is capable of uniting all ethnic, racial, and social strata. After the Spanish Conquest of Mexico and the disruption of the political, economic, religious, cultural, and ethnic order, the search for identity came to be of primary importance for New Spain. Uprooted populations of Indians, mestizos, and Creoles appropriated and nativized the image of the "new" Virgin of Guadalupe. Moreover, Guadalupe became a private saint, encompassing the functions of a mother-protectress-friend. But her role does not end here. Like the Mociuaquetzque, or Aztec women dead in childbirth, she emerges as a warrior who inspires courage in the national and regional struggles of colonial and contemporary Mexico.

The experiences of invasion, domination, and displacement have left in their wake an overwhelming sense of orphanhood and impotence for such Latin American nations as Mexico, Brazil, Cuba, or Haiti. They have long sought an icon of consolidation and protection. For Mexico, the Latino United States, and large portions of Latin America, this figure came to be the Virgin of Guadalupe, center of the all-pervading cult of Guadalupanismo. In the next chapter I discuss similar icons created in the Afro-Latin American areas of Brazil, Cuba, and Haiti.

Africa is our mother. All our strength comes from Africa.

—Maria-José, Mother of the Gods

⚜

Brazilian society is relational. A system where the basic, the fundamental value, is to relate, to mix, to blend, to conciliate. *To stay in the middle, to discover mediation and establish a gradation, to include (never exclude). To synthesize models and positions seems to constitute a central aspect of the predominant Brazilian ideology. I even say that it is its distinctive trait in opposition to other systems, especially those which inform the values of Protestant nations, such as the United States. Thus, in the United States there is exclusion and separation; in Brazil there is inclusion and organization into a hierarchy. In one case the creed says: equal, but separate; in the other it orders: different, but together.*

—Roberto DaMatta

⚜

[I]n the Caribbean the "foreign" interacts with the "traditional" like a ray of sun with a prism; that is, they produce phenomena of reflection, refraction, and decomposition.

—Antonio Benítez-Rojo

CHAPTER THREE

Brazil and the Caribbean

Afro-Indo-European Syncretism

❧❦

SYNCRETISM

My central focus in this book is the manifestation of the concept of cultural syncretism in the Black Madonna figure. I have examined pertinent examples in my discussion of the transformation of such signifiers as the Virgin Mary/Goddess and the crucifix/tree in chapters 1 and 2, focusing on central Europe and Mexico, respectively. This chapter continues the discussion of the Dark Goddess/Our Lady figures, looking at South America and the Caribbean. The discussion begins with an examination of the dynamics and variations of syncretism in these areas.

Syncretism can occur at a more accelerated, visible rate in societies that enter into contact with each other in sudden, dramatic ways, such as those of Latin America. In the Old World, familiar neighboring cultures interacted with each other over extremely long stretches of time; in Latin America, however, ethnically and racially disparate societies, totally unfamiliar with each other and inhabiting different continents, encountered immediate conflict during colonization and slave trade. As Fernando Ortiz observed: "All the cultural scale that Europe traversed in more than four millennia Cuba experienced in less than four centuries. . . . In one day in Cuba millennia and ages went by" (19, 22). The singular situation of Latin American cultures was brilliantly captured by the same author in his metaphor of Cuban society as the *ajiaco*:

What is an *ajiaco*? It is the most typical and complex stew, made out of various kinds of vegetables we call "tubers" and from pieces of diverse meats; all that is cooked with boiling water until a thick and succulent soup is produced and is seasoned with the most Cuban [*cubanísimo*] chili [*ají*], which gives it its name. . . . it always was a "sleeping" stew [*guiso "dormido"*]. The next day, the *ajiaco* was waking up to a new cooking; water was added, other tubers and animals were thrown in and it was boiled with more chili. And thus, day after day, without cleaning the casserole, with its bottom full of waste substances in pulpy and thick stock, in a sauce analogous to the one that constitutes the most typical, tasty, and succulent of our *ajiaco*, now with more purity, better seasoning, and less *ají*.

    The image of the Creole ajiaco symbolizes well the formation of the Cuban people. Let's follow the metaphor. . . .

    The characteristic of Cuba is that being an *ajiaco* it is not a finished stew, but one in constant brew. From the dawn of history until current times, in the Cuban casserole there is always a renewed entering into exogenous roots, fruits, and meats, an incessant bubbling of exogenous substances. That is why its composition changes and Cubanity [*cubanidad*] has different flavor and consistence. (15–16)

Two or more cultural components bring about a third new product, unlike either one of them. Following Malinowski in his introduction to Fernando Ortiz's *Cuban Counterpoint: Tobacco and Sugar* (xi), transculturation or syncretism can be defined as "an exchange between cultures, both of them active, both contributing their share, and both cooperating to bring about a new reality of civilization."

Such new reality is especially noticeable in the hybrid Latin American cultural expressions. Here, the alloyed cultures were not only Indian and European, but the predominant influence was African. For Latin America, such regions are mainly Brazil and the Caribbean. This is due to African slave trade, dating from the beginning of the sixteenth-century Conquest and continuing throughout colonization.[1] In the case of Brazil and Cuba, this trade started with the Bantu linguistic family of the Congo-Angola region (Barnet 73), and, from the second half of the eighteenth through the nineteenth century, centered on the Yoruba region of today's Nigeria and Benin. This relatively recent concentration of great quantities of individuals from one particular developed and clearly identifiable cultural region produced the conditions for intense syncretism in these areas of Latin America. According to Miguel Barnet: "[The Yoruba culture] has a richer and more complex superstructure than the [other African cultures brought to Cuba, and] provided the framework for the development and adaptation of the transculturated expressions that constitute Cuba's cultural heritage. Comparable in its richness and poetry to that of ancient Greece, Yoruban mythology offers the only consistent body of ideas about the creation of the world to be found among the treasures of Cuba's traditional popular culture" (17–18). Moreover, because of persecution, slaves were obliged to hide their religious practices and disguise them with Catholic symbols. They pretended to merely dance or play when in reality they were performing religious rituals, such as Candomblé, or practicing martial arts, such as Capoeira.[2] The cultural gap between sixteenth- to nineteenth-century Europe and Africa/Latin America facilitated this process. The continued necessity of disguise and subterfuge produced unique cultural expressions in Latin America.

For example, the Yoruba black Mother Goddess Yemoja was blended with the Virgin of the Immaculate Conception (see plate 5) and with the siren-like personifications of the Yoruba Mami Wata and the Amerindian Iara and appropriated by the Brazilian population as Iemanjá, a white, sensual Queen of the Seas figure, attired in blue (see plate 9). To the present day she is the persona most venerated in Brazil. On the other hand, the official Catholic patroness of Brazil became the black Our Lady Aparecida (see fig. 26). In addition, the African-influenced Candomblé religious communities in northeastern Brazil, led by older black priestesses and their female initiates, are contemporary examples of ancestral matriarchal organization.

In his 1996 analysis of Indo-Catholic religion in the Andes, Manuel Marzal states: "[T]rue syncretism [is] the result of a dialectic interaction of elements . . . of the two original religions, by which interaction certain elements persist in the new religion, others disappear altogether, still others synthesize with similar elements from the other religion or are reinterpreted and assume a new meaning" (17). On the other hand, Sergio Ferretti proposes the existence of the syncretic strategies of parallelism or juxtaposition, convergence or adaptation, and interpretation or linkage in Afro-Brazilian religions. In addition, in some areas of ritual, separation or no syncretism may exist ("Religious Syncretism" 91–93).

To illustrate these processes, I will use as examples three African water goddesses—Mami Wata, Yemoja (Yemaja), and Òṣun. Mami Wata, a goddess from the western coastal and central regions of Africa, is often represented as a beautiful white mermaid with long dark hair. This image, untypical of West African òrìṣà worship, may have originated from figureheads on European ships that traveled to the western coast of Africa.[3] Mami Wata, as such, disappeared in the Americas, but her representation as a beautiful white mermaid or woman with long black hair was adapted to (synthesized with) the most popular representation of the goddess of the salty waters, Iemanjá, in Brazil (see plate 10),[4] as well as with one of the images of the goddess of sweet waters, Oxum. Mami Wata's colors, red and white, were eliminated (disappeared), as Iemanjá kept the African Yemoja's blue and clear colors of the waters. Yemoja, who in Africa is "an avatar of Mama Wata" ("Goddesses of Africa"), acquired an extraordinary importance in the Americas, especially in Brazil, after the ocean crossing of African slaves. In Brazil and in Cuba, the Virgin Mary was linked to Iemanjá (Yemayá) in order to camouflage African worship, and Iemanjá was reinterpreted as the unofficial

Fig. 65. Oxum represented as a mermaid at the entrance to the Casa Branca *terreiro* in Salvador, Bahia, Brazil, 1996. (Photo by author.)

but also the most popular patroness of Brazil. Some of her traits, such as the blue color, her connection to the sea, and her life-giving and nurturing aspects, converged (synthesized) with those of the Catholic Virgin Mary. Nevertheless, we cannot say that Iemanjá is fully identified with Mary, as she possesses qualities that set her aside, such as her obvious sexuality and her destructive fury, characteristic of the oceans. Rather, some of Virgin Mary's attributes, for example, her day of worship—Saturday—were reinterpreted (linked) to Iemanjá. In fact, according to many Brazilian Candomblé leaders and scholars, the Iemanjá/Virgin Mary phenomenon should be seen as an example of juxtaposition or parallelism rather than synthesis or convergence.

After the Atlantic crossing to the New World, the African pantheon of gods was greatly reduced, and only the most significant òrìṣà persisted. They were linked to Catholic saints with similar traits. In Brazil, some of them were Iemanjá (goddess of salty waters) and Oxum (goddess of fresh waters), adapted to different representations of the Virgin Mary; Oxalá (creation god of universal love, peace, and justice) to Jesus Christ; Xangô (virile god of thunder and lightening) to Saint Jerome; Ogum (god of iron and war) to Saint Anthony; and Omolú (god of diseases and their cure) to Saint Lazarus. The adaptability and fluidity of their identities in the New World are

Fig. 67. The house of Oxum, with golden and yellow offerings, stands close to a pond with fresh water. Ilê Asé Orisanlá J'Omin *terreiro*, Itaparica Island, Bahia, Brazil, 1996. (Photo by author.)

Fig. 66. Iemanjá in trance at a Candomblé ceremony. Ilê Asé Orisanlá J'Omin *terreiro*, Itaparica Island, Bahia, Brazil, 1996. (Photo by author.)

Fig. 68. Oxalá in trance. Ilê Asé Orisanlá J'Omin *terreiro*, Itaparica Island, Bahia, Brazil, 1996. (Photo by author.)

Fig. 69. Altar for Changó, Cuba's equivalent to Brazilian Xangô, is adorned with his colors—red and white. Regla, Cuba, 1999. (Photo by author.)

Fig. 70. Two Omolús in trance accompany an *ogão* on his three-year ceremony. Ilê Asé Orisanlá J'Omin *terreiro*, Itaparica Island, Bahia, Brazil, 1996. (Photo by author.)

expressed not only by the fact that the corresponding saints may vary from region to region, but even the gender of the saint identified with a given *orixá* may be different. For example, some of the most important Brazilian male orixás are identified with female saints in Cuba; Changó (Xangô) becomes Saint Barbara and Obatalá (Oxalá) Our Lady of Mercy. In addition, in 1890, when Nina Rodrigues was studying Candomblé in Brazil, the correspondences of orixás and saints were still very fluid, varying from terreiro to terreiro, and there was a tendency to identify Xangô with Saint Barbara (Verger, "Esplendor e decadência" 27).

There is no conflict in reinterpreting a male *oricha* (orixá) as a female saint, as we are dealing with energies rather than gender per se. Therefore, a convergence of qualities in a given circumstance will determine which saint is apt to represent which oricha (orixá). According to Antonio Benítez-Rojo: "A syncretic artifact is not a synthesis, but rather a signifier made of differences. What happens is that in the melting pot of societies that the world provides, syncretic processes realize themselves through an economy in whose modality of exchange the signifier of *there*—of the other—is consumed ('read') according to local codes that are already in existence; that is, codes from *here*" (21). A good example is the Catholic Irmandade da Boa Morte,

Fig. 71. Women from the Irmandade da Boa Morte, or Sisterhood of the Good Death, a Catholic sisterhood at Cachoeira, Bahia, Brazil, wear white Candomblé attire and sacred necklaces to celebrate the Catholic holiday of the Good Death, 1996. (Photo by author.)

Fig. 72. Yoruba religious ritual, As Águas de Oxalá (the Waters of Oxalá). Procession by members of the Ilê Asé Orisanlá J'Omin *terreiro*, Asé Ilha Vera Cruz, Bahia, Brazil, 1997. (Photo by Ilê Asé Orisanlá J'Omin. Author's collection.)

or Sisterhood of the Good Death, of Cachoeira, an ancient town near Salvador, Bahia. This sisterhood is integrated exclusively by women over forty, who are also practitioners of the Candomblé religion. They celebrate Catholic ceremonies wearing white Candomblé attire and sacred necklaces. In Brazil and the Caribbean, Catholic saints were Africanized and adapted to the Yoruba religion. At the same time, the African òrìṣà became Europeanized and/or Indianized. For example, at Candomblé ceremonies, Iemanjá and other orixás appear dressed in sumptuous European Baroque-inspired clothes that do not exist in Africa (see fig. 7); only the *pano da costa* (cloth from the [African] coast), wrapped around the orixá's chest, is preserved.[5] At the same time, the most venerated representation of Jesus Christ in Salvador, Bahia is that of Nosso Senhor do Bomfim (Our Lord of the Good End), who is black. Christ is celebrated in a profuse annual ceremony, A Lavagem do Bomfim (the Washing of Bomfim), during which Candomblé practitioners, after parading with jars of water, wash the steps of the Bomfim Catholic Basilica. This tradition derives from a Yoruba religious ritual called As Águas de Oxalá (the Waters of Oxalá). As Benítez-Rojo observes, "Caribbean music did not become Anglo-Saxon [in the United States] but rather the latter became Caribbean within a play of differences" (21)

The extraordinary fluidity and adaptability of the Afro-Latin American orixás (orichas) is manifested not only in the transformations in appearance or the evanescence of certain gods or their traits from the pantheon, but also in the proliferation of paths or roads (caminos) of some orichas. For example, the most venerated and multidimensional Cuban oricha, Ochún, syncretized with the official patroness of Cuba, the Virgin of Charity of El Cobre (see plate 11), has a number of quite dissimilar paths through which she can be reached. She may be portrayed as "old and young, rich and impoverished, caring and spiteful" (Murphy and Sanford 7). According to Castellanos, Ochún's five ritually recognized paths are: Ochún Ibú-Akuaro, "hard-working, joyful, young, beautiful, and fond of music and dance"; Ochún Ololodí, "quite serious and . . . a good diviner . . . [who] rules over waterfalls and is a conscientious homemaker"; Ochún Ibú-Kolé, "powerful sorcerer who relies on the buzzard to bring her carrion to eat"; Ochún Yumú, "an old woman who lives in the depths of the river"; and Ochún Ibú-Dokó, "the patroness of the sexual act", or Ochún Ibú-Añá, "the queen of the drums." Nevertheless, "believers recognize [many] other manifestations of this oricha, such as Ochún Yeyé-Moró or Yeyé-Karí, the most coquettish, alluring, gorgeous, and joyful of them all. Despite the diversity of the caminos, the faithful insist there is but one Ochún" (35). Lydia Cabrera, in her Yemayá y Ochún: Kariocha, iyalorichas y olorichas, lists fourteen roads of Ochún .[6] The polysemous character of the orichas expresses the various contradictions of life in an intense constant flow: "The flexibility provided by the prototypical organization of Ochún and other orichas also promotes the incorporation, accentuation, or attenuation of meanings associated with changing physical and social realities" (Castellanos 36).

AFRO-BRAZILIAN RELIGIONS

Special manifestations of the new cultural expressions, which originated in the blending of cultures, are the diverse faces of Afro-Latin American religions. Roberto Motta distinguishes three main varieties of Afro-Indo-European religions in Brazil: Candomblé-Xangô, Catimbó, and Umbanda. The first is the most "classical" type, characterized by a preponderance of African, Yoruban (Nagô) elements. It is an urban religion that receives the name of Candomblé in the state of Bahia and Xangô in Pernambuco, Alagoas, and Sergipe; a variation that includes Fon (Jeje) elements, called Tambor de Mina, is found in Maranhão ("Ethnicity, Purity, the Market, and Syncretism" 72, 82–83). The second type, Catimbó, is the oldest (sixteenth century) and most Indian rural religion, practiced mainly in the northern states of Piauí, Ceará, and Rio Grande do Norte; the Pajelança of Pará and Amazonas also belongs to this category. The third type, Umbanda, is the newest and the most syncretic. It originated in the beginning of the twentieth century as an intent to "whiten" the African- and Indian-influenced religions. This was done through the theological "writings of Allan Kardec, the French codifier of nineteenth-century reinterpretation of Christianity in terms of both Asian beliefs and scientific lore that came to be known as Spiritism" (77).[7] Umbanda is practiced mainly in central Brazil—São Paulo, Rio de Janeiro, Minas Gerais, and Espírito Santo (Baamonde 26). In spite of the above typology, in Afro-Brazilian religions "there are continuities rather than sharply demarcated boundaries" (Motta, "Ethnicity, Purity, the Market, and Syncretism" 82); in addition, these religions include variations, different degrees of syncretism, and some of them, such as Macumba or Umbanda, are still very fluid. In fact, fluidity and flexibility are major traits of Brazilian society.

In this work I focus on Candomblé.[8] According to the spiritual leaders and practitioners of the most prestigious and orthodox Candomblé houses of Bahia, such as Ilê Asé Opô Afonjá, Ilê Asé Iyá Nassô Oká (Casa Branca do Engenho Velho da Federação), and Ilê Iyá Omí Asé Iyá Massê (Sociedade São Jorge do Gantois), Candomblé is a purely African religion that has been stripped from its transitory Catholic influence as part of the process of "re-Africanization" since the 1980s.[9] Nevertheless, as Sidney Greenfield points out:

> [E]ven though the Yoruba (or Nagô) houses were in fact organized by peoples from Yorubaland, they incorporated only a part of Yoruba religious culture, . . . which corresponded in meaning and practice to the beliefs and behaviors of the Luso-Brazilians to which it was adapted. Therefore, the Candomblés, *Xangôs*, *Batuques*, etc. of Brazil were not complete representations of Yoruba religion. They are better understood as a selection from Yoruba culture reinterpreted in terms of a parallelism or convergence between Yoruba and Brazilian Catholic assumptions about the universe and specifically the relationship between humanity and the supernatural as constrained by the social and political conditions that prevailed in Brazil at that time. The convergence between the role of the Yoruba òrìsà and the Catholic saints as intermediaries between humans and an all-powerful supreme being . . . made it possible for the founders of the Candomblés to seemingly adopt and practice Brazilian religious culture while still following their own beliefs and traditions. (115)

Fig. 73. Entrance to the Casa Branca *terreiro*, Salvador, Bahia, Brazil, 1996. (Photo by author.)

Fig. 74. Gantois *terreiro*, Salvador, Bahia, Brazil, 1996. (Photo by author.)

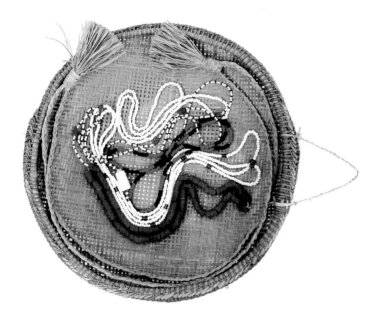

Fig. 75. *Contas*, or sacred necklaces, of the Brazilian *orixás*. (Author's collection and photo.)

In fact, rather than an exact continuation of African practices, what can be observed is a "reinvention of traditions" necessary to survive in a new setting. According to Roberto DaMatta (117), the above is part of the Brazilian characteristic of *relacionar*, or linking, constructing bridges, and staying in the middle of things.

Candomblé religion is of West African, Yoruban origin and follows a strict philosophy and organization. It is structured around the terreiro or *roça*, a physical space that symbolically re-creates a mythical African village community, facilitating regular ritual practice. The focus of Candomblé is on the life force, *axé*,[10] brought to earth in order to infuse all beings with divine energy. This is achieved primarily through possession trances that prepare the bodies of practitioners to receive the axé. Ritual drumming and dancing, sacrifices, and the consumption of sacred foods facilitate spreading this divine life energy among the people. The structure of the terreiro revolves around a ritual calendar of *festas*, or ceremonies; their specific purpose is to create optimum conditions for possession by the orixás, or gods. The orixá, or protective god/goddess of each person, sometimes referred to as *anjo da guarda*, or guardian angel, is determined during the *Jôgo de búzios*, or divination, performed by the iyalorixá (priestess) or *babalorixá* (priest) using sixteen cowry shells. Usually individuals have one primary, one secondary, and even a tertiary orixá they can identify with. They wear *contas*, especially "washed" sacred necklaces of beads representing the distinct colors of particular deities to honor them. Nonetheless, divination is not the only way to determine someone's orixá. Often, a given god or goddess may ask a person through a dream format to become initiated for him or her. Because this may

Fig. 76. Initiation ceremony *(confirmação)* of two *ékédes* led by the *iyalorixá* in trance. Ilê Asé Orisanlá J'Omin *terreiro,* Itaparica Island, Bahia, Brazil, 1996. (Photo by author.)

Fig. 77. Confirmed *ékédes* take seats at both sides of the *iyalorixá* throne in the *barracão*. Ilê Asé Orisanlá J'Omin *terreiro,* Itaparica Island, Bahia, Brazil, 1996. (Photo by author.)

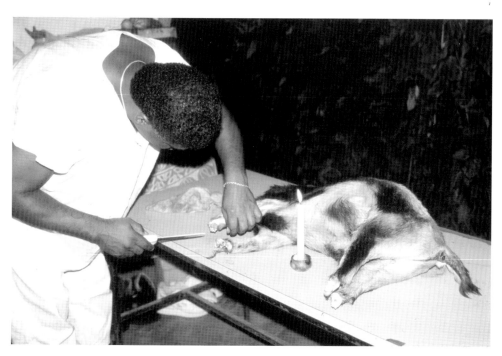

Fig. 78. A goat sacrificed by the *axôgún* is prepared at the Ilê Asé Orisanlá J'Omin *terreiro*, Itaparica Island, Bahia, Brazil, 1996. (Photo by author.)

Fig. 79. Offerings of sacred dishes at an *orixá* house. Ilê Asé Orisanlá J'Omin *terreiro*, Itaparica Island, Bahia, Brazil, 1996. (Photo by author.)

Fig. 80. The sacrificed goat's skin is used to elaborate an *atabaque*, or ritual drum. Ilê Asé Orisanlá J'Omin *terreiro,* Itaparica Island, Bahia, Brazil, 1996. (Photo by author.)

Fig. 81. Drums adorned for the *orixá* Ogum ceremony are being played at the Ilê Asé Orisanlá J'Omin *terreiro,* Itaparica Island, Bahia, Brazil, 1996. (Photo by author.)

happen before birth, as in the case of a woman receiving a message while pregnant, some children are born into the religion and grow up in the terreiros.

During my fieldwork in Salvador, Bahia, I participated in the initiation ceremony (*confirmação*) of two *ékédes*, a five-year-old girl named Dalinha and a twenty-eight-year-old accountant and university student, Celia, on 20 July 1996. Preparations for initiation start six months in advance with planning, study, and ritual baths. Starting on the twenty-first day before the public ceremony, the initiate is secluded in a special shack (*casa de força*) without contact with the external world, except for designated initiates; moreover, she may not be exposed to such elements as the sun or the dew. Every day she takes ritual baths, and a series of sacrifices, offerings, chants, and dances for the orixás are performed, including the *bori* and the *padê*.[11] All the activities of the roça are geared toward possession ceremonies, designed to bring the divine force axé to earth. The garden serves to grow herbs for healing ritual baths; the raising and subsequent ritual sacrifice of animals provides axé-full blood for blessing and initiation, as well as meat for sacred dishes to be offered to the orixás and shared at public ceremonies. The extremities, entrails, and blood (*partes de força* or "power parts") of a sacrificed goat are offered to the orixás, and the skin is dried to make a ritual drum used at the festas. Playing the drums, or *atabaques*, is an indispensable element of the ceremony and is believed to call the orixás with their axé to earth. The drums, to have power, ought to be made of natural elements, such as wood and animal skin from the terreiro, and they are named, blessed, fed, and adorned in a special manner. Only initiated men—the *ogãos*—are allowed to play ritual drums and to perform blood sacrifices. They also have organizational and protective functions in the terreiro, but the main ritual functions are the women's domain.

The spiritual leader or priestess of a traditional terreiro (terrain or religious community) has to be an older woman, a *mãe-de-santo* or iyalorixá.[12] Only after a minimum of seven years as a *iaô* or *filha-de-santo*[13] may an initiate be eligible to become the head priestess. This may occur after a dramatic life event such as an illness, a visionary episode, or a dream. The mother of gods is believed to be the intermediary between the orixás and humans and to have the ability to interpret divine will. She exercises absolute decision-making power about all matters concerning the terreiro and its members, from the most practical, such as economy and promotion, to the most esoteric, such as spiritual guidance, ceremonies, and divination. Her power comes from her healing and psychic abilities as well as from her practical knowledge and experience. She is the one to perform the *Jôgo de búzios*, or divination with sixteen cowry shells, and is versed in the *Jôgo de Odú* or *Ifá* oracle.[14] She prescribes the ritual baths and offerings (*oferendas*) to the gods, initiates new members of the

Fig. 82. Alda d'Alcántara Arruda, *iyalorixá* of the Ilê Asé Orisanlá J'Omin *terreiro*, dressed in her everyday white clothes. Itaparica Island, Bahia, Brazil, 1996. (Photo by author.)

terreiro, and even sews ritual clothes. One of her main functions involves entering into trances, during which she personifies different orixás in order to spread the blessings or axé among the people (see figs. 68 and 76).[15]

Other primary functions of a traditional Brazilian terreiro are also performed by women. The iyalorixá designates her "double"—a *iyá kêkêrê* or *mãe pequena* (little mother)—who helps her supervise all activities of the terreiro. The mãe-de-santo is the one to initiate the iaôs or filhas-de santo "putting the jackknife over the head" or "making the head" (*fazer a cabeça*) of the *abião* (aspirant). After the enclosure process, which can take anywhere from three weeks to three months, the abião becomes an initiate, or iaô. The iaô has to actively practice the religion for at least seven years before she can aspire to the *ébomin* category, which in turn makes her eligible for the iyalorixá position. If an initiate is not able to enter into trances or "receive the saint," she becomes an ékéde, her role during ceremonies being to help the ones in possession trances. They receive assistance with straightening their attire, cleaning off sweat, and changing into ritual clothes. The important function of cooking for terreiro ceremonies and for the offerings to the gods is also performed exclusively by women. The *iyá bassê*[16] is an older woman designated to direct these activities. The iyalorixá, the iaôs, the ékédes, and the ogãos constitute the família-de-santo (family of saint) or members of a given terreiro. This spiritual family surpasses in importance the blood family, although members of the same bloodline may belong to the same terreiro. The only restriction is that a mother cannot initiate her biological daughter or son into the religion.[17] Initiated and "confirmed" men (ogãos) are involved in separate activities in the terreiro, usually external to the religion, such as those of *axôgún* (performer of sacrifices) (see fig. 78), *alabê* (drummer) (see fig. 81), or *pêjigã* (maker of the altar). They may also be financial contributors. As the Brazilian anthropologist Edison Carneiro stated in 1948, "women hold all the permanent functions of the Candomblé, while the ones reserved to men are merely temporary or honorific. . . . This division of the hierarchy seems to confirm the opinion that Candomblé is a woman's trade" (*Candomblés da Bahia* 116–17).

Veneration of the Feminine

The woman-centered organization of the traditional Brazilian terreiro corresponds to ancient Yoruba beliefs in the great mystical power of older women. They receive the power *àjẹ* and are called *awọn ìyá wa* (our mothers), *iyámì* (my mother), and *iyá àgbà* (old and wise one). "The power of the mothers is equal or superior to that of the gods, for . . . the mothers own and control the gods" (Drewal and Drewal 8–9). According to Rowland Abiodun, "It is believed that from the beginning, the creator-God put women in charge of all the good things on earth. Without their sanction, no healing can take place, rain cannot fall, plants cannot bear fruits and children cannot come into the world."[18]

Older women are considered to be protective progenitors, healers, guardians of morality, social order, and the just redistribution of power and wealth. They are respected but also feared; they must be paid tribute and soothed in Gẹlẹdẹ festivals. Referring to Yorubaland, Drewal and Drewal explain the tripartite meaning of the word Gẹlẹdẹ: "'*Gẹ* means 'to soothe, to place, to pet or coddle'; *ẹlẹ* refers to a woman's private parts, those that symbolize women's secrets and their life-giving powers; and *dẹ* connotes 'to soften with care or gentleness'" (9, xv).

Juana Elbein dos Santos points out the existence of the feminine society Geledé in the Brazilian city of Salvador, Bahia and the corresponding festival that was performed every year on 8 December, the feast day of the Virgin of the Immaculate Conception, patron of Bahia. The festival was held annually until the death of Maria Júlia Figueiredo, Omóníké, *iyá-lase* or guardian of the oldest Nagô (Yoruba) terreiro of Bahia, Ilê Iyá-Nasô or Casa Branca (see fig. 73). Nowadays, the power of the *iyá-mi*, "our mothers," is kept by the *iabás*, or feminine orixás, such as Oxum, Iemanjá, Nanã,

Figs. 83 and 84. At Afro-Brazilian *terreiros* the important functions of handling food and cooking are performed exclusively by women. The preparation of sacred dishes for a ceremony takes several days and nights. Ilê Asé Orisanlá J'Omin *terreiro*, Itaparica Island, Bahia, Brazil, 1996. (Photos by author.)

Fig. 85. Members of the *família-de-santo* of the Ilê Asé Orisanlá J'Omin *terreiro* with author. Itaparica Island, Bahia, Brazil, 1996. (Photo by the Ilê Asé Orisanlá J'Omin. Author's collection.)

Oyá, and Ewa. All of them are also considered to be *iyá-eleye*, or owners of the gourd with a bird inside, which is a symbol of their power (*Os nàgô e a morte* 114–17). The great pumpkin symbolizes the egg-belly and the power of gestation and fecundity of the iyá-mi. Although in today's Brazil we cannot point to the practice of Geledé festivals, we can still observe the padê, a ritual restitution of feminine genitor power (*Iyá-mi Agbá*).

The above mythical beliefs are put into practice in the religious sphere of the terreiros but are also reflected in Brazilian society at large, especially in the African-influenced northwestern state of Bahia, where matrifocality is notable. This is mainly true for lower-class women of African descent, who are the heads of multigenerational households. They frequently have several and/or transitory sexual partners on whom they cannot rely materially, and the women are the ones to provide stability for the family. Consequently, children from different fathers receive the mother's last name, and daughters tend to be valued more than sons (Woortman 105).[19] This social structure originated during slavery, when the African family was abruptly dismantled and primarily single persons were brought to the New World. After obtaining their freedom, it was easier for women to find work and receive an income from domestic services or from trade (145, 105). According to Lloyd, trading is credited with allowing women in African Yoruba society to become economically independent of their husbands and accumulate greater wealth and prestige.[20] This situation was confirmed by the anthropologist Ruth Landes in her 1947 book on Bahia, *The City of Women*: "[S]tability is provided by black women. And the women have everything: they have the temples, the religion, the priestly offices, the bearing and rearing of children, and opportunities for self-support" (147).[21]

As I stated above, in the most traditional terreiros or Candomblé communities, the functions of iyalorixá or mãe-de-santo (priestess) and iaô or filha-de-santo (initiate who has the ability to enter into trances) can be performed only by women. In fact, during my stay in Salvador, Bahia in 1996, I frequented five terreiros of the Nagô (Yoruba) tradition (Ilê Asé Opô Afonjá; Ilê Asé Iyá-Nasô, or Casa Branca; Ilê Iyá Omí Asé Iyá Massê, or Sociedade São Jorge do Gantois; Ilê Asé Opô Aganjú; and Ilê Asé Orisanlá J'Omin, or São Bento), one of the Angola tradition (Mãe Bebê), and one of the Caboclo tradition. Only one of the seven (Ilê Asé Opô Aganjú) was directed by a man. But there also exists a great fluidity of gender roles in the milieu of Afro-Brazilian religious practices. Less orthodox terreiros initiate and admit male *filhos-de-santo* and may be directed by male priests (babalorixás or *pais-de-santo*). It is also common knowledge in Brazil that the pais-de-santo and the filhos-de-santo, or men who enter into trances incorporating orixás, tend to be homosexuals. Of the

136 Candomblé communities studied by the anthropologist Vivaldo da Costa Lima in the 1970s, only 34 were guided by pais-de-santo, of whom 28 were homosexuals ("A família-de-santo" 171). This is symbolically expressed by the fact that while being possessed, a person becomes the "horse" mounted by the orixá, as in a sexual act. In this way, regardless of the sex of the orixá, the person ridden by it becomes "structurally feminine." This is confirmed by the attire worn by male priests, which reinforces the ambiguity of gender identity. They wear sumptuous seventeenth-century-inspired women's gowns, pants, and headdresses. The clothes reflect the character and sex of the god/goddess and not of the person who wears them. In Africa, the priests of the Yoruba cults are also always women or men dressed in women's nineteenth-century nuptial attire (Matory 222–23). As Miguel A. De La Torre affirms, in relation to Cuban Santería and its orichas, "*los santos* (the saints) fail to fit into any male/female, black/white, or major/minor category. They inhabit a sacred area where borders are fluid and opposites are subverted and perpetually put in disarray" (8).

In northern and northeastern Brazil, where the matrilineal tradition is much more powerful than in other regions, there is a strong interdependence between the Candomblé and other areas of daily life. The symbolic gender system of the Afro-Brazilian religions, based on activity and passivity rather than on hetero- and homosexuality, also influenced the broader society, creating the categories of *homen* (active element) and *bicha* (passive element). "Homen" is used indiscriminately for those who sexually penetrate women and bichas. The social identity of the homen is not affected by the gender of his partner (Matory 226–27).

It is important to note that originally in Africa, and other places with strong African influence, such as Cuba, divination was a male domain. The *olúo*, or *olúwo*, was the foremost chief of the *babalawo* community of Ifá diviners (Barnet 27–8, 157). Both functions, the olúwo and the babalawo, have disappeared in Brazil, and divination has become absorbed by the female iyalorixá. There also are male babalorixás, but they are not as highly respected as the female. In Cuba, a country very similar to Brazil in its ethnic, cultural, and religious Yoruba-Catholic components, this process of feminization did not occur. Conversely, today in Cuba there is a strong male dominance in Afro-Cuban religions, such as Regla de Ocha (Santería). The paramount role in the hierarchy of diviners is taken by the babalawo (father of the secrets), who "rules the practice of Santería" (Barnet 28, 157). Another eminent role is held by the *oriaté*—an authority in divination and initiatory rites, versed in the philosophy of the religion, the ancient Yoruba myths, and their interpretation.[22] During my fieldwork in Cuba, I also observed vestiges of Spiritism and Indian beliefs in the placement of glasses of water for the spirits (*bóveda espiritual*), ritual cigar smoking, and the

Fig. 86. *Bóveda espiritual*, or Spiritist altar, made of seven glasses filled with water for the spirits of the dead. On the higher shelf there are images of Jesus Christ and Catholic saints. Havana, 1999. (Photo by author.)

Fig. 87. Regla de Palo altar in a Havana house. In Afro-Cuban religions, *orichas* and ancestors' spirits are frequently represented by dolls, 1999. (Photo by author.)

presence of Regla de Palo altars in the same space as the *canastilleros* for the orichas.[23] In Havana, altars were placed and divination happened inside private apartments, probably because of space constraints and previous censure of such practices.[24] Santería practice was persecuted as a crime in Cuba until 1940, and later restrictions resumed in 1962, until they were softened in the 1980s. Santería even received financial backing by the Cuban government in the 1990s. In the United States, Santería was not recognized as a legitimate religion until 1992 (De La Torre 4).

DARK VIRGINS AND WHITE GODDESSES

In comparison with east-central European and Mexican milieus discussed in previous chapters, the Virgin Mary/Goddess figure underwent even greater modifications and exchanges in areas of Latin America strongly influenced by African (mostly Yoruba) cultures. In this section I examine the development and transformation of symbolic functions played by particular Afro-Latin American female deities, such as the goddess Iemanjá in Brazil. The holy figure brought to the New World last tends to

Figs. 88 and 89. Cuban *canastilleros*, with attributes of the *orichas* placed on different shelves. Regla and Havana, 1999. (Photos by author.)

Fig. 90. Sanctuary of the Virgin of Regla, Cuba, 1999. (Photo by author.)

be the one to absorb or give a new name to the deities worshipped in preexistent religions. Such was the case of the Catholic Virgin of Guadalupe (see plate 2), who replaced Tonantzin–Ciuacoatl and a whole gamut of Aztec and pre-Aztec goddesses. This phenomenon also occurred in Brazil, where the Yoruba goddesses Iemanjá (see plate 9 and fig 66) and Oxum incorporated the Catholic Virgin of the Immaculate Conception (see plate 5), the African Mami Wata, and the Indian Siren Iara,[25] in spite of the simultaneous presence of the official national patroness, Our Lady Aparecida (see fig. 26). In Cuba, a country similar to Brazil in its cultural and racial substratum, Yemayá and Ochún reign at par value with the Virgin of Regla and the Virgin of Charity of El Cobre (see plate 11), while in Haiti Ezili Dantò is identified with the image of the Polish Black Madonna of Częstochowa. Moreover, similar to previously described east-central European and Mexican milieus, these goddesses are assembled in triads in a way that corresponds to Neolithic female deities. In Brazil, this trinity is constituted by Oxum, Iemanjá, and Nanã, in Cuba by their counterparts Ochún, Yemayá, and Naná Burukú,[26] and in Haiti by Lasyrenn, Ezili Dantò, and Ezili Freda. Carol Ochs, in her excellent study *Behind the Sex of God*, discusses the notion of the triple goddess as one of the two great mysteries of matriarchal religions. The maiden, the mother, and the old woman are actually aspects of the same entity with her waxing, full, and waning aspects. The "patriarchal adaptation of the three-in-one theme . . . is . . . the Christian Holy Trinity, where the Father, Son, and Holy Spirit are mystically united in one 'being'" (78) (see fig. 27).

In Brazil, an all-encompassing function is performed by the goddess Iemanjá, who is the utmost maternal and protective symbol and serves as a unifying force in the

Fig. 91. Virgin of Regla, Cuba, 1999. (Photo by author.)

Fig. 92. Ezili Dantò, or Mater Salvatoris, identified with the Polish Black Madonna of Częstochowa. Port-au-Prince, Haiti, 1980. (Photo by Judith Gleason. Reproduced with permission.)

Fig. 93. Women dancing at a Voodoo ceremony, with Ezili Dantò represented as the Black Madonna of Częstochowa in the background. Port-au-Prince, Haiti, 1980. (Photo by Judith Gleason. Reproduced with permission.)

Fig. 94. Nossa Senhora da Conceição da Praia (Our Lady of Immaculate Conception of the Beach), patron of Bahia. Salvador, Bahia, Brazil, 1996. (Photo by author.)

Fig. 95. Nossa Senhora da Conceição da Praia Church in Salvador, Bahia, Brazil, 1996. (Photo by author.)

life of different groups of Brazilians, greatly diversified by their economic, racial, and cultural status. Some see her as the Virgin of the Immaculate Conception, patroness of the sailors and of Bahia, the Virgin of the Glory or Assumption, and as Our Lady of Sailors—the Candlemas Virgin;[27] others, as the Yoruba Mother Goddess of the salty waters. In her different incarnations, she is present in the Catholic Mass as well as in Candomblé, Umbanda, and Caboclo ceremonies.[28]

The most popular image of Iemanjá in today's Brazil is related to the representation of the Virgin of the Immaculate Conception from the Baroque era. Already in the Middle Ages, the Virgin as *stella maris,*[29] or sea star, was associated with nautical imagery. In 1142 Alfonso Henriques, founder of the Portuguese dynasty, consecrated Portugal to the Mother of God, and during the Renaissance, the role of Mary as Queen of the Seas acquired a practical application for Spanish and Portuguese sailors. As Virgen de los Mareantes (Virgin of the Sailors) (see fig. 46), she became their protectress during maritime crossings. The Virgin of the Immaculate Conception was specially associated with the moon, the sky, and the sea (Warner 262, 267). Before his Atlantic crossings, Christopher Columbus named one of his caravels Santa María

Fig. 96. [left] Church of Sant' Anna (Saint Anne), Salvador, Bahia, Brazil, 1996. (Photo by author.)

Fig. 97. [right] Casa de Iemanjá (House of Iemanjá) is a gathering place for Salvador, Bahia fishermen, 1996. (Photo by author.)

(Holy Mary), and he gave the same name to one of the first Western Hemisphere islands he "discovered." In 1640 João IV proclaimed Our Lady of the Immaculate Conception as patroness of all Portuguese possessions, including Brazil (Boff 9, 11). Nossa Senhora da Conceição da Praia was also proclaimed "the only patroness" of the first capital of Brazil, Salvador, Bahia. Her sculpted image, as represented in the monumental church vis-à-vis Salvador's harbor, is similar to the seventeenth-century Spanish paintings by Velázquez, Zurbarán, Rivera, and Murillo (see plate 5).

Nonetheless, this is only the beginning of Mary's "career" in Brazil. The Immaculate Conception constitutes just one of the ingredients in the complex process of syncretisms and appropriations leading to the creation of very particular icons and cults. In Rio Vermelho, another Salvadorean shore, we can find the Igreja de Sant' Anna (Church of Saint Anne) next to the tiny Casa de Iemanjá (House of Iemanjá). Saint Anne, the Virgin Mary's mother, by whom Mary was "immaculately" conceived, is the protagonist of the first known representation of the Immaculate Conception,[30] and Iemanjá is the Yoruban goddess of the seas. The Casa de Iemanjá, where fishermen and other devotees gather to pray and leave offerings all year round, is also an annual point of embarkation on 31 December for boats full of flowers and

Fig. 98. Iemanjá with offerings inside Casa de Iemanjá, Salvador, Bahia, Brazil, 1996. (Photo by author.)

Fig. 99. Offerings inside Casa de Iemanjá, Salvador, Bahia, Brazil, 1996. (Photo by author.)

gifts dedicated to the goddess of the sea. That date is designated as Iemanjá's national holiday. In addition, in Brazil the two most important holidays dedicated to the main Yoruban deities of the waters are 8 December—to Oxum—and 15 August—to Iemanjá (D'Oxum 14). In this manner, the main Catholic Marian holidays, that of the Immaculate Conception (8 December) and that of the Assumption (15 August), became "distributed" between the orixás or goddesses equivalent to the Virgin Mary in Afro-Brazilian syncretic religions. These two days also correspond to two images from the seventeenth century that merged to create the icon of the Immaculate Conception: the Virgin of the Assumption, based on the description of the Woman of the Apocalypse, and the Immaculata Tota Pulcra.

Iemanjá is the Yoruban goddess of the salty waters and of fertility and was popularized in Brazil by West African slaves in the second half of the eighteenth century; as with the Virgin Mary, her color is blue and her day is Saturday. Today Iemanjá is a very important orixá in the Afro-Brazilian religion Candomblé. She is the goddess of the sea and the mother of almost all gods or orixás as well as of humans. Her name, Yeyé omo ejá, means Mother Whose Children Are Fish (Verger, *Orixás: Deuses iorubás* 190). She is also one of the wives of the god Oxalá, who is syncretized with Jesus Christ in a similar manner to Mary's or "Notre Dame's" identification with the Church as the Bride of Christ. In the Scriptures, Mary is described as a "highly favored daughter" of the Lord (Luke 1: 28), mother of the "Son of God" (Luke 1: 32), and bride of the Holy Spirit.[31] But since God is three equal persons: "Father, Son, and Holy Spirit" (Ripalta 15–16), Mary is also the Bride of Christ: "Daughter of God, Mother of God, Wife / of the Holy Spirit, from Nazareth" (García Nieto 39). "Scripture portrays the Church as the Bride of Christ. . . . The association of Mary with the Church allowed for her to take on the 'Bride of God' image from Ecclesia. . . . She is [Jesus's] physical Mother because she bore and raised Him according to the flesh, and His mystical Bride because she is the Image and preeminent member of the Church, who is the Bride of Christ. . . . Saint Germanus of Constantinople called Mary Theonymphos, a Greek term meaning 'God-wed' or 'Wedded to God'" ("Mary, the Bride of God"). According to myth, Iemanjá is the wife of her brother Aganjú, with whom she had the son-sun Orungán. She was raped by Orungán and gave birth to the waters and to the orixás.[32] Although in Christianity the notion of a Holy Matrimony (Hieros Gamos) between Mary and Jesus was sublimated through her identification with the church, the idea of the Virgin Earth-Moon giving birth to the son-sun has been preserved. In the same way that Christ appears with a crown in the form of a cross behind his head, the sun is designed with a four-point star in the Babylonian *kudurrus* (stelae), and a similar hieroglyph is used to designate the sun among the Maya, giving continuity to the universal archetype of the sun god (Pascual Blázquez 8). We can find analogies in different ancient cultures, as in the case of the Aztec Virgin Mother Goddess, Coatlicue, who gives birth to her sun-son god, Huitzilopochtli, or the Egyptian goddess Isis, who bears the god Horus. In addition, this figure, linked to social movements and religious causes, is the mother/source of a savior or advocate for the people.

An even more peculiar development occurred in the consciously syncretic, urban religion Umbanda, which began on 15 November 1908 (*Hail Umbanda*) and became widespread in Brazil. The Iemanjá image, as represented in Umbanda, became so popular that it created a national cult—Iemanjismo. This image, the result of multiple syncretic borrowings, conserves many similarities with that of the Immaculate Conception but is free of her contradictions. As in the traditional representation of the Immaculate Conception (see plate 5), Iemanjá, dressed in a blue robe, is portrayed as a white woman with long hair in a standing position. Some elements that frequently accompany both figures are the moon, the stars, and the crown. Nevertheless, as the Immaculate Conception becomes transformed into Iemanjá, she is liberated from the "pure" whiteness of her tunic, from her mantle, and from her waistband (see plate 9 and fig. 98).[33] Her blue dress is now fitted and low-necked, revealing the attributes of a sexual, fertile woman with wide hips and full breasts. The mirror, one of the six symbols of the purity of the Virgin Tota Pulcra, is reconceptualized as a symbol of Iemanjá's and Oxum's vanity (see plate 10). Interestingly, in Cuba, the ritual fan, or *abebe/agbebe*, is adorned with peacock feathers, which are a symbol of Ochún.[34] Similar to the case of Guadalupe–Tonantzin, Virgin Mary–Iemanjá's ancient connection with death is uncovered, as she is also the siren and the *calunga*,[35] who attracts sailors to the bottom of the sea.

The Virgin Mary in Christian tradition is reduced to only two female attributes— virginal purity and motherly love—(D'Ancona 5) although, as Ochs argues, the "basic duality that reflects the contradictory characteristics of all things" is also preserved by Mary, who "is the inversion of Eve" (81). "Building on the biblical image of Christ as the 'New Adam,' early Christians spoke of a 'New Eve,' a feminine cooperator with Jesus in the economy of the redemption." Mary was perceived as the second Eve who reverses the sin of the first one. "Later Church Fathers . . . identified the New Eve with the Church" ("Mary, the Bride of God"). In her Afro-Latin American incarnations, Mary recovers her ancient dominion over the whole cycle of birth, life, and death as well as her full humanity. The Virgin, in her Iemanjá form, claims her original role as a protector of fertility, life, and death, as in the archetype of the Magna Mater. This connection can be confirmed by the fact that until recently in Bahia, on 8 December, the day of the Immaculate Conception, the festival of the feminine society Geledé was celebrated in order to placate the "terrible ancestral mothers" (Augras 15). The Virgin Mary also recovers her humanity by becoming the incarnation of both the reality and the fantasy of a genuine Haitian woman in the complementary figures of Ezili Dantò and Ezili Freda.

As the Brazilian iabás (orixás, or goddesses connected to the waters) are represented by the trinity Oxum–Iemanjá–Nanã, or young woman–mature mother–old woman, so the Haitian *ezili* (*loas*, or goddesses) constitute the trinity Lasyrenn–Ezili Dantò–Ezili Freda. Lasyrenn, the siren/whale figure of West Africa, is identified with the patron saint of Cuba, Nuestra Señora de la Caridad del Cobre (Our Lady of Charity of El Cobre), syncretized with Ochún. Ezili Dantò, the most loved Mater Salvatoris, plays the role of protector as well as friend. She is portrayed by the image of the Polish Black Madonna of Częstochowa (see plate 1, fig. 9, and fig. 92).[36] Images of this famous Byzantine icon were most likely brought to Haiti by Polish soldiers sent by Napoleon Bonaparte to quell the Haitian slave rebellion. The Poles, used to fighting "for our and your freedom," joined the cause of Haiti's independence from France, which led to the creation of the first sovereign Latin American state in 1804. They remained in Haiti, and with them remained the sacred icon of the Madonna

Fig. 100. New Orleans Voodoo altar with the goddess Ezili Dantò as the Polish Black Madonna of Częstochowa, 2002. (Photo by author.)

of Częstochowa. This icon, which portrays a black, older Mother of God with three symbolic wounds resembling African tribal marks on her right cheek, is called Mater Salvatoris (Mother of the Savior) in Haiti and became fused with the African Mother Goddess Ezili Dantò. Subsequently, she was brought to the United States by the slaves of the French colonists who were escaping the Haitian war of independence at the beginning of the nineteenth century, and to this day she may be seen on New Orleans' Voodoo altars. Ezili Dantò is considered to be a goddess of unconventional sexuality, independence, and hard work; has various sexual partners, probably of both sexes; and is a single mother, her Christ-child is recognized as female.[37] The third goddess is Ezili Freda, represented by María Dolorosa del Monte Calvario. Surprisingly, she is not incarnated as an old wise woman figure, analogous to the Old European Neolithic as well as contemporary Brazilian trinity. Instead, she is represented by a white Haitian elite woman, beautiful, vain, and inclined to romance (Brown, *Mama Lola* 221–47). In both Brazilian and Haitian cultures, their most popular Goddess/Virgin Mary figures have been transformed by changing contexts and adapted to contemporary needs. Ezili Dantò is a persona with which the majority of Haitian women can easily identify. She is a single mother and a survivor, hard working but without the security of a stable man in her life. Such grim reality calls for a fantasy escape. This is provided by Ezili Freda, who resembles a soap opera character of a white elite woman concerned only with her own pleasures. In the case of Brazil, the transformation of Iemanjá from a West African faceless container for the orixá of the salty waters into the whitened, Virgin of the Immaculate Conception–like, sensual figure, reflects in part the superimposition of the image of a typical Brazilian woman with her abiding dream of wealth/whiteness.

Ilê Asé Orisanlá J'Omin Terreiro

During my research in Salvador, Bahia in 1996, I conducted meticulous fieldwork at the Ilê Asé Orisanlá J'Omin religious community. Placed in the contexts of other terreiros and the African-influenced society of northeastern Brazil and the Caribbean, it will serve as a case study on syncretism and hybridity in Latin America.

Although Bahia's Candomblé practitioners make claims as to the African purity of their religion, even in the most orthodox terreiros, Catholic and Indian influences are obvious. In the new sociopolitical colonial setting, preexisting religions had to be reformulated, reinterpreted, and reorganized in order to survive (Greenfield 120). In the Ilê Asé Orisanlá J'Omin terreiro, whose Catholic name is Terreiro de São Bento, there are crucifixes hanging over the iyalorixá throne in the *barracão*, or ritual space,[38] and the *eguns'*, or ancestors', house. There are also two *aldeias*, or "villages," honoring *caboclos*, or Indian spirits. These are specially designated places of the terreiro, dedicated to the caboclos Sultão das Matas and Gentileiro, similar to the houses of the particular orixás. The difference is that the caboclos are housed outside, and offerings to them are placed near or hung from the trees, re-creating the native Brazilian tradition.

The mythical space of the Ilê Asé Orisanlá J'Omin terreiro is located on the Itaparica Island, far away from urban distractions. There is no running water or electricity, and the members of the terreiro travel there from their homes in Salvador, usually a three-hour trip by bus and ferry, which involves crossing the All Saints Bay (Bahia de Todos os Santos). They stay at the roça or terreiro anywhere from a few days to a few weeks at a time, depending on their function within the religious community and their outside occupations. But the life and influence of the roça does not end at the Itaparica Island. When I visited the iyalorixá Alda d'Alcántara Arruda's house in Salvador, it was full of terreiro members and aspirants, and terreiro-related activities continued there. In her city home, Alda sews ritual clothes and performs divination for outside clients. She is well versed in the Jôgo de búzios, as well as in the Jôgo de Odú or the Ifá oracle.[39]

During our conversations, both the iyalorixá and other members of the terreiro

Fig. 101. Entrance to the Ilê Asé Orisanlá J'Omin *terreiro*, Itaparica Island, Bahia, Brazil, 1996. (Photo by author.)

Fig. 102. *Barracão*, or ritual space, at the Ilê Asé Orisanlá J'Omin *terreiro*, Itaparica Island, Bahia, Brazil, 1996. (Photo by author.)

Fig. 103. The entrance to the *barracão* is adorned by palm branches (*marió*), specially prepared by men, in order to prevent negative spirits from entering the ritual space. (Photo by author.)

Fig. 104. A crucifix hangs over the *iyalorixá* throne in the *barracão* at the Ilê Asé Orisanlá J'Omin *terreiro*, Itaparica Island, Bahia, Brazil, 1996. (Photo by author.)

Fig. 105. A crucifix hangs on the *eguns*', or ancestors', house at the Ilê Asé Orisanlá J'Omin *terreiro*, Itaparica Island, Bahia, Brazil, 1996. Only men have access to this house. (Photo by author.)

Fig. 106. At the *aldeias de caboclos* (villages of the Indian spirits), and for the *orixá* Ossain, offerings hang from or are placed near trees. Ilê Asé Orisanlá J'Omin *terreiro*, Itaparica Island, Bahia, Brazil, 1996. (Photo by author.)

always insisted that their religion comes from Africa and their intent is to keep it as purely African as possible. When I inquired about the Catholic symbol of the crucifix, which was placed both above the chair of the iyalorixá in the barracão and on the eguns' house, it was explained to me that they were there only as a tribute to Alcides, who founded the terreiro in 1934.[40] At that time Catholic symbols were necessary to cover up forbidden African religious practices. In the same fashion, African orixás were camouflaged as Catholic saints possessing similar powers and attributes. This was facilitated by the similarities between Yoruba worship and popular pre-Reformation Catholicism.[41] For example, the Virgin of the Immaculate Conception became Iemanjá, Saint Anne became Nanã, Saint Lazarus became Omolú, and Jesus Christ became Oxalá. Those and other orixás share personal characteristics, colors, and feast days with their respective saints. In spite of their claims to African purity, until today even some of the most traditional and orthodox terreiros of Bahia order Catholic Masses on days of important Candomblé ceremonies. A good example is the celebration for the orixá Nanã, the old wise woman, on 28 July, the feast day of Saint

Fig. 107. The Ilê Asé Orisanlá J'Omin *terreiro* is located on Itaparica Island, across All Saints Bay from the city of Salvador, Bahia, Brazil, 1996. (Photo by author.)

Anne, mother of the Virgin Mary.

On 28 July 1996 I participated in the Sant'Anna celebrations organized by the Sociedade São Jorge do Gantois, or Ilê Iyá Omí Asé Iyá Massê, one of the three oldest and most traditional Candomblé communities in Bahia (see fig. 74). Wearing white ritual attire, two female practitioners, one old and one young, began the celebration by bringing a statue of Saint Anne, adorned with pink roses, to the church Igreja de Sant' Anna (see fig. 96). A ceremonial blessing of the statue followed. After the Mass, everyone returned to the terreiro for breakfast and ritual dancing and drumming. The blessed statue of Saint Anne was deposited in an honorific place[42] next to the iyalorixá, *mãe* Cleusa; there was also a statue of Saint George, identified with the orixá Oxossi, patron of the terreiro. Nevertheless, there was no indication of any liturgical mixture with Catholicism during this "African" ceremony.

The consensus among Candomblé priestesses (Mãe Stella 45) and Catholic priests, such as the archbishop of Bahia, Dom Lucas Moreira Neves, seems to be that there is nothing wrong with this parallel practice of religions, provided they do not mix with each other and are maintained as separate cults. Pierre Verger, one of the main authorities on Candomblé,[43] quoted a similar opinion by *pai* Balbino of the Opô Aganjú terreiro: "Candomblé and Catholicism are like water and oil. You can pour them into the same container, but they will remain separate" ("Syncrétisme" 45). That is, according to Ferretti's classification ("Religious Syncretism" 91–93), they accept the existence only of parallelism or juxtaposition in Afro-Brazilian religions, rejecting the

Fig. 108. The house of Oxalá, identified with Jesus Christ, is adorned by the symbol of the dove. Ilê Asé Orisanlá J'Omin *terreiro*, Itaparica Island, Bahia, Brazil, 1996. (Photo by author.)

other strategies of convergence or adaptation (Marzal's "synthesis") and interpretation or linkage (Marzal's "reinterpretation").[44] Nevertheless, Verger also reminds us of the paradox that the African gods and the Catholic saints are simultaneously identical and separate, but equally revered (45).

In the Ilê Asé Orisanlá J'Omin terreiro, much smaller and newer, but no less strict or orthodox than the Gantois terreiro, we can see the symbol of the crucifix in the barracão and on the house of the eguns, or ancestors. We also notice the symbol of the dove on the house of Oxalá, identified with Jesus Christ. No Catholic Masses are held for this terreiro. Among the houses of the African orixás, we can find two aldeias, or "villages," for Sultão das Matas and for Gentileiro, both representing Indian ancestral spirits, or caboclos. It was explained to me that they were celebrated in ceremonies separate from those of the orixás, and nothing else was revealed until I attended the Mesa Branca ceremony for the caboclo Cacique Pedra Branca (Chief White Stone) at the city home of iyalorixá Alda. I was strongly discouraged from participating in this ceremony, under the pretext that it was quite unimportant and not as nice as the festas for the orixás.[45] In fact, I did not find out about the ceremonies until shortly before leaving Salvador.

Contrary to predictions, Mesa Branca turned out to be a most interesting ceremony. In comparison with all the public Candomblé festas, which lasted a minimum of three to four hours and were usually performed on a Saturday night,[46] this was a much shorter and smaller event. It lasted from 7:00 p.m. to 9:30 p.m. on a Thursday, with the attendance of only some of the terreiro members and no outsiders.[47] As in Candomblé rituals, the dress color was white, but conversely, women's heads were uncovered. This ceremony, dedicated to a *dono da terra* (lord of the land), or Indian ancestor, opened and closed with a Catholic "Our Father" in Portuguese. The name of the ceremony, Mesa Branca, or White Table, is derived from the central presence of a white cloth-covered table on which all white offerings (like those for the orixá Oxalá)—flowers, grapes, water, and an Oxalá necklace—are placed. An oratory included Bible reading and comments about Jesus Christ and his Yoruba counterpart Oxalá. Mãe Alda experienced the embodiment of the caboclo Cacique Pedra Branca through a trance. As Pedra Branca, the priestess blessed, gave advice, and cleaned the energy fields of those present. The ceremony was performed without the drumbeats and Yoruba chants of the Candomblé and without the cigars and beer drinking of the Caboclo ceremonies. All communication, including chants, was conducted in Portuguese.[48]

This curious ceremony was neither traditional Candomblé, nor Candomblé de Caboclo, nor a strict Spiritist session, nor a Catholic prayer gathering. Simultaneously, it had elements of all four. The African, the European, and the Indian ingredients were celebrated in the figures of Oxalá, Jesus Christ, and Perda Branca, respectively. Despite appearances, there was no contradiction but rather parallelism and identification of all of them. Indeed, they all three share the similar characteristics of being warriors for peace, being "deified ancestors" (Barnet 24), and being symbolized by the color white. In this context, there was no problem in having the Indian caboclo Cacique Pedra Branca celebrated in an African way as an ancestor of the Brazilian land (or the Yoruba egun), or in a Spiritist way as one of the deceased. Jesus Christ, introduced as a religious icon by the Portuguese, was viewed as part of the same archetype.

The Mesa Branca was mainly a Spiritist ceremony with Caboclo elements, similar to the ones I observed at Mãe Aída's Candomblé de Caboclo terreiro on 31 July 1996, where the focus was the divination and advice given to the participants by the mãe-de-santo in trance. Conversely, in the Ilê Asé Orisanlá J'Omin ceremony, there was no dancing, drumming, drinking, or cigar smoking, and it communicated a definitely more Spiritist and Catholic character. We can conclude that the collective spirit of the warrior of peace identified with each one of the three main Brazilian ancestries was celebrated that evening. The belief that cigar smoke, used in Candomblé de Caboclo ceremonies, helps to access the future and hidden knowledge comes from

Fig. 109. At Candomblé *terreiros* everyone dresses in white, and ceremonies may take place at all hours of day and night. Ilê Asé Orisanlá J'Omin *terreiro*, Itaparica Island, Bahia, Brazil, 1996. (Photo by author.)

Fig. 110. Syncretic altar with Catholic, Indian, and African elements at the Ilê Asé Orisanlá J'Omin *terreiro*, Itaparica Island, Bahia, Brazil, 1996. (Photo by author.)

the Amerindian tradition, and is also widely used for divination by the santeros in Cuba.[49] In fact, Cuban Santería has a much more syncretic character than Brazilian Candomblé, as Spiritist, Indian, Kardecist, and Catholic elements are present. Its mixture recalls the highly crossbred Brazilian Umbanda religion.

The Mesa Branca ceremony brings to mind a spatial arrangement I observed at the center of the only house serving the needs of people (and not orixás, caboclos, or eguns[50]) at the Ilê Asé Orisanlá J'Omin terreiro. This was a hybrid altar that included the Catholic images of Saint John and Saint Lucia, several Indian caboclos, and Yoruba orixás, such as Xangô and Oxum. This spatial arrangement, where figures and symbols of each tradition were placed one on top of another on several separate shelves, echoed the Cuban canastillero (see figs. 88 and 89)[51] and *bóveda de aguas* Spiritist altars (see fig. 86). It also echoed the endless conglomeration of Catholic saints, African gods, and Indian ancestors seen in botánicas all over Latin America, the Caribbean, and the Latino United States (see plate 12).[52] Such stores may contain objects, remedies, and services from a wide range of popular religious manifestations representing the diverse practices of Catholicism, Spiritism, orixá worship, Indian ritual, and Occultism to New Age, depending on local need. As they serve mainly people from popular extraction, they tend to be located in U.S. Latino inner cities and Latin American popular barrios. Nonetheless, this is no longer true for places like New Orleans or Salvador, Bahia, where cultural mixture is so preponderant that the syncretic worship spread to other neighborhoods and became commodified as a tourist attraction. In such places, the assemblage of diverse, seemingly contradictory and exaggerated objects became metamorphosed from "kitsch" into "chic."

Symbols of National Identity and Social Justice in Brazil and in Cuba

In chapters 1 and 2, I analyzed the role of the Our Lady of Częstochowa and the Virgin of Guadalupe as symbols of national identity and social justice. In this section, I will discuss the construction of national Catholic icons in Brazil and in Cuba. In Brazil, in spite of the existence of the all-encompassing Iemanjá, the official symbol of nationality became Our Lady Aparecida, a thirty-six-centimeter statue of a black Virgin of the Immaculate Conception, found in 1717 by humble fishermen in the Paraíba River (see fig. 26).[53] This finding was followed by a series of miracles and homages. The year 1745 marked the construction of the first chapel, 1888 of the first church, and 1980 of the New Basilica. In 1904 Aparecida was crowned, in 1930 she was declared Patroness of Brazil by Pope Pious XI, and in 1931 she was designated Queen of Brazil. With the 1980 papal visit to her sanctuary, 12 October was declared a national holiday honoring Aparecida. While consecrating the New Basilica, the Polish pope John Paul II compared the black Virgin Aparecida to his native country's black patroness, Our Lady of Częstochowa:

> Lady Aparecida, a son of yours
> that belongs to you without any reservations—totus tuus!—
> . . .
> wants to speak to you, at this moment.
> He remembers with emotion, because of the dark color
> of this image of yours, another
> representation of yours,
> the Black Virgin of Jasna Góra![54]

Nevertheless, according to Rubem Fernandes: "Where the Polish Patroness integrates all of Mary's titles [of Mother, Lady, and Queen] under the royal crown, the Brazilian Patroness . . . has not accomplished that feat. . . . the Black Lady Aparecida does not enjoy the same significance and value as the Black Lady of Częstochowa. . . . Aparecida is only recognized in the center-south of the country as the number-one devotion center [with] the states of São Paulo, Rio de Janeiro, and Minas Geraïs . . . [as] the basic sphere of Aparecida's influence" (799–801). This significance was taken over by the goddess Iemanjá. The appearance of the Virgin Aparecida in the early 1700s coincides with the emergence of Brazilian nationalism since the Emboabas War (1708–9).

As I discussed earlier, the widespread image of Iemanjá from Umbanda portrays her as a beautiful white woman with long hair. On the other hand, Frei Clodovis Boff points out that in some songs used by the CEBs (Comunidades Eclesiásticas de Base)—popular Catholicism congregations—such as "Mãe negra Aparecida," Our Lady Aparecida is addressed as *Soberana quilombana* (sovereign of a free area composed of runaway slaves), *Menina Yaô* (girl initiated in an Afro-Brazilian religion), and *Olodum nosso Deus* (Olodum our God) (87–88); she is perceived as a liberating power for the oppressed in her role as goddess mother/father:

> Come, Mary woman,
> To teach us your new song
> A God with a woman's face
> Come to announce to the poor! ("Vem, Maria Mulher")

> Women oppressed through history,
> Great discrimination
> Raise their voice and proclaim:
> Is time for liberation! ("Eu te saúdo Maria," Boff 83).

The Cuban Virgin of Charity of El Cobre (see plate 11) on the other hand, according to tradition was found floating in the sea near the Oriente, or Eastern Province, in the early 1600s (different accounts mention 1606–8, 1611–12, and the 1620s as the dates of her appearance). From 1640 she became the focus of devotion in the town of El Cobre, and during the nineteenth-century war for independence from Spain (1868–78) and subsequent struggles until Cuban independence in 1902, she became "the rebel Virgin, the patriot Virgin, the national Virgin" (Tweed 19, 22–23). In 1936 she was crowned the Mother and Patron of Cuba; in 1959 a Mass for her was celebrated on Havana's Revolution Square in honor of Castro's triumphant revolution; and in 1998 Pope John Paul II crowned her in Santiago de Cuba as the Patron and Queen of Cuba

("Virgen de la Caridad Patrona de Cuba"). According to legend, the Virgin of Charity was found by the Indian brothers Juan and Rodrigo de Hoyos and the black slave boy Juan Moreno in the Nipe bay while searching for salt.

The fact that the men she appeared to are portrayed as being of Indian and African races, rowing a small boat during a storm, symbolizes the emergence of a nationalist sentiment based on native and dispossessed populations, similar to Mexico and Brazil. Yet the colors of the two Indians and of the Virgin have since been bleached, and one of the Indians in present-day popular representations appears as a bearded European. He was renamed Juan, thus creating *los tres Juanes* (the three Johns), representing the African, the Amerindian, and the European components of Cuba. The Virgin of El Cobre/Ochún was also adopted by exilic Cubans, who built a shrine for her in Miami, Florida in 1973, after her statue was smuggled out of Cuba in a suitcase. By the 1990s, this shrine became the most popular Catholic pilgrimage site in the United States. The history of this Virgin parallels events from Cuban history: in the early 1600s she was found floating in the sea on a wooden board and rescued like a contemporary *balsera* (rafter) (De La Torre 5–8); she fought for Cuban independence and for Castro's revolution; and, more recently, like so many of her compatriots, one of her statues "escaped" illegally through the border and ended up in Miami. Similar to so many Cubans, she is of multiracial origin.

As Ivor L. Miller observes, besides the image of the Virgin of Charity of El Cobre/ Ochún, other symbols from Catholic and Afro-Cuban religions have been widely used in Cuban politics. Castro's revolutionary colors—red and black—correspond to the oricha Elegguá (syncretized with El Santo Niño de Atocha), who dwells on the crossroads and opens the way for any enterprise. Castro's revolutionary army came from Sierra Maestra on 1 January 1959; this is the ritual date of El Niño de Atocha/ Elegguá as well as of San Miguel/Oddùa. It is also the day when babalawos perform prophecy for the new year. During Fidel Castro's inaugural speech in 1959, a white dove landed and remained on his body the entire time. The white dove is a powerful symbol for Catholics as well as for practitioners of all Afro-Cuban religions. For Catholics it represents the Holy Spirit; for the Yoruba (Lukumí) Santería, Obatalá or Our Lady of Mercy; for the Palo Monte, Nsámbi; for the Abakuá, Abasí. In addition, at the beginning of his speeches Castro salutes the martyrs of the revolution, giving them the reverence shown for Afro-Cuban eguns, or ancestors, and monuments to different heroes around the country are structured as huge altars. Another ambiguous element are the white suits worn by the Cuban presidents Machado and Batista and Castro's white outfit used during his visit to Guinea's President Touré in 1972, as they may suggest adherence to Afro-Cuban religions, whose members wear

Fig. 111. Santería offerings to *oricha* Elegguá, represented by a coconut shell, with the face made out of cowry shells, and by a doll dressed in white ritual attire. San Antonio, 2005. (Photo by April D. Johns. Reproduced with permission.)

Fig. 112. El Santo Niño de Atocha, syncretized with Elegguá. (Author's collection.)

Fig. 113. During Fidel Castro's inaugural speech in Havana, 1959, a white dove landed and remained on his body the entire time. (Fidel Castro Photographs Collection. Manuscripts Division. Department of Rare Books and Special Collections, Princeton University Library. Reproduced with permission.)

only white for one year after initiation. The colors, symbols, and spatial arrangements may be read at many levels, because they signify something different in the cultural code of Catholics, Afro-Cubans, and Westerners. When politicians display these symbols, diverse sectors of a multicultural population read them in distinct ways. These multiple superimposed symbols usually reinforce each other (35–47).

A particular use of Afro-Catholic symbology was displayed in the saga of Elián González, a Cuban boy who appeared in the waters near the coast of Florida on Thanksgiving Day 1999. He came to be seen as Jesus by the Catholic community and as Elegguá by the Santería community. According to Miami rumors, as Jesus and as Elegguá, he was destined to save the Cubans by overthrowing Castro's rule (De La Torre 5).

The Virgin of Charity of El Cobre (see plate 11), identified with Ochún, is usually portrayed as a dark-skinned triangular figure, dressed in gold like Ochún, holding a white baby Jesus. Similarly, the Virgin of Regla (see fig. 91), syncretized with Ochún's sister Yemayá, is also black and holds a white baby Jesus, but the color of her clothes is blue, as it corresponds to Yemayá. The prototypes of both these figures are identifiable in Spain (see fig. 25).[55] The Peninsular Virgin of Regla at her sanctuary in Chipiona in southern Spain is also a small (sixty-two centimeters) black statue holding a white baby Jesus. Although the two figures were made from one piece of wood, Jesus was stripped from the Virgin and replaced with a white one in the sixteenth century.[56] In Brazil, some images of Our Lady Aparecida are depicted above a small boat rowed by the three humble fishermen who found her in the Paraíba River, similarly to the case of the Virgin of Charity of El Cobre. Aparecida is of intense black complexion and is identified with the Virgin of the Immaculate Conception as are Iemanjá (in Bahia) and Oxum (in Rio de Janeiro) (Fernandes 812).

SUMMARY

The phenomena discussed in this chapter constitute an example of the extraordinary fluidity of appropriation, reconceptualization, and exchange of color, gender, meaning, and religious and cultural identity that occurred both in the Atlantic transitions and in the context of the new hybridity of emerging Latin America. Here, traditional values and needs had to be renegotiated on a continual basis. As Roberto Motta notes, "In contrast with most Western traditions [Candomblé] is not a salvation religion." Rather, it helps the devotees to "survive in this world" ("Ethnicity, Purity, the Market, and Syncretism" 75). Through revision and interpretation, Candomblé practitioners accommodated elements of Yoruba tradition to the structure of Brazilian society (Greenfield 122). These processes were more intense in coastal areas such as the

Caribbean and Brazil, where Indian, European, and African populations collided with full strength.

However, as with Brazilian, Cuban, and Haitian Africans, the results of the above transformations are sometimes surprising—the entire society, including the dominant classes, feels the impact of the group that was the most dispossessed and abused. Nowadays, all Brazilians, Cubans, and Haitians, whether they are aware of it or not, are under the influence of the culture of African slaves that over time permeated daily life in those countries, and it is mainly because of the cultural expressions of this group, originally at the lowest level of society, that they are known to the world.[57] And yet, this process has not been unilateral. While the Africans lent the Europeans the name and the characteristics of their goddess Yemoja, the Portuguese provided the consecrated image of the Virgin of the Immaculate Conception with her erect posture and her blue color. The result of these exchanges is Iemanjismo, an all-encompassing national cult of the "new" Yemoja.

Although the original images of the phenomena of Guadalupe, Iemanjá, Yemayá, and Ezili Dantò exist in Spain, Portugal, Poland, and Africa, they have not evolved in the same way in the new territories as in their places of origin. In Spain, in Portugal, in Poland, and to a lesser degree in Africa and in Mexico, their representations are petrified. It is within the porous borders between different races, languages, and cultures in the New World that these effigies acquire a new dynamic life carrying out multiple functions. This encourages an analysis of modes of survival developed by populations as a response to fluctuating circumstances. Strategies may include irony, mockery, playfulness, and improvisation, developed by black slaves brought to American shores. Along with other coastal societies, the latter were constantly exposed to new contexts and their existence endangered. Their resilience provided unforeseen creative possibilities. Parallel to the transformation of these human groups, their symbols also undergo modifications, fulfilling new roles in these difficult transitions. These symbols, ever fluid and adaptable, reflect the identity and strength of individuals who live in hybrid circumstances. In the next chapter I discuss further transfigurations of the syncretic Virgin of Guadalupe figure in the Latino United States.

Plate 1. Our Lady of Częstochowa, Jasna Góra, Poland. Icon dating from sixth–ninth century AD, of the type *Hodegetria*, or "Indicator of the Way."

Plate 2: The Virgin of Guadalupe, Basilica of Guadalupe, Mexico City.

Plate 3: Procession for the Black Madonna of Częstochowa in the southern town of Poronin, Poland, 1991. Copies of sacred icons travel across the country visiting different locations. (Photo by author.)

Plate 4: Matachines—Danza Guadalupana de Pablo Olivarez, Sr., dancing in front of Our Lady of Guadalupe Church on El Paso Street. First and third figures from the left represent the China Poblana, San Antonio, 12 December 2005. (Photo by author.)

Plate 5: *The Virgin of the Immaculate Conception of El Escorial* by Bartolomé Esteban Murillo. Mary is represented as a young virgin. (Reproduced with permission of the El Prado Museum, Madrid, Spain.)

Plate 6: Our Lady of Guadalupe, Cáceres, Spain. (From the archives of the late Antonio D. Portago.)

Plate 7: "Estandarte de Cortés con la Virgen de la Inmaculada Concepción." Banner with the Virgin of the Immaculate Conception wearing a crown with twelve stars used by Hernán Cortés during the conquest of Mexico. The image bears a striking resemblance to the Mexican Virgin of Guadalupe. (Museo Nacional de Historia, Mexico City. Reproduced with permission of the Instituto Nacional de Antopología e Historia, Mexico City.)

Plate 8: *Verdadero retrato de santa María Virgen de Guadalupe, patrona principal de la Nueva España jurada en México* (Real Portrait of Holy Mary Virgin of Guadalupe, Main Patron of New Spain Sworn in Mexico) by Josefus de Ribera i Argomanis, 1778. (Reproduced with permission of the Museo de la Basílica de Guadalupe, Mexico City.)

Plate 9: Multiple Iemanjá statues at a Salvador, Bahia *botánica*, Brazil, 1996. (Photo by author.)

Plate 10: Iemanjá and Oxum represented as mermaids at the Casa de Iemanjá in Salvador, Bahia, Brazil, 1996. (Photo by author.)

Plate 11: Our Lady of Charity of El Cobre, syncretized with Ochún, wears yellow and gold. Havana, Cuba, 1999. (Photo by author.)

Plate 12: *Botánica* in Salvador, Bahia, Brazil. Sacred necklaces for the *orixás* hang over statues of Catholic saints and Indian ancestors' spirits, or *caboclos*. In front, a highly syncretized figure from the Umbanda religion, the Pomba Gira, a female form of the trickster *orixá*, Exú. She may be perceived as a devil or a protectress, 1996. (Photo by author.)

Plate 13: Lowrider car with a mural of the Virgin of Guadalupe by Milton Chávez on the hood, Albuquerque. (Photo by Jacqueline Orsini Dunnington. Reproduced with permission.)

Plate 14: Blending of two Mexican icons: the Virgin of Guadalupe and Frida Kahlo, Santa Fe, New Mexico. (Photo by Charles Mann. Reproduced with permission.)

Plate 15: *Portrait of the Artist as the Virgin of Guadalupe*, 1978, by Yolanda M. López. (Reproduced with permission of the artist.)

Before the world, before all of North America, before all our brothers in the bronze continent, we are a nation, we are a union of free pueblos, we are Aztlán.

—RUDOLFO ANAYA

❧

Today we are witnessing la migración de los pueblos mexicanos, *the return odyssey to the historical/ mythological Aztlán.*

—GLORIA ANZALDÚA

❧

I'm going to Aztlán, where I wanna be.

—EL VEZ

CHAPTER FOUR

Aztlán

The Subversion of the Virgin in the Mexican American Southwest

ॐ

The transformation of religious symbols through syncretism, the superimposed layers of meanings, reaches its peak in contemporary borderland areas, such as those of the southwestern United States.[1] Here, the dark Virgin of Guadalupe, which replaced Indian goddesses during the Spanish Conquest and colonization of Mexico, reemerges with a vengeance, acquiring unexpected hybrid forms and messages.

Border spaces between cultures reflect a dynamic identity, hybridity, adaptability, creativity, and ambiguity. *Nepantla,* or "place at the frontier," (Anzaldúa, "Chicana Artists" 163) also means transgression of cultural and judicial norms. People who find themselves in these circumstances lose their context of origin and have to adapt to new conditions. Those who resist assimilation may find themselves in countercultures. Whether they desire it or not, they are subject to absorption by the dominant culture, the group that has the most economic and, consequently, political power. In these circumstances, "*la Virgen de Guadalupe* is the single most potent religious, political and cultural image of the Chicano/ *mexicano.* She . . . is a synthesis of the old world and the new, of the religion and culture of the two races in our psyche, the conquerors and the conquered. She is the symbol of the mestizo true to his or her Indian values. *La cultura chicana* identifies with the mother (Indian) rather than with the father (Spanish)" (Anzaldúa, "Coatlalopeuh" 53–54).

The subversive role of the Virgin, discussed in previous chapters in accordance with her description in the "Song of Songs,"[2] has been further developed in present times. Most recently, in Mexico, Nicaragua, and the United States, the Zapatistas, the Sandinistas, and the California vineyard workers have carried her on standards during struggles for social justice.[3] In the demonstrations against the U.S. war in Iraq, starting in 2003, and against the criminalization of immigrant workers in 2006, the Virgin of Guadalupe has been proudly displayed on the banners of protesters in many U.S. cities.

Fig. 114. *The Legacy of César Chávez*, 1997, mural by Emigdio Vasquez, Rancho Santiago College, Santa Ana, CA. (Reproduced with permission of the artist.)

This process of "appropriation" of the Virgin Mary has been especially developed and adapted to local needs in the Mexican territories that became part of the United States in 1848 and are now the states of Texas, New Mexico, Arizona, and California. Here, far from the official centers of power, the fluidity and adaptability of the image of Guadalupe is prominent. In the liminal spaces of the borderlands, "the levels of resignification" (García Canclini 278) are multiple, and the image of the Virgin of Guadalupe is charged with special significance as an ally of the dispossessed and immigrant populations. The symbol of Guadalupe also acquires new functions along with new meanings in these fluctuating circumstances. Converted into a signature of resistance against the dominant Anglo-Saxon culture, she achieves new status as the Virgin of the "crossing," the "pollution," and the "identity crisis" (Gómez-Peña 180–82). Her role as an emblem of Chicano identity and dignity became most obvious in its association with the vineyard workers' strike organized by César Chávez in 1965. This act of Mexican American assertion, which had tremendous sociopolitical significance for Hispanic populations in North America, also paved the way for a new application of the Guadalupe figure. Emigdio Vasquez's 1997 mural *The Legacy of César Chávez* illustrates this period of Chicano struggles. Besides being a tribute to United Farm Workers Union leaders, César Chávez, Fred Ross, and Dolores Huerta, the mural includes many anonymous farm workers and the founder of Teatro Campesino, Luis Valdez (Dunitz and Prigoff, *California Murals*). It also features a red banner with the black eagle, symbol

Fig. 115. *Tradicion Cultura,* San Antonio's West Side Mexican American mural featuring symbols of identity, such as a lowrider car and the Virgin of Guadalupe, placed in front of the San Antonio cityscape. (Photo by author.)

Fig. 116. Pachucos are a frequent motif on Mexican American murals. Parking lot in the San Francisco Mission District. (Photo by author.)

of the United Farm Workers Union, the Virgin of Guadalupe, and the Mexican and U.S. flags.

The United Farm Workers strike did more than secure more humane treatment for manual immigrant labor. It also served as a catalyst for the Movimiento Chicano of the 1960s, which embraced broader themes of "militant struggles for civil rights, cultural equity, and self-determination" for Chicanos/as (Ybarra-Frausto xv). Their declared homeland Aztlán was a mythical region located in today's southwestern United States from which the Aztecs migrated south to settle in central Mexico in the early 1300s. Aztlán "symbolized the spiritual union of the Chicanos" (Leal 8). "Aztlán" and "Chicano/a" were thus open spheres in need of definition, and they found their elucidation in a variety of fluid icons and rituals. As Tomás Ybarra-Frausto states in his foreword to *Velvet Barrios*: "Chicano culture was articulated as an open category with creators negotiating its form and content, derived from multiple sources such as Anglo American, Mexican, and European traditions. This fluid transculturation freed the imagination to create haunting and hallucinatory hybrid cultural expressions" (xv). The core of these expressions is manifested through *Rasquachismo,* or the esthetic of the poor,[4] "a dynamic sensibility of amalgamation and transculturation that subverts the consumer ethic of mainline culture with strategies of appropriation, reversal, and inversion" (xviii). Conceptual articulations of this phenomenon are expressed in diverse ways: calendar art, lowrider cars, Pachuco dress, velvet paintings, tattoos, murals, posters, and *quinceañera* rituals. Lowriders are automobiles or other vehicles lowered to the ground and meant to go "low and slow" in order to display customized lacquer jobs and hydraulics, murals, and luxury details (see plate 13). The lowrider culture, as well as the Pachuco/zoot suiter of the forties and the contemporary Cholo, can be seen "as part of the historical negotiation of Chicano identity in response to social oppression within the dominant society through the creation of oppositional spaces that are part of the Mexican American experience in the United States" (Sandoval 181–82, 195).

Among other Chicano/a cultural icons are the Virgin of Guadalupe, the Thunderbird or United Farm Workers Union eagle, the Mestizo Head, the Pachuco, Emiliano Zapata, César Chávez, the crucifix, the Sacred Heart symbol, pre-Columbian motifs and, since 1975, Frida Kahlo (Gaspar de Alba, *Chicano Art* 47, 50, 148). In fact, Frida Kahlo has become ubiquitous in the Mexican American/Latino community as a symbol, complementary to Guadalupe, that stands for female empowerment, independence, and bold creativity. Her image is sold along with that of Guadalupe, and sometimes it is blended with the Mexican national icon, as in the *arte de paño* piece "Fridalupe," in which Guadalupe is portrayed with Frida Kahlo's

Fig. 117. Velvet painting featuring the ill-fated lovers Mixtli or Ixta (Ixtacihuátl) and Popo or Popoca (Popocatépetl) from the pre-Columbian Legend of the Volcanos. San Antonio. (Photo by author.)

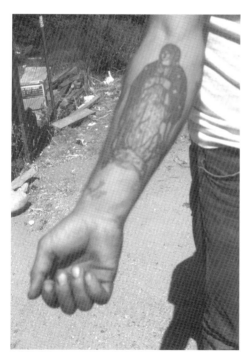

Fig. 118. Tattoo with the Virgin of Guadalupe from La Española, New Mexico. (Photo by Jacqueline Orsini Dunnington. Reproduced with permission.)

Fig. 119. Pilgrim to Chimayó, New Mexico, with a tattoo featuring the Virgin of Guadalupe. (Photo by Jacqueline Orsini Dunnington. Reproduced with permission.)

Fig. 120. Pre-Columbian motifs, such as the plumed serpent Quetzalcoatl, the pyramid, and the ill-fated lovers Ixtacihuátl and Popocatépetl, with their correspondent volcanoes, dominate this mural on a house in the San Francisco Mission District. (Photo by author.)

face (see plate 14). The list is multifaceted and contradictory, but we should not forget that the origins of this paradox have their roots in the violent *mestizaje* and syncretism of the Spanish Conquest of America and the ensuing colonial era. After Mexico (at least superficially) reconciled its multiple cultural components following independence in 1821, the territories in question were taken over by the United States as a consequence of the 1848 Guadalupe-Hidalgo Treaty, adding yet another layer to the complex identity of Mexicans. They became Mexican Americans, "foreigners in their own land," once again avidly searching for identity. In the words of Alicia Gaspar de Alba, "Chicano identity is, ultimately, a border identity; neither side wants you and you can't go home" ("Rights of Passage" 200). This sentiment has been expressed in a poem by Gloria Anzaldúa: "Que la Virgen de Guadalupe me cuide / Ay, ay, ay soy mexicana de este lado" (May the Virgin of Guadalupe look after me / Ay, ay, ay I am a Mexican from this side) (*Borderlands* 3). The inevitable result of this psychological displacement is a seemingly contradictory conglomeration of symbols and rituals with which they are bound to identify.[5]

One of the modalities in which these symbols appear is public art. In the Americas, its long trajectory[6] peaks with the muralists of the Mexican Revolution (1910–18).

Figs. 121 and 122. At the Mexican *Mercado* (Market) in San Antonio, shopping bags and other objects with the image of Guadalupe are sold along with those representing Frida Kahlo, 2005. (Photos by author.)

Known as *Los tres grandes*, Diego Rivera, David Alfaro Siqueiros, and Clemente Orozco displayed their works on public buildings and in common spaces. This art form was continued and is still vibrant in Mexico and in U.S. cities with major Mexican American or other Latino influences. The murals of California, concentrated in the Mexican American/Latino barrios, are among the most impressive. They serve as "the symbolic representation of collective beliefs as well as a continuing re-affirmation of the collective sense of self" (Cockcroft and Barnet-Sánchez 5). In accordance with their mission as an expression of communal life and history, they are usually collectively elaborated and exhibited in public spaces accessible to all, rather than in exclusive museums or galleries.

The mural *Mexico-Tenochtitlan–"The Wall That Talks"*, completed in 1996 by the Quetzalcoatl Mural Project collective in the Highland Park neighborhood of Los Angeles, deserves mention here. Employing the full range of Aztec, Mayan, Native American, African, and mestizo elements, it weaves the history of Mexico and the southwestern United States. Some specific figures and events chosen for this historical panorama are the Aztec migration from Aztlán to Tenochtitlan (Mexico City), the apparition of the Virgin of Guadalupe, Emiliano Zapata and the Mexican

Fig. 123. *End Barrio Warfare,* 1998. Mural led by Augustine Villa, Lisa Mendiola, and Sonny Mendiola, located on the corner of Guadalupe and Chupaderas streets in San Antonio. (Photo by author.)

Revolution, César Chávez and the grape harvesters' strike, and the struggle of the Zapatistas led by Subcomandante Marcos. The Aztec civilizing god, the feathered serpent Quetzalcoatl, unifies all of them. According to Jerry Ortega, one of this mural's painters, "The mural emphasizes the political significance of cultural self-definition of 'el Chicano'" (Dunitz and Prigoff, *Painting the Towns* 186).

The San Antonio mural *End Barrio Warfare* (1998) deals with the barrio problem of violence and the senseless use of guns. It situates the narrative of the mural in time and space by providing the San Antonio cityscape in the background and the Chicano identity icons of Pachucos and a lowrider on each side of the mural. Hidden Aztec figures provide another cultural point of reference. In the central plane a beautiful and peaceful Mexican American female face emerges like a lily from the desolation and fire that surround her, pointing out an alternative to the existing situation.[7] These and similar murals emphasize community collaboration, create a record of people's stories, and provide an affirmation of Chicano/a cultural roots. As Armando Duron, president of the Social and Public Art Resource Center (SPARC) in Los Angeles, states, the murals express "the coming together of peoples who have heretofore had no voice, no images, no monuments. Through this process

Fig. 124. *Nicho/Mural para la Virgen de Guadalupe*, 2001. Mural led by Mary Agnes Rodriguez and Janie Tabares Orneles, located at El Paso Street in San Antonio. (Photo by author.)

Fig. 125. *Our Lady of Guadalupe Veladora*, 2003. Sculptural mosaic in the form of an enormous *veladora* candle with the image of Guadalupe, by Jesse Treviño. Guadalupe Street, San Antonio. (Photo by author.)

Fig. 126. *The Last Supper of the Chicano Heroes*, detail of the mural *Mythology and History of Maiz*, 1986–89, by José Antonio Burciaga. Stanford University, California. (Reproduced with permission of Cecilia P. Burciaga.)

they express their history, their frustrations, their dreams" (Dunitz and Prigoff, *Painting the Towns* 25).

The Virgin of Guadalupe is a pervasive presence in mural art. Although many images present her in traditional ways, such as the one on the mural *Nicho/ Mural para la Virgen de Guadalupe,* located on the San Jacinto Senior Home at El Paso Street in San Antonio, and *Our Lady of Guadalupe Veladora*, a three-dimensional sculptural mosaic in the form of an enormous votive candle on Guadalupe Street, other works have deconstructed customary renderings. This process occurs either by the juxtaposition of unusual elements, as in *The Last Supper of the Chicano Heroes*,[8] or by a radical transformation of the image itself, as in the works of Alma Lopez. In *The Last Supper of the Chicano Heroes*, Guadalupe dominates a gathering of forty historical heroes from the Americas chosen in 1988 in a poll of one hundred Chicano/a students from Stanford University and one hundred Chicano/a activists from the 1960s. Ernesto "Che" Guevara presides over the group.[9] Guadalupe governs over life and death, represented by corn and a *calavera* (skeleton), recuperating the all-encompassing, cosmic dimensions of the Aztec goddess Tonantzin– Coatlicue. In this mural she conserves her traditional dress and posture but wears an "America" band, thus being identified with the whole continent.

Conversely, in the murals conceived by California artist Alma Lopez, such as *Heaven*, the traditional religious elements are entirely deconstructed. *Heaven* is created in the image of an ex-voto or a traditional Mexican devotional painting used to offer thanks for a favor granted by a saint. Nevertheless, the content of Alma Lopez's version of the *retablo* is quite subversive. It represents a woman in heaven who "rejects the institutionalized religious patriarchal system and gazes at her female lover's image in the golden heart brought to her by an angel" ("Heaven, Digital Billboard"). Two additional images in this mural are equally provocative. One scene depicts the same lesbian couple in love sitting on a moon against a starry night background; a second pieta-like scene shows one of the lovers bending over the other's fallen body. Beneath the body appear images of the Mexico-U.S. border fence. In the background, two volcanoes named after the ill-fated lovers Popocatépetl and his beloved princess Ixtacihuátl form an intertextual reference (see fig. 117).[10] The moon, the stars, the sky, the sacred heart, the angel, the roses, and the pieta-like posture are expropriated from the traditional Virgin Mary iconography and applied to the Chicana lesbiana context.

Another work by Alma Lopez, *Las Four* (1997), dethrones traditional values, in this case those of *La Causa Chicana*. This mural, commissioned for the Estrada Courts Community Center, represents four great Latina women: Dolores Huerta,

Fig. 127. Graffiti combined with mural art chronicle the violence in the barrio. San Antonio's West Side. (Photo by author.)

Fig. 128. T-shirts with the Virgin of Guadalupe for sale. Stand with religious articles on El Paso Street, San Antonio, 2005. (Photo by author.)

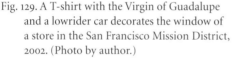

Fig. 129. A T-shirt with the Virgin of Guadalupe and a lowrider car decorates the window of a store in the San Francisco Mission District, 2002. (Photo by author.)

Fig. 130. The Virgin of Guadalupe advertises a coffee shop in Las Cruces, New Mexico. (Photo by Jacqueline Orsini Dunnington. Reproduced with permission.)

cofounder of the United Farm Workers Union; Sor Juana Inés de la Cruz, famous seventeenth-century Mexican nun/poet; Adelita, soldier in the Mexican Revolution; and Rigoberta Menchú, Guatemalan activist and Nobel Peace Price winner. Seated in front of them are four young barrio women, the possibility of the unfolding of their greatness suggested. Behind these figures is a disc with the Aztec moon goddess Coyolxauhqui. In this case, the chosen symbol for the feminine energy was a pre-Columbian goddess rather than the Catholic Virgin. This mural may be considered a counterbalancing response to another Estrada Courts mural, designed by Ernesto de la Loza and named *Los Cuatros Grandes* (1993). It represents four Mexican and Chicano male heroes: Pancho Villa, Emiliano Zapata, César Chávez, and Mario Moreno Cantinflas, flanked by Quetzalcoatl, an Aztec warrior, and an almost naked princess Ixta.[11] As Alma Lopez explains, her intention was to "go beyond the sexualized images of Ixta and the tattoo women [and] create images of women parallel in presence to Zapata, Villa, and the Aztec warriors."[12]

In the life and art of Chicanos, La Guadalupana is appropriated and adapted to changing needs and situations. She is omnipresent, appearing in different forms and in different places, such as paintings, murals, billboards, graffiti, T-shirts, shopping

Fig. 131. *Guadalupe Defending Xicano Rights*, 1976, by Ester Hernandez. (© 1976 Ester Hernandez. All rights reserved. Reproduced with permission of the artist.)

Fig. 132. *The Walking Guadalupe*, 1978, by Yolanda M. López. (Reproduced with permission of the artist.)

Fig. 133. *Margaret F. Stewart: Our Lady of
Guadalupe*, 1978, by Yolanda M. López.
(Reproduced with permission of the artist.)

Fig. 134. *Victoria F. Franco: Our Lady of
Guadalupe*, 1978, by Yolanda M. López.
(Reproduced with permission of the artist.)

bags (see fig. 121), store windows, advertisements, painted prisoners' handkerchiefs
(see fig. 40), medallions, and tattoos (see figs. 118 and 119). Liberated from her static
pose, she is transformed into a truly active woman who works, walks, dances, jogs,
even practices martial arts, as in Ester Hernandez's 1976 pioneer work, *Guadalupe
Defending Xicano Rights*. Other examples of this postmodern madonna are found
in the paintings of Yolanda M. López, which represent Guadalupe in a triptych of
women of different generations jogging, working, participating in daily life, and
even walking the street wearing a short skirt and high heels, as in *The Walking
Guadalupe*.[13] In the first painting of the triptych, *Portrait of the Artist as the Virgin
of Guadalupe* (see plate 15), the artist herself is portrayed as a jogger with muscular
legs. The traditional Virgin Mary/Guadalupe elements—the cloak, the angel, and
the serpent—are present but are reinvented. The statically hanging mantle is now
free-flowing in the wind created by the jogger's movement; the runner is stepping
on an angel whose wings are the colors of the American flag, and in her hand she
holds a serpent. Thus, the jogger rejects U.S. politics and reclaims her power by
reappropriating the serpent, an ancient symbol of goddess wisdom and immortality.
The other two paintings, *Margaret F. Stewart: Our Lady of Guadalupe* and *Victoria
F. Franco: Our Lady of Guadalupe*, represent respectively the artist's mother sewing
a Guadalupe mantle and her grandmother sitting on a Guadalupe mantle while

Fig. 135. *La Sirena* (The Siren). Image from the Mexican Lotería (Lottery) game. (Author's collection and photo.)

holding a serpent skin. Symbolically, the cyclic passage of time is embodied by the shed serpent skin held by this old woman. The older the generation, the more static the image and the less light emanates from the halo. Roses and an angel with Mexican flag-colored wings, indicating their place of origin, accompany both the artist's mother and grandmother. In these paintings, a number of Guadalupe's elements, such as the mantle, the angel, and the serpent, were retained, but recontextualized and infused with a new message.

In *Our Lady*, a digital print produced by Alma Lopez in 1999, the Virgin is deconstructed even further. The artist, portraying herself as Guadalupe, wears a bikini made of Guadalupe's roses, her mantle with Aztec motifs barely covers her shoulders, and she is held by a female angel with bare breasts. The traditional starry mantle is folded beneath the image, and Guadalupe's reddish robe serves as a backdrop. The artist's defiant facial expression and posture are the antithesis of the humility and reserve projected by Guadalupe. Another image, *Latina in the Land of Hollywood* (1999) was created for the cover of a book with the same name by Angharad N. Valdivia. In a mini dress, the artist swings bare feet and legs while sitting on the moon in a starry sky above Hollywood. Her red nail polish, lack of jewelry, and long, flowing hair give her an air of naïve sensuality. As in traditional Virgin Mary renderings, a garland of roses held by two angels frames her. This element, as well as the starry mantle backdrop of sky and moon, clearly alludes to Guadalupe's figure but is reconfigured as an exposé of the distorted Latina representations promoted by Hollywood. This is clearly a reference to the stereotypical portrayal of Latinas as sexy and wild yet virginal, naïve, and girlish.

Alma Lopez has also produced *Lupe & Sirena*, a series with the titles *Encuentro* (1999), *Lupe & Sirena in Love* (1999), and *Lupe & Sirena in Aztlán* (2000). This series shows the traditional icon of Guadalupe embracing a sexy, bare-breasted mermaid— an image from the Mexican Lotería game. Both figures are surrounded by traditional Catholic elements, such as angels, roses, the blue sky, the heart, and by Los Angeles and border imagery. The figures stand on the moon but are supported by a viceroy butterfly instead of the anticipated angel. This exchange serves a distinct purpose. The butterfly constitutes a metaphor illustrating the resilience found among Mexican American border communities.[14]

The deconstruction of female icons sometimes adopts a cartoon format. This is the case of *Citlali, La Xicana Super Hero* (see fig.12), created by the San Antonio artist deborah kuetzpalin vasquez. Citlali is a sort of Wonder Woman and an "Avenger of the Bronze Gente de Aztlan." This sexy and muscular figure is presented as a warrior for Chicano/a rights. Although the accompanying Aztec symbols evoke strong allusions to the Aztlán theme, the central identifying element imprinted on her chest is the traditional image of the Virgin of Guadalupe. Once again, we see the identification of Guadalupe as a brave warrior for social justice.

These Chicana paintings exemplify the new reality that the Virgin of Guadalupe, as "one of the first and most enduring icons of Chicano popular culture[,] is . . . re-visioned and re-presented . . . as a symbol of female empowerment rather than feminine submission" (Gaspar de Alba, *Chicano Art* 139). In fact, as Chicana lesbiana scholar and writer Alicia Gaspar de Alba points out, "the trinity of female roles by which Chicana and Mexicana womanhood has been socially constructed—the mother, the virgin, and the whore" (*Velvet Barrios* xxiv), corresponding to the archetypical trinity of the three Marys of Christ's crucifixion, has been subverted and charged with new significance: "Rather than the chaste virgin, the weeping mother, and the treacherous whore, La Lupita [Guadalupe], La Llorona, and La Malinche are now configured as powerful icons of Chicana resistance to cultural hegemony and patriarchal domination. La Lupita can be a karate expert, a marathon runner, or a seamstress . . . La Llorona's weeping is now interpreted as an oppositional scream against patriarchal inscriptions of womanhood, and among Chicana lesbians she symbolizes defiance to compulsory heterosexuality; La Malinche, once the Mexican Eve accused of the downfall of the Aztec empire, is now an affirmation of *la india*"

Fig. 136. *Water Lady* by Michael Isaac Cardenas. (Photo by author. Reproduced with permission of Isaac Alvarez Cardenas and the artist.)

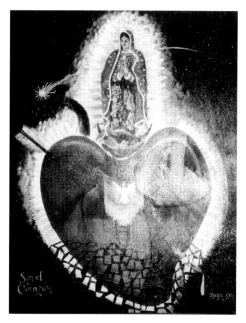

Fig. 137. *Soy el Corazón* by Ramón Vásquez y Sanchez. (Photo by author. Reproduced with permission of the artist.)

(*Chicano Art* 143). The revised and de-stereotyped myth of La Malinche as traitor, as well as the new icon of Frida Kahlo, became models for Chicanas and Chicana lesbians as marginalized members of La Causa Chicana (50, 144).

As these icons are renewed, the La Llorona myth also "continues to evolve throughout time." The prototypical story, which is certainly much older, tells about a rich Spanish hidalgo who exploits a native Mexican woman during the sixteenth-century Conquest of America. After she bears him two sons, he abandons her and goes to Spain to marry a woman of his aristocratic social class. The desperate Indian woman throws her two sons into the river and then follows them in death by also drowning herself. Local tradition holds that her tormented ghost still wanders along riverbanks, weeping and looking for her children. This legend mimics the historical account of the Spanish conqueror Cortés and the Indian princess Malinalli (Malinche), as retained in collective memory. The newer versions of this myth address the themes of the forced repatriation of Mexican Americans from the United States in the 1950s, prostitution and AIDS, and the abuses of a factory owner who pollutes the river with waste. In the latter case, the wealthy businessman rejects the woman who, after drinking from the river poisoned by his factory waste, bears him two disfigured sons. The tale of "the river of life that became the river of death," "the destruction of the fertile feminine . . . [and] the deterioration of the creative flow" reflects the issues of each generation of Mexicans and Mexican Americans (Pinkola Estés 300–2). For example, in Alicia Gaspar de Alba's poem "Kyrie Eleyson for la Llorona," La Llorona is the "Patron saint of bus stops and turnstiles / . . . / Mother of the dispossessed" (*Velvet Barrios* 223).

The Mexican mothers Guadalupe, La Malinche, and La Llorona blend and become interchangeable. Malinche–La Llorona is also the Virgin Mother. The myth of La Llorona has fueled the imagination and has been revised and re-created by the Chicana writers Sandra Cisneros (*Woman Hollering Creek*), Alma Villanueva (*Weeping Woman*), Ana Castillo (*So Far from God*), and Gloria Anzaldúa and Maya Christina Gonzalez (*Prietita and the Ghost Woman/Prietita y la Llorona*), among others. This is also true for Guadalupe, who is invoked in multiple Chicano/a literary works, such as Rudolfo Anaya's *Bless Me, Ultima*.

Besides the incarnations of Guadalupe as a liberated woman, another of her functions revived by Chicanos/as is her all-encompassing goddess aspect as a mother of all creation and a ruler of the elements of earth, water, fire, and air. Various Chicano/a paintings from San Antonio allude to Guadalupe's connection with ancient Indian cultures. In *Water Lady*, a work by Michael Isaac Cardenas, Guadalupe as Mother Earth carries water at a peyote ceremony, while in *Soy el Corazón* (I Am the Heart) by Ramón Vásquez y Sanchez, she is represented as a cosmic, compassionate lady, adored by an Indian shaman. Her importance in Chicano/a life becomes extraordinary. As Ramón Vásquez y Sanchez explains, "[Being] foreigners in our own country . . . what unites us is the Virgin of Guadalupe . . . we want her to take us out of bondage. . . . We sing *mañanitas* for her, we offer her flowers, and she is always present with us in all important life passages: birth, quinceañera, marriage, and death. The people need to believe in something. We pray to her before we pray to Christ, because she is the mother who gives life and has a heart. She is not a religious figure; she belongs to the people, the home, the family" (4 February 2000).

In this evocation of the Virgin's role, we hear an echo of the idea of tlapialli, or an indigenous personal cult. Guadalupe is "expropriated" from the Catholic religion and accommodated to various contexts with heterogeneous meanings. As Ana Castillo explains, "Men call upon Her and carry her banner to lead them out to war . . . we [women] call upon Her privately, quietly in prayer, from our kitchens and bedrooms" ("Extraordinary Woman" 78). Amalia Mesa-Bains discusses the esthetics of feminist *Rasquachismo* or *Domesticana* in home altars and yard shrines:[15] "[P]re-Hispanic in nature, the family altar functions for women as a counterpoint to male-dominated rituals in Catholicism. . . . Set in domestic sites, altars become the domain of women and are a powerful tool in expressing the family's spirituality. The image of the Virgin of Guadalupe, a female deity, is a common icon in the home altar and creates a connection to women in their role of spiritual leadership" (303–4).

Nowadays, one can observe that certain Chicano/a groups and individuals reject their imposed Anglo and Spanish cultural heritage in order to rediscover their indigenous roots. This can be seen in the ease with which Guadalupe is associated with Indian goddesses, the earth, and the cult of the female. Mexican Americans live in a multireligious society with no emphasis on a unique tradition, often feeling as "foreigners in their own land."[16] Once again, there is a need to reinvent an identity and an ancestry. Guadalupe, stripped in part of her Hispano-Catholic associations and ready to be used as a protective mother by this new cause, is being transformed into a patroness and a symbol of the Indian heritage of Chicanos/as. She becomes one of the identifiers of Aztlán, the mythical land of the Aztecs, appearing on murals and paintings next to other Chicano/a symbols, such as the pyramid, the eagle, the feathered serpent Quetzalcoatl, and the Indian warrior. To a certain extent, the Spanish-Catholic religion may be seen as an imposition of the enemy, and identity is sought in pre-Christian images, as in the case of some descendants of Texas Coahuiltec Indians.[17]

Summary

Mexico is a liminal place where the European, the Indian, and the African races have intersected since the sixteenth century. From the mid-nineteenth century until the present, the southwestern United States has provided both a geographical and a cultural focal point for vigorous transformations. Each cultural entity contributed its preexistent ethnic and linguistic multiplicity by creating circumstances that produced amazingly hybrid exchanges. In this context: "*Guadalupe* unites people of different races, religions, languages: Chicano protestants, American Indians and Whites. . . . [She] is the symbol of ethnic identity and of the tolerance for ambiguity that Chicanos/ *mexicanos*, people of mixed race, people who have Indian blood, people who cross cultures, by necessity posses" (Anzaldúa, "Coatlalopeuh" 54). It is in these conditions that the most fertile possibilities for transformation, adaptation, and ambiguity are created. Here, consecrated symbols may be emptied of their habitual meaning and be refilled with new content (Gómez-Peña 183). It is interesting that the symbol of Guadalupe, as a protective and combative mother and a source of empowerment and hope, was able to transcend religions, races, and languages to become a universal patroness of groups with divergent interests: both Catholics and those who oppose organized religion, both the straight and the gay.[18]

As in any syncretic process, disparate cultural ingredients engender new creations.

Thus Chicanos/as subvert, reinvent and activate the familiar myths and images as they endow them with new meanings until their prototypes often become unrecognizable. Guadalupe, through her syncretic origin, teaches us how to incorporate cross-cultural elements harmoniously into our lives and how to coexist with them. She exemplifies acceptance and generosity, at the same time exuding power. She is also a hybrid visual symbol that has been recognized since colonial times as one that unites all segments of the Mexican population. This tradition continues in the present day, as Guadalupe's influence transcends national and religious boundaries and becomes universal, a part of the human consciousness that is unconstricted by country or faith.

Conclusion

ॐ

This work traces the dynamic process of the development and transformation of religious symbols by which, over the course of millennia and through commingling of cultures, an ancient African Mother Goddess may be reflected in the Black Madonna, a ubiquitous and central symbol in Catholicism. It is the ongoing story of the veneration of the dark feminine. The story begins with the cult of the primeval African Mother/Fertility Goddess, which spread by means of migrations to other lands.[1] The study follows the story up to the present day, tracing a cross-cultural analysis of the figure of the Black Madonna, examining her different avatars and their transformations and parallelisms across time in four cultural areas: east-central Europe, Brazil and the Caribbean, Mexico, and Greater Mexico (parts of the United States). Each of these regions is characterized by distinct racial, ethnic, and cultural components: Caucasian-European, Afro-Latin American, Indo-Latin American, and Indo-Latino-Anglo-American. Strikingly, in all these apparently dissimilar cultures, the most venerated and popular image is that of a Dark Madonna. In Poland it is the icon of Our Lady of Częstochowa. As we move to the supersyncretic space of the Americas, the Dark Virgin becomes a more complex symbol. The syncretic processes of convergence or adaptation, interpretation or linkage, and parallelism or juxtaposition (Greenfield and Droogers 91) produce particular versions of the goddess Iemanjá and Our Lady Aparecida in Brazil, the goddess Ochún and the Virgin of Charity of El Cobre in Cuba, and the goddess Tonantzin and the Virgin of Guadalupe in Mexico. The manifold and dynamic nature of these exchanges is due to fluctuating life conditions and experiences in the colonies and other border areas with intense intercultural contact. The extraordinary hardships in which large sectors of the New World population had to subsist triggered the development of remarkable survival and adaptation mechanisms, such as the extreme flexibility of individuals expressed through play (*galhofa*), mockery, irony, and improvisation in the coastal and insular Afro-Latin American areas of Brazil and of the Caribbean, and the more passive resistance in the Indo-Latin American mountain areas of Mesoamerica and the Andean region. As Benítez-Rojo remarks, "the violence of plantation/colonial/ neocolonial society, on being processed by the carnival's machine, has been converted into the Caribbean's travestying mirror that at once reflects the tragic and the comic, the sacred and the profane, the historical and the aesthetic" (311). The greater the intensity and speed of societal changes, the greater the contradictions and possibilities they engender. This process is especially visible in the seeming ambiguity of hybrid, multilayered symbols in Latin America and the Latino United States.

The comparative analysis contained in this book demonstrates that the ancient African and European symbol of the dark feminine has not disappeared but has both resisted historical, political, economic, and geographical changes through millennia and found ways to transform and adapt to new conditions. At the same time, we are also observing an unprecedented ongoing development. In the past, cult objects gained special significance by means of the religious or civil construction of symbolic meaning; today commerce, through the idolization of youth, beauty, and brand names, matches or even supersedes the symbolic influence of religion (Sarlo 31–32). Given this new context, what is the place of inherited sacred symbols, like the Black Madonna, that humanity has carried in collective memory for thousands of years? Will those symbols resist the exposure to the global market in a world where culture is treated as an investment, a resource that has to bring value (Yúdice), where fragmentation and hybridity coexist with growing homogeneity? If they adapt, what form will that adaptation take?

Besides the devotional and creative uses of the Dark Madonna, we have seen the commodification of her image as part of the cultural tourism industry in Salvador, Bahia and in New Orleans. All around the world, but particularly in Brazil, the religious consumer market is expanding. Devotional centers are proliferating and competing with each other for followers. As Peter Berger states, "the religious tradition, which previously could be authoritatively imposed, now has to be *marketed*. It must be 'sold' to a clientele that is no longer constrained to 'buy.' The pluralistic situation is, above all, a *market situation*. In it, the religious traditions become consumer commodities" (138).

Although there are considerable differences in the size, character, affluence, and influence among Brazilian terreiros, many of them are connected to the Internet, which expands their national and international relations and services. Prominent priestesses and priests appear on television and participate in conferences. On Saturdays, days of their public ceremonies, the terreiros are open to visitors from any religion, social class, race, and country, which is in tune with their all-inclusive nature.

Fig. 138. *Botánica* in Salvador, Bahia, Brazil, 1996. (Photo by author.)

They are also open to initiating anyone that the religious leaders consider suitable, following a traditional process. According to Roberto Motta, "Ethnicity no longer is a characteristic of the worshippers, but it remains as a hallmark of the authenticity of the commodity being offered to persons of all racial and national origins" ("Ethnicity, Purity, the Market, and Syncretism" 79). The tourism industry in Bahia also benefits from the re-Africanization of the terreiros. For example, the tourism information organization Bahiatursa publishes lists of different religious communities, classified by type (Candomblé nagô, Candomblé de Angola, Candomblé de Caboclo, and so on) and location, including the name of the main priest or priestess, address and phone number, and posts them in the information booths in key locations of the city. Although anyone is welcome to participate in the free public ceremonies on Saturday nights, some terreiros admit international tours, charging them a considerable amount of money (fifteen dollars per person in 1996) to attend the ceremony. I observed such a phenomenon at the Ilê Axé Opô Afonjá, one of the oldest and most powerful terreiros in Bahia, during a ceremony dedicated to the orixá Xangô, on 29 June 1996.

What are the consequences of opening a roça to this type of commodification? Bringing in buses of tourists who do not even know what the ceremonies are about and who perceive them as some kind of scary entertainment seems to demean the reputation of Candomblé. Are the religious leaders harming their worship or their business through such practices? Perhaps this religion has such a strong and long-standing foundation in northeastern Brazil that no number of visitors could harm it as long as they keep their place as spectators, and the initiates keep their religious secrets. Is the fact that people are paying to attend changing the character of the sacred, ceremonial space, which is meant to be equally accessible for all? The custom of Candomblé calls for an exchange. Although generally there is no set price for services, such as divination, the client must leave something, usually money, in exchange for what she or he receives. At the public ceremonies everyone receives plenty, the sacred energy axé, food, and music, among other things. It could be argued that people who make an effort to come on their own already contribute their desire and readiness to participate, and they go about spreading the sacred axé they receive, while uninformed onlookers do not really contribute anything, thus they have to pay. Why, then, is this practice being accepted? Perhaps because it promotes international tourism and private enterprise, and it represents financial gain for the terreiros that go along with it. The paradox is that Mãe Stella, the iyalorixá of the Axé Opô Afonjá, is a very strong advocate for the re-Africanization of Candomblé. She claims, as do many others, that Candomblé is a purely African religion now that it is free from the constraints of the forced influence of Catholicism that originated during slavery. Why,

Fig. 139. A variety of devotional objects for sale near the Basilica of Our Lady of Guadalupe in Mexico City. (Photo by Jacqueline Orsini Dunnington. Reproduced with permission.)

then, alter it, bringing in uninformed foreigners as spectators? This phenomenon is an example of what is seen by Roberto Motta as the "Brazilian paradox," in which "the search for ethnic authenticity leads to its concomitant de-ethnicization" ("Ethnicity, Purity, the Market, and Syncretism" 81). But perhaps the re-Africanization movement, which wants to eliminate the colonial European-Catholic impositions, is yet another layer of transculturation. Indeed, the clock cannot be turned back, and inhabitants of Latin America are no longer purely African, at least not culturally. In addition, from the sixteenth to the nineteenth century, religion and life in Africa also underwent substantial transformation. As a consequence, we can find a number of more ancient and strict religious rituals in Brazil than in the parts of Africa that originated them. Another "Brazilian paradox," this phenomenon confirms that culture is never static.

Even the traditionalist Mexico has not escaped the commodification of the Virgin of Guadalupe. Her spiritual ubiquity seems to be reflected in material ways, as she is for sale in all imaginable forms, from T-shirts, wedding gowns, hats, boots, shopping bags, and tattoos to computer mouse pads. This commerce has transcended national borders, and plastic and metal Virgin of Guadalupe statuettes, pendants, and pins manufactured in China are now being sold in Mexico and other parts of the world as authentic devotional objects. Moreover, her image is used to market products in

Fig. 140. Devotional stores in the vicinity of the Black Madonna of Częstochowa Sanctuary at Jasna Góra, Poland, resemble Latin American *botánicas*, except they are devoted exclusively to Catholic objects.

magazine advertisements. The above is allowed as long as it does not transform the image of Guadalupe in any way that could be considered sacrilegious.

Although in Poland the Black Madonna appears on calendars, pendants, key chains, and similar objects, I have not seen her image imprinted on garments or as ads in shops or in magazines. In fact, the monastery store at Jasna Góra, which carries books and reproductions of the image of Our Lady, rejects commercialization to the point that even today it does not accept credit cards, in spite of the fact that the sanctuary is visited every year by millions of people from all over the world. The same is true of small shops and stands in the proximity of the sanctuary that sell religious articles. The "House of the Pilgrim" (Dom Pielgrzyma), the only place to stay at Jasna Góra itself, does not accept guests for more than two or three nights at a time between May and October, and until the late 1990s was also outside of the international financial network. During my 2005 stay in Warsaw, it was harder to find Black Madonna images than ever before. Is this utmost religious and national symbol being superseded by the more urgent material needs of the emerging capitalist market of postsocialist Poland?

Is there a possibility of a shielded space for the Black Madonna in the unfolding twenty-first century? Catholics in Poland and Mexico have guarded her image against any change or nonreligious use. Should cultural policy also attempt to contain the appropriation of the regional and particular by the global economy? As Jean Franco observes, "What has . . . changed over the last decades is not only the dualistic way of understanding culture as 'high' or 'low,' 'avant-garde' or 'traditional' but also a change of values so that hybridity is now seen as creative and enriching while purity unhappily evokes ethnic cleansing" (209–10). This revaluing of hybridity, which shares much with what is known as "political correctness" in the United States, does not apply to all contexts. In the same way that traditional Catholics want to keep their icons sacred and pure, Brazilian iyalorixás and Cuban babalawos refuse to dilute the Africanness of their religion through the incorporation of Catholic elements.

As cultural property increasingly becomes part of the market economy, the image of the Black Madonna becomes saleable. Is she going to be reduced to just another commodity? Will this diminish or enhance her spiritual and social impact and appeal? Because there has been a relationship between money and religion throughout the ages, it is hard to imagine that the market economy will deprive this figure of the significance she has accrued through millennia, for the dark feminine is the symbol of wisdom, love, nurture, protection, and transformation and the messenger of peace and justice all over the world. These endangered values, which have been at the core of intrinsic human yearnings across time and space, today need representation as much as ever.

We can expect the process of "updating" and enrichment of the figure of the Black Madonna/Virgin Mary to continue. As our world becomes more complex, and as cultures come together through global exchanges, we are likely to see the symbols of the sacred dark feminine reemerge in various unexpected, even surprising new forms. Further studies, examining developments in the regions discussed in the previous chapters and in other areas, such as the Andes, the Balkans, and Anatolia, can be expected to reveal the continuing evolution of the Black Madonna as a cross-cultural symbol.

Notes

Introduction

1. Old Europe was a native European civilization, dating from 7,000 to 3,500 BC. In today's geographical terms, this area includes either all or part of Russia, Ukraine, Bulgaria, Slovakia, Poland, Serbia, Croatia, Slovenia, Italy, Greece, Hungary, Rumania, and Turkey (Gimbutas, *Goddesses and Gods* 16).

2. My fieldwork in Vilnius, 12 July 1997.

3. *Candombe* drum music is performed by Afro-Uruguayans. Although the name shares a common root with Brazilian Candomblé religion, candombe is a musical style and does not include religious practice.

4. Some Matachines groups, like the Danza Guadalupana de Pablo Olivarez, Sr., dress in Mexican national colors—red, green, and white—(see plate 4), and wear other insignia of Mexican identity, such as the eagle on the nopal cactus on the front of their dress and Our Lady of Guadalupe on the back and on their headdress. Most of the dancers dress as Indians, and others impersonate another Mexican national symbol—La China Poblana (see chapter 2). We can also notice U.S. flags on some dancers, as an indication of their official nationality.

5. Although this phenomenon is most concentrated in the Southwest, it is no longer merely regional; it extends throughout many cities and regions of the United States, therefore called Greater Mexico or Latino United States.

Chapter One

Part of the material included in this chapter was presented at the 2003 Hawaii International Conference on Arts and Humanities, 13 Jan. 2003, and published in the *Conference Proceedings* CD-ROM.

1. Baba Yaga (Baba Jaga)—old witch in the Slavic folk tradition; Coatlicue—Aztec Mother Goddess associated with death; Nanã—Yoruba goddess representing the old wise woman, one of the trinity Oxum–Iemanjá–Nanã.

2. As represented in the Dynasty 22 ornament at the Louvre Museum, Paris. Image reproduced in Wilkinson 142–43.

3. Although Mary is clearly part of this horizontal trinity, there is also a suggestion of a vertical trinity in the figures of the dove–Holy Ghost and God the Father high in heaven, above Jesus.

4. See also section "The Serpent and the Bird" in chapter 2.

5. An example may be the Basque, the Etruscan, and the Baltic regions (Gimbutas, *Living Goddesses* 122).

6. *Wiedźma* comes from the Polish *wiedzieć*—"to know," *wiedza*—"knowledge."

7. In fact, a "fervent worship of the Virgin Mother" already existed in pagan Europe, pointing to the independent and influential position of women (Briffault 499).

8. *Baba* (pl. *baby*)—a derogative name for a married, old, or peasant woman in Poland and Russia; originally pertinent to the goddess Złota Baba. Also see explanations in the section "Mother Earth and Mother of God" of this chapter.

9. I refer to the works of Chicana painters Yolanda M. López and Ester Hernandez, discussed in chapter 4. Comparable latitude in the representation of Our Lady does not exist in Poland.

10. In the subsequent discussion of the Old European civilization I am indebted to Marija Gimbutas's *The Living Goddesses*.

11. In the Polish region of Kujawy, the Neolithic sites of Brześć Kujawski and Krusza Zamkowa have produced a grave containing rich offerings and the remains of a woman with a child as well as numerous figurines and other graves of women buried in the fetal position. It was believed that the fetal position would facilitate the woman's rebirth from the earth's fertile womb (Głosik 43–44).

12. During my 2002 fieldwork in the Kurpie region of Poland, it was apparent that all traditional nineteenth-century wooden houses were "crowned" by the image of two crossed birds. The images of the bird and of the Tree of Life definitely dominate Polish folklore imagery. Interestingly, in both Viking and Mesoamerican Indian structures the image of the birds was substituted by the one of snakes.

13. In several folk pieces during a performance by the Georgian State Dance Company (18 Sept. 2002), the female dancers wore enormous, triangular, metal breastplate-like necklaces and earrings as well as crowns and long gowns with flowing sleeves—attire that strongly resembled that of the Old European goddess.

14. Flowery Quetzal Feather–Our Mother–Our Grandmother (Soustelle 102; Durán 229; Sullivan 17).

15. When Vasilisa asks questions, Baba Yaga answers, "[I]f you know a lot, you will become old soon" (Afanasiev, "Vasilisa prekrasnaia." 161), thus confirming the connection of wisdom to old age.

16. Jacques Huynen, in his *El enigma de las vírgenes negras* (33, 115), confirms the use of white, red, and navy blue (perceived as black) as an essential characteristic of medieval Black Virgins.

17. Other versions of this tale are Afanasiev's "Bajka o żabie i bohatyrze" and "Czarevna liagushka."

18. The frog, as a creature that undergoes transformation, was one of the regenerative symbols of the goddess (Gimbutas, *Living Goddesses* 26). As a symbol of fertility, the frog was Isis's and Hecate's attribute and it was used as offering to Hera and Artemis (Kopaliński 503).

19. Feminine form of Światowid/Świętowit, an important Slavic god before Christianity (Urbańczyk 34–35).

20. Marzanna or *panna moru* (death maiden), also called Morena, Murena, Morana, Mara, Marzaniok, Śmiertka, Śmiercicha, or Śmierć (Death), was probably connected to sacrificial spring rituals (Szyjewski 4–5; Ogrodowska 148, 150).

21. Hair and circular objects like the necklace, the belt, the ring, and the gown symbolize the feminine divinity and are imbued with magic powers (Perkowska 48). According to Lucian of Samosata (*De dea Syria*, vi, qtd. in Briffault 220), "at Byblos, the surrender of a woman's virginity to a stranger could be commuted by her cutting off her hair, as is done at the present day by Catholic nuns when becoming mystically married to the Divine Bridegroom." In Slavic cultures, the cutting of the bride's long braids symbolizes the taming of her personal freedom and power, while unleashing her fertility.

22. Rusałki, as well as Topielice, Wodnice, Panny Wodne, Panny Morskie, and Boginki, are perceived as female demons (Bartmiński 171).

23. Despite being relegated to folklore, ancient figures like the Rusałka have strongly influenced the imagination of the Slavs. They appear in literature, music, and art. A good example is the application of the Rusałka to the cause of Czech national identity in the 1901 romantic opera *Rusalka* by Antonin Dvorák (1841–1904). At the time, Bohemia (today's Czech Republic) was a province of the Austro-Hungarian Empire (Naib).

24. According to Orgelbrand (2:624), such an effigy existed on the bank of the Obdora River in Russia.

25. Four such kamienne baby dating from the eleventh century may be seen today on display in the park surrounding the Nieborów Palace in central Poland.

26. The artist commented on the close connection of woman and dough, which can be shaped as "enormous, squarebuilt, husky [and] hides under dresses, aprons. At the same time it is nice to burrow oneself into such body" (*Alicja Łukasiak Baba*). The body made out of yeast dough is "alive" and connects life with the transiency of time (Łukasiak, "Baba").

27. "Sermones Polonici," qtd. in Hubbs 118.

28. G. Vernadsky, *Kievan Russia* (London, 1943) 155, qtd. in Hubbs 243. In this context, an occurrence from the past comes to mind. When we were four to five years old, my brother, my cousin, and I had a conversation in which it was pointed out that "in our family, only women count." This comment by my cousin prompted a discussion. We discovered that we could name four generations of our female lineage who at the time lived together or in close proximity in Warsaw, while we knew very little or nothing at all about the families of the male relatives who had integrated themselves into this matrilineal and matrilocal family. Needless to say, women were the pivotal hands and heads of their households that wove the family network.

29. According to a traditional peasant tale from Poland, "Sometime, centuries ago Mother of God spun very beautifully, she spun thin, long thread" ("Ongi, przed wiekami Matka Boska bardzo pięknie przędła, przędła nici cieniuchne, długie") ("Podania, przesądy, gadki i nazwy ludowe w dziedzinie przyrody," *Zbiór Wiadomości do Antropologii Krajowej (ZWAK)* 5 (1881): 152, qtd. in Eisele and Renik 38.

30. Examples are the twelfth-century fresco from the church in Sorpe, Catalonia, and the fifteenth-century German painting *Virgin Mary with a Distaff* (see fig. 29).

31. The *Merriam-Webster Online Dictionary*'s definition of "distaff" is quite revealing. This word not only means "a staff for holding flax, tow, or wool in spinning," but it is also intrinsically connected to women, meaning: "woman's work or domain" and "the female branch or side of a family."

32. This ancient song was re-created as a poem by Joan Alcover to music by Amadeu Vives in 1903 and adopted as a hymn of Mallorca in 1996, usually performed by the singer Maria del Mar Bonet ("Gèneres: La poesia Modernista," "Mallorca un país enmig de la mar: Els Símbols," "Institut Joan Alcover"). As we have seen in many instances, ancient figures and rituals have often been relegated to folklore, children's tales, or games.

33. The same tradition prevailed for political reasons—i.e., the Crusaders erecting a church on top of the temple in Jerusalem, and later, the Ottomans placing the dome on top of the church, the Dome on the Mount (Samelson).

34. Information engraved on one of the walls of the Święty Krzyż sanctuary (my fieldwork, 7 July 2002).

35. Słupecki (19) discusses the names of these deities cited in several sources. Łada and her twin sons Boda and Leli persisted in the song "Łada, Łada, Ileli, Ileli, Poleli," As well as in the popular saying "Lelum polelum."

36. According to Bartmiński (87), *łysa* means *czarna,* or black.

37. Pressured by the Benedictine order, in 1478 King Kazimierz Jagiellończyk proclaimed a ban on the Sobótki ceremonies, called "witches' sabbaths," performed on the Łysiec mountain (Ogrodowska 262–63).

38. The sacred stone and tree was believed to be inhabited by god and was identified with god himself (Whittick 335).

39. My fieldwork in this region on 7 July 2002; Bartmiński 141.

40. "Przygarnęli mnie ludzie/ziemia wykarmiła/jak mam jej nie kochać/matką dla mnie była" (Bartmiński 54).

41. "I kiedy śmierć ci skłoni głowę umęczoną,/ta matka-ziemia ciebie nigdy nie odrzuci,/ale cię chętnie przyjmie w swe matczyne łono" (Bartmiński 55).

42. "Ziemia jak matka utulila ich w swym wnętrzu, jednako szlachcica, chłopa i rzemieślnika" (Bartmiński 46).

43. "2 XI 1830 roku Chopin opuścił Warszawę. . . . Opowiadano i pisano, że na wyjezdnym wręczono Chopinowi urnę z ziemią ojczystą, którą podobno miano mu włożyć do grobu" (J.M. Chomiński, *Chopin* [Cracow, 1978], 53, qtd. in Bartmiński 25).

44. "A potem ukląkł [chłop] na czarnej jej [ziemi] piersi/pełnej słońca i wilgoci/i począł szeptać ciche błaganie . . . / obdarz nas ziemio—matulu kochana/chlebem czarnym smacznym"(Bartmiński 54).

45. Of all the Slavic countries, only Poland, the Czech Republic, Slovakia, Slovenia, and Croatia are predominantly Catholic.

46. Image #76 in Lazarev.

47. "Zanim tę ziemię Bóg stworzył/Jam już była poczęta" and "Jeszcze w swym szyku nieba nie stanęły,/Ani w swych brzegach morza zatonęły,/Gdy Boska mądrość pagórki ważyła,/Tyś przy niej była!," qtd. in Zowczak 74–75.

48. In the following account of Polish popular religiosity, I am indebted to Eisele and Renik.

49. My fieldwork in the streets and churches of Warsaw on 15 Aug. 1998.

50. In ancient times, "virgin" only meant that a woman was unmarried, connoting the reverse of what it means today. For example, "The virgin Ishtar is also frequently addressed as 'The Prostitute.' . . . The hierodules, or sacred prostitutes of her temples, were also called 'the holy virgins.'" (S. Langdon, *Tammuz and Ishtar* [Oxford, 1914], 18, 75–76, qtd. in Briffault 169). In reality, *hierodulai* (Gr. "sacred women") were high-ranked priestesses. The Roman Catholic Church did not recognize such status in women and classified them as whores and sorceresses. Thus, the venerated hierodulai, who were entitled to wear red robes, were transformed into "harlots" or "scarlet women" (Gardner 103).

51. The term *Matka Polka* symbolizes the qualities of fortitude, bravery, devotion, sacrifice, and heroism of Polish women who had to take care of family and society while their husbands were fighting for the freedom of Poland on the battlefield, or when they were deported to Siberia from the eighteenth-century partitions of Poland through the First and Second World Wars (Olbryś).

52. Poem "Strażniczko granic" by priest F. Ochała (1995), qtd. in Rakoczy 277.

53. W. Smoleń, *Ilustracje świąt kościelnych w polskiej sztuce* (Lublin, 1987), 268–69, qtd. in Rakoczy 21.

54. J. Zbudniewek, *Dzieje kultu Matki Boskiej Zwycięskiej w Brdowie* (Jasna Góra, 1983) 5–6, qtd. in Rakoczy 24.

55. A. Krynicki, "Rola pielgrzymki w życiu religijnym katolików," typescript AJG (Lublin, 1972) 76, qtd. in Rakoczy 25.

56. The image of the Black Madonna of Częstochowa wearing a gas mask appeared on the cover of the Polish magazine *Wprost* on 21 Aug. 1994, as a protest against air pollution. It provoked heated protests against the use of sacred images for nondevotional purposes ("Przeor Jasnej Góry"). To my knowledge, this is the only such radical transformation of the image of the Black Madonna in Poland.

Chapter Two

Parts of the information contained in this chapter appeared in my article "Fluidez y transformación."

1. "Song of Teteo innan," Sahagún, *Florentine Codex* [1981] 2: app. 226.

2. Fray Juan de Torquemada, *Monarquía indiana* 2 245b and Francisco Javier Clavijero, *Historia antigua de México* 2: 82, qtd. in Lafaye 211.

3. Francisco Mateos, SJ, "Constituciones para los indios del primer concilio limense," *Missionalia hispanica* 7.19 (1950): 554, qtd. in Lafaye 215.

4. In this chapter as well as in chapter 4, I explain paradoxes related to the use and functions of the Virgin of Guadalupe icon to the present day.

5. The Nahuatl account of the apparitions, entitled *Nican Mopohua* (Here Is Being Said), attributed to the learned Indian Antonio Valeriano, was published by Lasso de la Vega in 1649 (included in Torre Villar and Navarro de Anda 26–35).

6. "The first of these goddesses [the most important] was called *Cihuacoatl*, . . . which means the wife of the serpent; they also called her *Tonantzin*, which means our mother" (Sahagún, *Historia general* [1956] 1: 46).

7. In 1648 appeared *Imagen de la Virgen María Madre de Dios de Guadalupe, milagrosamente aparecida en la ciudad de México* by Miguel Sánchez, and in 1649 the *Nican Mopohua*. As Enrique Florescano comments, "The creation of a literature dedicated to giving a foundation of the appearances of the Virgin of Guadalupe was the work of a group of priests and Creole scholars obsessed by the need to give roots and identity to those born in New Spain" (*Memory, Myth, and Time* 136).

8. "Le parecía que la devoción que esta ciudad ha tomado en una ermita o casa de nuestra Sra., que han intitulado de Guadalupe, (es) en gran perjuicio de los naturales, porque les daban a entender que hacía milagros aquella imagen que pintó un indio [Marcos] . . . y que ahora decirles [a los indios] que una imagen pintada por un indio hacía milagros, que sería gran confusión y deshacer lo bueno que estaba plantado, porque otras devociones que había, como nuestra Sra. de Loreto y otras, tenían grandes principios y que *ésta se levantase tan sin fundamento*, estaba admirado" (emphasis mine). "Información que el Arzobispo de México Don Fray Alonso de Montúfar mandó practicar con motivo de un sermón que en la fiesta de la Natividad de Nuestra Señora (8 de Septiembre de 1556) predicó en la capilla de San José de Naturales del convento de San Francisco de Méjico, el provincial Fray Francisco de Bustamante acerca de la devoción y culto de Nuestra Señora de Guadalupe," qtd. in Torre Villar and Navarro de Anda 38–44. The Indian Marcos de Aquino was a renowned painter recognized by Bernal Díaz del Castillo in his *Historia de la conquista de Nueva España* (169–70).

9. *Apparitionists* and *Antiapparitionists*—those who support the supernatural origin of the image of the Virgin of Guadalupe and those who oppose it, affirming that it is a painting by the Indian Marcos Cipac de Aquino, and the cult is a social construct. The banned Mexican film *Nuevo mundo* illustrates the latter version of events.

10. See my articles "El ciclo de la muerte de Atahualpa" and "La danza de la pluma."

11. The Virgin Mary, as heiress to the Great Goddess, is also the lady of the waters; her name, *Maria*, signifies "the seas" in Latin. In several maritime regions of the Spanish-speaking world, girls are often named María del Mar (Mary of the Sea). A contemporary expression of the connection between the Virgin Mary (in this case the Virgin of Guadalupe) and the sea is her stylized image, proclaimed as La Reina de los Mares (the Queen of the Seas). It was blessed by Pope John Paul II at the Guadalupe Basilica and submerged in the Pacific Ocean next to the islet La Hierbabuena on the feast day of Guadalupe, 12 Dec. 2002. This image substituted a forty-four-years-old one, which was part of the first submarine altar on the American continent ("Nueva imagen submarina").

12. Among the more than six thousand Extremaduram conquerors of the New World were the well-known figures of Francisco Pizarro, Vasco Núñez de Balboa, Pedro de Alvarado, and Pedro de Valdivia.

13. This Cortés's banner is kept in Mexico City's Chapultepec Castle museum. Only one (Tlapoyawa's) of the innumerable sources that discuss the image of the Mexican Guadalupe and its origin I reviewed mentions this resemblance. María Guevara from the Universidad de Guanajuato first pointed out to me the existence of this banner in July 2000.

14. Reproduced in Chavasse 151.

15. Francisco de San José, *Historia universal de la primitiva y milagrosa imagen de Nra. Señora de Guadalupe* (Madrid, 1743) 145, qtd. in Peterson, *Creating the Virgin of Guadalupe* 604; Nebel 127.

16. 8 Dec. was the day of the feast of the Virgin of Guadalupe of Villuercas, Spain, as well as that of the Virgin of the Immaculate Conception.

17. In native Mexican languages, like Nathuatl, the same word designates blue and green. Blue-green, jade, or turquoise was a sacred color and it was worn by the high priest of Huitzilopochtli (Soustelle 81–82).

18. I discuss the Virgin of the Immaculate Conception figure in chapter 3.

19. It was either a nose adornment, *yacametztli*, or a design on the skirt and *huipil*. Images from Codex Borgia, Borbonicus, and Magliabechiano, reproduced in Sullivan 10, 17, 19, 20, 21, 25, 27, and image from Durán, plate 25, illustrate the usage of the crescent moon by Mexican goddesses. English names of goddesses were provided by Sullivan 15–30. Rubén Vargas Ugarte translated Cihuapilli as "La amable Señora"—"Fair Lady" (180).

20. "Song of Ciuacoatl," Sahagún, *Florentine Codex* [1981] 2: app. 236. Women who gave birth, seen as brave warriors, were addressed in the following manner: "My beloved maiden, brave woman, thou hast worked like a slave, thou hast labored, thou hast become an eagle warrior, thou hast become as an ocelot warrior; thou hast raised up, thou hast taken to the shield, the small shield. Thou hast exerted thyself, thou hast encountered, imitated our mother Ciuacoatl, Quilaztli" (Sahagún, *Florentine Codex* [1976] 6: 179). In addition, "Cuauhcihuatl, Eagle Woman, who appears in times of war, is a primary manifestation of Cihuacoatl/Quilaztli" ("Where Does the Name Guadalupe Come From?").

21. Image included on the cover of the first written reference to the apparitions of the Virgin of Guadalupe, titled *Imagen de la Virgen María Madre de Dios de Guadalupe, milagrosamente aparecida en la ciudad de México*. For a selection of Mexican patriotic imagery see Cuadriello, "Mirada apocalíptica" 10–19.

22. Paintings reproduced in Cuadriello, "Mirada apocalíptica" 12 and 13.

23. See similar statement referring to Our Lady of Częstochowa by the German governor of Poland during WW II, Hans Frank, included in chapter 1.

24. Examples of other eighteenth-century paintings are *La Virgen sobre el Aguila* (Maza, plate 7) and *Virgen de Guadalupe posada sobre las armas mexicanas y guarnecida por san Juan Evangelista y Juan Diego* by Miguel de Villavicencio (Cuadriello, "Mirada apocalíptica" 18).

25. See images in Zerón-Medina 134–35.

26. Malintzin "is represented twenty-four times in the first forty-eight scenes of the *Lienzo de Tlaxcala*" (Gillespie 2) and is usually placed in a central position.

27. McBride-Limaye identifies La Llorona with Cihuateteo, as "the weeping woman who laments her people's fate after the Conquest" (11). In the Aztec culture the Mociuaquetzque were the women who died in childbirth, considered equal to brave warriors who perished in battle. "[T]hey brought down the sun [and] carried it with a litter of quetzal feathers." They descended on earth as the "Goddess Women" or Cihuateteo, looking for artifacts to spin, weave, and plow the earth (Sahagún, *Florentine Codex* [1969] 6: 61, 163). Once again, women die while giving birth and are reborn to weave anew the fabric of life, perpetuating the eternal cycle of birth, death, and

regeneration. The *Florentine Codex* also says that the goddess Ciuacoatl (Snake Woman) "walked weeping and wailing [by night], a dread phantom foreboding war (1: 3), and describes a howl of a wild animal, similar to the sound of a weeping old woman, as an evil omen ([1979] 5: 151).

28. These notions have been reevaluated by contemporary Chicana lesbiana community. For detailed discussion on this topic, see chapter 4.

29. *China*—Spanish for "Chinese"; woman with Asian or Indian features. In the South American Indian language Quechua—"female" or "servant woman." Poblana—from the Puebla state of Mexico.

30. *Chinaca*—young Mexican country girl.

31. Pantaleón—a popular Mexican male first name in the nineteenth and beginning of the twentieth century.

32. "Con su escolta de rancheros, / diez fornidos guerrilleros, y en su *cuaco* retozón/que la rienda mal aplaca,/Guadalupe la *chinaca* va a buscar a Pantaleón. / . . . /Guadalupe va de prisa, de retorno de la misa: / que, en las fiestas de guardar, / nunca faltan las rancheras/con sus flores y sus ceras a la iglesia del lugar; / . . . / se dirige al campamento donde reina el movimiento/y hay mitote y hay licor; / porque ayer fue bueno el día, / pues cayó en la serranía un convoy del invasor. / Qué mañana tan hermosa: ¡cuánto verde cuánta rosa! / ¡Y qué linda en la extensión / rosa y verde, se destaca / con su escolta, la *chinaca* que va a ver a Pantaleón!" (Nervo, *Poesías completas* 308–10).

33. The double snake symbol was used in Mesopotamia to represent the medicinal god Ningishzida and in Greece for the god Asclepius. A similar healing emblem was known by the East Indians as well as by the Aztecs and other North American Indians (Campbell, *Mythic Image* 283–90).

34. Testimony and writings by Lithuanian-born anthropologist Marija Gimbutas as well as by my father, Eligiusz Oleszkiewicz, born and raised in Wilno, capital of today's Lithuania, Vilnius.

35. For example, in the Lithuanian tale "Eglė žalčių karalienė" (Queen of the Snakes) (Miłosz 91–98) and in the Polish "O wężowej wdzięczności" (About Snake's Gratitude) (Wortman 123–30).

36. Examples are Saint Columba of Iona, England, from the sixth century, of Cordoba, Spain, from the ninth century, and from Sens, France (dates unknown) (Attawater 91–92).

37. My fieldwork, Necropolis Puig des Molins, Ibiza, Spain, 20 June 2003.

38. Reprinted in Taylor 22.

39. I observed this phenomenon especially in Polish and Mexican shrines sculpted of wood. In a contemporary painting by Father John Giuliani, *Our Parent above, and His Son, the one with pierced hands, and Holy Spirit*, pertaining to *The Madonna Series*, "inspired by Native American culture and art," the Holy Trinity is depicted as an old male/female Indian figure above an eagle and a young Indian man ("Our Parent above").

40. She was also named Heart of the Earth (Tlalli yiollo) and Our Grandmother (Toci). "Eagle feathers were strewn over her skirt—it was strewn with eagle [feathers]; it had white eagle feathers, pointed eagle feathers." Other goddesses, like Ciuacoatl (Snake Woman), had a headdress of eagle feathers (Sahagún, *Florentine Codex* 1: 3–5).

41. I discuss theatricality in Andean society in my *Teatro popular peruano*.

42. Especially famous are the Los Angeles, San Diego, and San Francisco murals, but other cities with a large Latino population, like New York, Chicago, Santa Fe, and San Antonio, have a

considerable number of murals made by community collectives as well as by individual artists. I further discuss the topic of mural art in chapter 4.

43. M. E. Descourtilz, *Voyages d'un naturaliste et ses observations faites sur les trois règnes de la Nature* (Paris: Defart, 1809).

CHAPTER THREE

Parts of this chapter were previously published in Spanish in my articles "Los cultos marianos nacionales en América Latina," "Fluidez y transformación," and "Color, género y poder" as well as in essays in conference proceedings, "Ilê Asé Orisanlá J'Omin" and "El papel de la mujer en el Candomblé."

1. The first African slaves were brought to Brazil in 1516 (Seljan 72), and in 1517 Spanish emperor Carlos V officially permitted the introduction of black slaves in the Antilles. In Cuba, slavery persisted until its abolition in 1880, and in Brazil until 1888.

2. Capoeira, developed in Brazil by Angolan slaves, thanks to its gracious movements and the use of music, was seen by the colonial authorities as a form of dance, when in fact it was a contest of strength and agility, a preparation for battle.

3. Henning and Oberländer 216; "Permanent Collection: Sub-Saharan African Art"; "Goddesses of Africa." In Haiti Mami Wata became Lasyrenn (Mermaid), discussed later in this chapter.

4. For a more extensive discussion of Iemanjá, see section "Dark Virgins and White Goddesses" in this chapter.

5. During my fieldwork in Bahia, it was stressed to me time and again that the pano da costa, often the only African element in the orixá dress, was the most important one. One of the very few orixás that preserved the African character of their attire is Omolú (Saint Lazarus) (see fig. 70).

6. These roads are: Ochún Yeyé Moró o Yeyé Kari, Ochún Kayode, Ochún Miwá, Ochún Aña, Ochún Yumú, Gumí, Bomó or Bumí, Ochún Sekesé, Ochún Akuara or Ibú, Ochún Fumiké, Ochún Ololodí or Olodí, Ochún Funké, Ochún Edé, Ochún Niwé, Ochún Kolé-Kolé or Akalá-kalá, Ikolé, Bankolé or Ibú Kolé, and Ochún Awé (Cabrera, *Yemayá y Ochún* 70–72). It is interesting to note that in Catholicism there also are many manifestations of the Virgin Mary, with such different names as " Mary of the Immaculate Conception," "of Charity," "of the Assumption," "of the Pilar," "of the Candles," etc. This multiplicity is reflected in popular female first names.

7. The name Umbanda was previously used to designate Rio de Janeiro's version of such Indian-influenced religions as Catimbó (Recife) or Candomblé de Caboclo (Bahia), and today it is known in Rio as Macumba (Motta, "Ethnicity, Purity, the Market, and Syncretism" 77).

8. I conducted intense fieldwork on Candomblé in Salvador, Bahia during May–Aug., 1996, focusing mainly on the Ilê Asé Orisanlá J'Omin or Terreiro de São Bento.

9. African religious practices were forbidden and persecuted by Brazilian police until the 1980s. In spite of the re-Africanization process, colonial influences, such as the sumptuous Baroque attires, are an intrinsic component of this Brazilian religion and do not exist in Africa. It is also true that some aspects of ancient Yoruba worship have been preserved so well here that people of African descent, such as those from the United States, come to Brazil to study these cultural expressions. On the other hand, groups of Afro-Brazilians who established themselves in

Africa practice forms of Candomblé that preserve ancient Yoruba elements lost in contemporary local worship.

10. The word *axé* is also used to signify terreiro or spiritual community.

11. Padê for the orixá Exú is a ritual involving the placing of offerings and dancing at the center of the ritual space where the public ceremony is going to take place (barracão) in order to prevent the negative forces of other Exús from entering the ceremony. Bori is a ritual performed in the *camarinha*, or seclusion shack, in order to "strengthen" the head of the person being initiated. It involves animal offerings, chants, and dances (Gomes Arruda).

12. *Iyalorixá* means "wife of the orixá" (god) in Yoruban, and *mãe-de-santo*—"mother of saint" in Portuguese. She should usually be over forty years old, but there is no rigid rule. Mãe Alda of the Terreiro de São Bento became a iyalorixá at twenty-seven.

13. *Iaô* means "the youngest wife" in Yoruban, and *filha-de-santo*—"daughter of saint" in Portuguese.

14. *Ifá*—An African divination system with a traditional tray, based on sixteen numbers.

15. The iyalorixá of the Terreiro de São Bento or Ilê Asé Orisanlá J'Omin, mãe Alda d'Alcántara Arruda, was able to incorporate several orixás, including Oxum and Oxagião (a young facet of Oxalá/Jesus Christ).

16. From the Yoruban iyágba-sê, iabá-sê—"old woman who cooks" (Costa Lima, "Organização" 101).

17. Although Ilê Asé Orisanlá J'Omin was structured as a blood family terreiro with the mother, Alda d'Alcántara Arruda, being the iyalorixá, her husband, Dílson Gomes Arruda, the main ogão, and her two initiated daughters, Celeste (Oxairanlé) an ékéde (not entering into trances) and mãe pequena, and Marcia (Najise) an iaô (entering into trances), this in no way is typical for the larger terreiros. As my interviews with twenty-two members of this religious community demonstrated, they had stronger ties to the terreiro's spiritual family of choice than to their own blood families (personal interviews 19 and 20 July 1996 and 1 Aug. 1996).

18. Rowland Abiodun, "The Concept of Women in Traditional Yoruba Religion and Art," Conference on Nigerian Women and Development in Relation to Changing Family Structure, University of Ibadan, Apr. 26–30, 1975, 1, qtd. in Drewal and Drewal 9.

19. Ochs lists naming the child and inheritance through the mother as intrinsic characteristics of matriarchal religions (87).

20. P.C. Lloyd, "The Status of the Yoruba Wife," *Sudan Society* 2 (1963): 39 and *Power and Independence* (London: Routledge & Kegan Paul, 1974), 38, qtd. in Drewal and Dreawal 10.

21. Peter Fry in *Para inglês ver* disagrees with the position of Ruth Landes. According to him, the bicha, or homosexual, embodies the key aspects of the feminine and the masculine roles, which he can use to his own advantage. For example, he is in a better position than a woman to deal with the police (76).

22. There are three main divination systems in Santería: *obí* (four pieces of coconut), *diloggún* (sixteen-cowry divination), and Ifá divining tray and chain *opele* (*oguele*) (Barnet 28, 30, 158). According to the santero Raúl Chaveco and to Barnet (28), there are also women (*santeras* or *iyalochas*) who practice the diloggún.

23. The Regla de Palo, Palo Monte, Regla Conga, or Mayombe tradition comes from the Congo region (Barnet 90, 73). *Canastillero*—an altar with religious attributes of the orichas, structured as a cabinet with several shelves. See also note 51.

24. My fieldwork in Havana 7–14 Nov. 1999, including interviews with and divination by oriaté René Delgado Oquendo and santero (*babalocha*) Raúl Chaveco, on 12 Nov. 1999, as well as an interview with Natalia Bolívar Aróstegui, the female *akpetebí* (helper) of a babalawo and initiate of Regla de Palo, author of various books on Afro-Cuban religions, on 13 Nov. 1999.

25. From *Igpupiara—ig* (water) and *iara* (lord) (Iwashita 58).

26. In Cuba Naná Burukú is a male oricha who is "old and highly respected . . . and is 'the mother of the St. Lazaruses.' . . . His Catholic counterpart is the Virgin of Mount Carmel" (Barnet 65).

27. As Nossa Senhora da Gloria, or Our Lady of the Assumption, Iemanjá is celebrated on 15 Aug.; as Nossa Senhora das Candeias (in the Bantu terreiros of Pôrto Alegre), on 2 Feb. (Iwashita 34; Boff 54–55).

28. For a discussion of these religions see "Afro-Brazilian Religions" earlier in this chapter.

29. The term *stella maris* originated as an error of the copyists who wrongly interpreted the name *stilla maris,* or "drop of the sea," that Saint Jerome gave to Miriam (Warner 262).

30. In eighth-century iconography, the Immaculate Conception was represented as the moment of Anna's and Joachim's embrace at the Golden Gate of Jerusalem.

31. "[I]t is by the Holy Spirit that she has conceived this child" Matthew 1:18 (*The New American Bible* 966, 1020–21).

32. Nestor Ortiz Oderico, *Macumba: Culturas africanas en el Brasil* (Buenos Aires: Plus Ultra, 1970), qtd. in Bolívar Aróstegui and Porras Potts 103.

33. The waistband in the images of the Virgin Mary indicates that she is pregnant, *en cinta.*

34. Bolívar Aróstegui 155; Hernandez. On some illustrations, Oxum is portrayed as carrying a vulture and a peacock (Fatunmbi 26). The dove is a ritual bird of the female orichas: Yemayá, Ochún, Oyá, and Obá, as well as of Obatalá, syncretized with Our Lady of Mercy ("Regla de Ocha"). According to Cabrera (*Yemayá y Ochún* 277), the duck is the main sacrificial bird for Yemayá, and her ex-messenger. The duck represented the goddess as early as in the Neolithic (Gimbutas, *Language of the Goddess* 10, 25). As an aquatic bird it unites the three realms of water, sky, and earth. See my discussion on the identification of the bird with the goddess in chapter 2.

35. "Bantu goddess of the sea and of death" (Bastide 472).

36. For more information about the Polish icon and its functions throughout the centuries, see chapter 1.

37. Earlier in this chapter I pointed out similar characteristics while describing black women in colonial and contemporary Brazil. According to Brown, this girl is identified with "Anaise, the daughter of Erzulie Dantor and St. Jacques Majeur" ("Olina and Erzulie" 114).

38. *Barracão* (Port.)—literally, "large cabin." The word most likely comes from the place where slaves were housed. Today it is used for a ritual space where Afro-Brazilian ceremonies are performed.

39. During my visit to Alda's house on 1 Aug.1996, a complete one-and-one-half-hour session involving both types of divination took place. My three orixás, the numbers that lead my life, and my present and future were determined.

40. Alda d'Alcántara Arruda and Dílson Gomes Arruda, personal interviews, 19 July 1996.

41. As God in Catholicism, Yoruban Olodumaré is abstract and remote, and he is approached by his intermediaries, the òrìṣà (orixá in Brazil), in a similar fashion as the Catholic God is represented by the saints.

42. I observed a strikingly similar ritual while participating in a Mexican American quinceañera celebration for Giovana del Villar on 20 Dec. 2000 in San Antonio, Texas.

43. The French photographer Pierre Verger (1902–96) became fascinated with Candomblé after he came to Salvador, Bahia in 1946. He was initiated in Nigeria as Fatumbi and devoted his life to the study and documentation of Afro-Brazilian religions and the relationship between Bahia and Africa. After his death, his house in a popular neighborhood of Salvador was converted into a library and a resource center.

44. See the "Syncretism" section of this chapter.

45. Indian and African ancestors (caboclos and *prêtos velhos* respectively) are often regarded as inferior spirits.

46. Although public Candomblé ceremonies originally took place from midnight till daybreak at 5:00 a.m., and in the city nowadays they are usually performed from 7:00 or 8:00 p.m. till 11:00 p.m., these restrictions do not apply at more rural terreiros, such as the Ilê Asé Orisanlá J'Omin at the Itaparica Island, where ceremonies may be performed at all times of night and day.

47. I was the only outsider, although after three months of close contact with the terreiro, I was considered an abião (aspirant).

48. At Candomblé ceremonies chants are performed in Yoruban.

49. I had a spontaneous reading inspired by a cigar smoke while conducting an interview with the santero Raúl Chaveco in his Havana apartment on 12 Nov. 1999.

50. *Eguns*—spirits of dead ancestors. *Egungun*—bone, skeleton (Bolivar Aróstegui and Porras Potts 261). Here, as in popular Iberian Catholicism, we can observe a continuum between the world of the living, of the dead, and of the saints (Greenfield 120).

51. This altar, as well as the Cuban canastilleros where attributes of the orichas are placed, was highly reminiscent of sixteenth–seventeenth century New World Catholic churches' central altar-pieces. They were structured as rectilinear arrangements of sculptures and paintings of holy figures. Examples are the main altars of the San Francisco church in Tlaxcala (sixteenth century), the church at Huecotzingo (sixteenth century), and the Santo Domingo convent church in Puebla (seventeenth century) (McIntyre). According to Bolívar Aróstegui, canastilleros developed from nineteenth-century display cabinets, which were adapted to hold the attributes of the orichas (270).

52. I conducted fieldwork in botánicas in Salvador, Bahia, Brazil; San Juan, Puerto Rico; San Antonio, San Francisco, New Orleans, and New York City from the 1980s to the 2000s.

53. The following discussion of Our Lady Aparecida draws on Boff (19–29, 39) and Fernandes (802–3).

54. "Senhora Aparecida, um filho vosso / que vos pertenece sem reserva—totus tuus!— / . . . / quer dirigir-se a vós, neste momento. / Ele lembra com emoção, pela cor morena / dessa vossa imagem, uma outra/representação vossa, / a Virgem Negra de Jasna Góra!" (Silva Lima 36).

55. The Virgin of El Cobre is identified with Nuestra Señora de la Caridad y de los Remedios, brought to the American continent by Cortés's comrade Ildefonso Rodríguez around 1550. She

is also the seventy-centimeter Virgin of Remedios brought by Cortés in his Conquest of Mexico, and during Mexico's wars for independence she was the symbol of the Spaniards. According to tradition, she appeared to a humble shepherd boy around 1370–90 in Abades, Spain ("Historia de la Virgen de Remedios de la Villa de Abades"). Some scholars have suggested that the Our Lady of Charity statue from Illescas, province of Toledo, Spain, popular in the sixteenth and seventeenth centuries, was the prototype of the Cuban image (Tweed 20–21). The black statue of the Virgin of Regla, on the other hand, has her origins in the fourth century, and according to legend the image was built on order of Saint Agustín, bishop of Hipona in North Africa. When the Vandals plundered Hipona, the image was brought to Spain and placed in front of the sea ("La Virgen de Regla: Fiesta"). In 713 it was hidden from the Moors, until it reappeared in 1330 to a canon of the León Cathedral ("Santuario Virgen de Regla").

56. My fieldwork in Chipiona, Spain, 9 June 2004. See image in Buey and Vallecillo.

57. I refer to such dance and musical expressions as son, rumba, cha-cha-chá, mambo, bolero, bossa nova, samba, merengue, or salsa, which spread around the world, becoming the "legacy of humanity." Afro-Latin American culture is also present in literature and the visual arts, among other arts.

Chapter Four

Another version of this chapter was presented at the Twenty-fifth Congress of the Latin American Studies Association, Las Vegas, 7 Oct. 2004, and included in the *Congress Proceedings* CD-ROM. Part of this material was previously published in Spanish in my "Fluidez y transformación."

1. By "borderlands," I not only mean the geopolitical border between Mexico and the United States, since 1848, but also an economic, cultural, and psychological frontier, which extends thorough "Greater Mexico," or areas of the United States densely populated by Mexican Americans and other Latinos.

2. "Who is this that rises as the dawn, / beautiful as the moon, / brilliant as the sun, / fearsome as an army?" (*La Biblia* 1141).

3. For Mexico, see video *Mayan Uprizing in Chiapas*; for the Nicaraguan Sandinistas, see Randall 121. I refer to the famous strike of the California vineyard workers organized by César Chávez in 1965 as well as to subsequent protests by Mexican and Chicano agricultural workers in the United States.

4. Similar esthetic expressions, related to the colonial Baroque proliferation of excess, such as the Peruvian *barroco de la pobreza,* exist in Latin American countries. As the oxymoronic name indicates, they are paradoxes, in that the apparent opulence is made out of the affluent society's waste materials juxtaposed in a way contrary to that society's esthetic norms.

5. While I am writing this text in San Antonio, Texas, on a May afternoon in 2003, I see in front of me the ever-present U.S. flag (in fact, two flags, one in the shape of a heart) on the house of my Mexican American neighbor. It is the only flag on my street.

6. Prehistoric cave paintings of Africa, Asia, Australia, Europe, and the Americas may be considered manifestations of public art.

7. "Mural # 10"; San Antonio Mural Tour.

8. This scene is part of the Stanford University mural *The Mythology and History of Maiz* (1986–89) by José Antonio Burciaga.

9. The top thirteen Chicano heroes chosen were: César Chávez, Emiliano Zapata, Dolores Huerta, Frida Kahlo, Luis Valdez, Ernesto "Che" Guevara, Joaquín Murrieta, Tomás Rivera, Sor Juana Inés de la Cruz, and Dr. Martin Luther King, Jr.

10. This scene alludes to Chicano velvet paintings and calendar art that the artist de-mythifies.

11. Mural reproduced in Dunitz and Prigoff, *Painting the Towns* 173.

12. Estrada Courts is one of the oldest housing projects in Los Angeles. It contains a large collection of murals from the 1970s ("*Las Four* by Alma Lopez").

13. This image provoked a scandal in Mexico after being published in the journal *Fem* in 1984 (Lippard).

14. Alma Lopez sees the viceroy as vulnerable and "pretending to be something it is not just to be able to exist" (*Alma Lopez*).

15. "Defiance of an imposed Anglo-American cultural identity and of restrictive gender identity within Chicano culture have inspired a female rasquachismo or domesticana. . . . Techniques of subversion through play with traditional imagery and cultural material are characteristic of domesticana" (Mesa-Bains 305).

16. In addition, Christianization was less strongly enforced in the northern region of New Spain than in the rest of the viceroyalty. According to the Jesuit Francisco de Florencia in his 1755 book *Zodiaco Mexicano*, out of 106 images of the Virgin distributed in New Spain, only 7 were destined for the Northern Diocese (Ortiz Echaniz 2).

17. During two interviews, Ramón Vásquez y Sanchez, "Xagu Kaí," painter and director of the arts program at the Centro Cultural Aztlán in San Antonio, explained to me that as a Coahuiltec he also serves as director of the Native American Church, which practices peyote ceremonies in one of the San Antonio missions. This does not makes him any less Catholic, as he participates in Mass every Sunday (Vásquez y Sanchez, 4 Feb. and 7 Feb. 2000). This Indian-Catholic syncretism is analogous to the one practiced in Afro-Catholic religions, such as Brazilian Candomblé, Cuban Santería, and Haitian Voodoo, described in chapter 3.

18. Examples of Guadalupe serving the gay community are the works of the Chicana lesbiana painters Yolanda M. López, Ester Hernandez, and Alma Lopez of California.

CONCLUSION

1. Birnbaum, among other scholars, argues that humanity started in Africa and the world's oldest divinity is an African dark mother (*dark mother* xxv).

Glossary

Abakuá Afro-Cuban mutual aid society for men.

Abebe or **agbebe** Ritual fan used by female **orixás Iemanjá** and **Oxum** in Afro-Brazilian religions.

Adelita Legendary woman soldier of the Mexican Revolution (1910–18).

Ajiaco (Sp.) From **ají**—"chili." Complex stew, used by Fernando Ortiz as a metaphor for the different layers and mixtures of Cuban society.

Alabê Male drummer in Afro-Brazilian religions.

Aldeia (Port.) "Village." Used in reference to places dedicated to the worship of Indian ancestors or **Caboclos** at a Brazilian **terreiro**.

Arte de paño (Sp.) "Cloth art." Art embroidered or painted on cloth, made by Chicanos/as and Mexicans, including prisoners, in which the Virgin of Guadalupe is frequently represented.

Atabaque (Port.) Ritual drum in Afro-Brazilian religions.

Awọn ìyá wa (Yor.) "Our mothers."

Axé (Braz.), **aché** (Cuba), or **àjẹ** (W. Afr.) Divine life force brought to earth during ceremonial drumming and dancing. Human beings are infused with this energy through possession trances, sacrifices, and the consumption of sacred foods, among other practices. Also name given to a **terreiro** or **roça**.

Axôgún Male performer of sacrifices in Afro-Brazilian religions.

Aztec or **Mexica** Postclassical Indian culture. Its members migrated south from the territories of today's southwestern United States, built Tenochtitlan (today's Mexico City) in the fourteenth century AD, conquered local cultures, and established themselves in this area.

Aztlán Mythical homeland of the **Aztecs**, located in the areas of today's southwestern United States, from where the **Mexica** migrated south to establish themselves on Texcoco Lake in central Mexico.

Baba (pl. **baby**) (Pol.) Derogative name for a married, old, or peasant woman in Poland and Russia; originally pertinent to the goddess Złota Baba, or Golden Woman.

Babalawo (Yor.) "Father of the secrets." High priest in the Yoruba and Afro-Cuban tradition.

Babalorixá (Yor.) or **pai-de-santo** (Port., "father of a saint") Spiritual leader or priest of an Afro-Brazilian **terreiro**.

Baba Yaga (**Baba Jaga**) (Pol.) Also called **Baba Jędza, Jędza, Wiedźma, Czarownica, Języ Baba, Zalęta**. Old witch with magical powers of transformation in the Slavic tradition. Corresponds to the old wise woman aspect of the triple goddess.

Bachiller (Sp.) Holder of a bachelor's degree.

Balsero/a (Sp.) "Rafter." From **balsa**—"raft." Popular name for a Cuban citizen who leaves the country illegally on a raft or boat in order to reach the United States.

Barracão (Port.) "Large cabin." Ritual space in an Afro-Brazilian **terreiro** where ceremonies are performed. Comes from the cabins African slaves were housed in.

Barrio (Sp.) "Neighborhood." Word used in the United States for popular, usually inner city, neighborhoods inhabited by Latinos.

Bicha Passive homosexual in Brazil.

Boguroditsa or **Bogomater'** (Russ.) "God Birth-Giver." Title used for the Virgin Mary in Russia.

Bori Ritual performed in the **camarinha** or seclusion shack in order to "strengthen" the head of the person being initiated. Involves animal offerings, chants, and dances.

Botánica (Sp.) Devotional store that offers objects, remedies, and services from a wide range of popular religious manifestations, such as Catholicism, Spiritism, **oricha** worship, Indian ritual, and New Age.

Bóveda espiritual or **bóveda de aguas** (Sp.) "Spiritual vault" or "water vault." Spiritist altar composed of seven glasses filled with water, to honor spirits of the dead in Cuban Spiritism.

Caboclo or **Dono da Terra** (Port.) "Owner of the Land." An ancestral Indian spirit in Afro-Brazilian religions.

Calavera (Sp.) Skull or skeleton used in the Mexican syncretic tradition of the Day of the Dead. Also, a poem for that occasion.

Calunga Bantu goddess of the sea and of death.

Camarinha (Port.) "Little room" or **casa de força** (Port.) "house of strength." Seclusion shack in a **terreiro** where an **abião** or aspirant must stay for twenty-one days without contact with the external world, performing special rituals, before being initiated into an Afro-Brazilian religion as a **iaô**.

Caminos (Sp.) "Roads" or aspects of an Afro-Cuban **oricha**.

Canastillero (Sp.) Afro-Cuban altar with religious attributes of the **orichas**, structured as a cabinet with shelves.

Candombe Drum music performed by Afro-Uruguayans. The name shares a common root with Brazilian **Candomblé** religion. Notwithstanding, **Candombe** is a musical style and does not include religious practice.

Candomberos Drummers who perform **Candombe** music.

Candomblé Afro-Brazilian religion from Bahia, Brazil, in which Yoruban elements are syncretized with Catholic ones. It is gradually becoming more and more "purely African" through the process of re-Africanization since the 1980s, a conscious effort to free the religion from Catholic elements imposed during colonial times. It receives the name of **Xangô** in the states of Pernambuco, Alagoas, and Sergipe.

Capoeira Martial art developed by Angolan slaves in colonial Brazil. Thanks to its gracious movements and the use of music, it was disguised as a form of dance, when in fact it was a training for battle.

Catimbó Syncretic, most Indian Brazilian rural religion, strongly influenced by Indian beliefs and rituals, practiced mainly in the northern states.

Ceiba or **yaxche** (kapok) tree. Sacred silk-cotton tree with magical properties of the Mayan culture, also venerated in Cuban Santería. In Afro-Brazilian religions called **iroko** and in Haitian Voodoo **mapou**.

Chalchutlicue "The One with a Skirt of Green Stones." Aztec water and fertility goddess.

Chicano/a (**Xicano/a**) From the Nahuatl **Mexica** or **Aztec**. Self-denomination term used by part of the Mexican American population, usually connected to their political stance. It springs from the self-determination movement of the 1960s.

China (Sp.) "Chinese." Woman with Asian or Indian features. In the South American language Quechua—"female" or "servant woman."

La China Poblana Mexican archetype of a virtuous Mexican woman and an identity symbol. Originally a slave brought from seventeenth-century India to serve a wealthy Mexican family.

La chingada Approximates "the violated woman."

Cholo Contemporary figure, analogous to the **Pachuco** of the 1940s.

Cihuateteo Aztec "Goddess Women" who descended on earth after dying during childbirth. Considered equal to brave warriors.

Citlalicue "The One with a Starry Skirt." Aztec goddess, also called **Tonacaciuatl**, or "Lady of Our Nutrition."

Ciuacoatl "Snake Woman" or "Wife of the Serpent." Aztec goddess identified with **Tonantzin**.

Coahuiltec Indian from the area of Texas and northern Mexico.

Coatlicue "Lady of the Serpent Skirt." Aztec Mother Goddess associated with death; mother of the god **Huitzilopochtli**.

Comunidades Eclesiásticas de Base (**CEBs**) (Sp. and Port.) Popular Catholicism congregations in Latin America.

Conquistador (Sp.) Spanish conqueror of the New World.

Contas (Port.) "Beads." Especially "washed" sacred necklaces worn in Afro-Brazilian religions.

Coyolxauhqui Aztec moon goddess.

Derroche (Sp.) Waste, excess, extravagance.

Diana/Artemis Roman/Greek black virgin goddess of fertility and regeneration.

Diloggún Sixteen-cowry divination system used in Santería.

Domesticana Female **Rasquachismo** esthetics, characterized by defiance and subversion of Anglo-American esthetic norms.

Dvoievierie (Russ.) "Two faiths." Coexistence of two or more religious systems during transition periods, as when in Russia official Christianity was paralleled by pre-Christian peasant practices.

Ébomin Category to which a **iaô** may ascend seven years after initiation, and which makes her eligible to become an **iyalorixá**, or head priestess, in a Brazilian **Candomblé terreiro**.

Egun Spirit of an African ancestor in the Brazilian **Candomblé** tradition.

Ékéde Initiate in Afro-Brazilian religions who does not enter into trances. Her role during ceremonies is to help those in possession trances.

Elegguá (Cuba) or **Exú** (Braz.) **orixá** (**oricha**) or god of the crossroads, "the trickster," syncretized in Cuba with **El Niño de Atocha**, a particular representation of Baby Jesus. His colors are red and black.

Ewa Afro-Brazilian female **orixá**, one of the **iyá-mi**.

La Extremeña (Sp.) Black, triangular Virgin of Guadalupe from the Spanish region of Extremadura.

Ex-voto (Lat.) Votive offering. A traditional painting, carving, or personal object used to offer thanks for a favor granted by a saint.

Ezili Dantò Haitian Mother Goddess identified with Mater Salvatoris (Lat.), "Mother of the Savior," and the Polish Our Lady of Częstochowa.

Ezili Freda One of a trinity of Haitian goddesses, represented as a vain, white, elite woman. Identified with María Dolorosa del Monte Calvario.

Família-de-santo (Port.) "Family of saint." Spiritual family or members of a given **terreiro** in Brazil.

Festas (Port.) "Feasts." Ceremonies. The structure of the **terreiro** revolves around a ritual calendar of **festas**.

Freya Scandinavian goddess whose sacred day was Friday.

Gẹlẹdẹ Festival to honor older women, performed in Yorubaland.

Geledé Feminine society and festival that used to be celebrated every 8 December in Salvador, Bahia, Brazil, in order to placate the ancestral mothers.

Gringo (Sp.) Foreigner, usually Anglo-American. Used in Mexico and other parts of Latin America.

La Guadalupana (Sp.) Mexican Virgin of Guadalupe.

Guadalupanismo (Sp.) Cult of the Virgin of Guadalupe in Mexico.

Hidalgo (Sp.) Spanish nobleman.

Hieros Gamos (Gr.) "Holy Matrimony," or union of the God and Goddess, and their representatives on earth.

Hodegetria (Gr.) "Indicator of the Way." Type of icon, already known in the fourth century AD, which represents the Mother of God holding the infant Jesus in her left arm and pointing to him as the path of salvation with her right hand. Very popular in the Christian Orthodox world.

Homen (Port.) "Man." Term applied in Brazil to both heterosexual and active homosexual men.

Huitzilopochtli Aztec fire and war god of the south, immaculately conceived by the goddess **Coatlicue**.

Huixtocihuatl Aztec Goddess of Salt.

Iabás Feminine **orixás** or goddesses, such as **Oxum, Iemanjá, Nanā, Oyá,** and **Ewa,** in Afro-Brazilian religions.

Iaô (Yor.) "The youngest wife" or **filha-de-santo** (Port.) "daughter of saint." Initiate in an Afro-Brazilian religion. After seven years she may be eligible to become a head priestess or **iyalorixá.**

Iemanjá (Braz.) or **Yemayá** (Cuba) Mother Goddess of the salty waters, patron of sailors and fishermen. Syncretized with Our Lady of Immaculate Conception in Brazil and with the Virgin of Regla in Cuba. Her colors are blue and silver.

Iemanjismo (Port.) Widespread cult of the goddess **Iemanjá** in Brazil.

Ifá Divining Tray Divination system with the chain **opele** used in **Santería.**

La India An Indian woman.

Iroko Kind of **ceiba** tree that grows in Africa and Latin America. Sacred tree with magical powers in Brazil. Also an Afro-Brazilian **orixá.**

Ixiptla (Nah.) Aztec representation of a divinity, called "idol" by the colonial Spaniards.

Iyá àgbà (Yor.) "Old and wise one."

Iyá bassê From the Yoruban *iyágba-sê* or *iaba-sê,* "old woman who cooks." An older woman in charge of cooking and of the offerings to the gods at an Afro-Brazilian **terreiro.**

Iyá kêkêrê (Yor.) or **mãe pequena** (Port.) "Little mother." Initiate who helps the **iyalorixá** or **mãe-de-santo** supervise all activities of the **terreiro.**

Iyalorixá (Yor.) "Wife of the orixá" or **mãe-de-santo** (Port) "mother of saint." Spiritual leader or priestess of an Afro-Brazilian **terreiro.** Usually a woman over forty.

Ìyámì (Yor.), **Iyá-mi** (Braz.) "My mother" or "Our mothers."

Jeje African Fon culture.

Jôgo de búzios Afro-Brazilian divination system performed by the **iyalorixás** (priestesses) or **babalorixás** (priests), using sixteen cowry shells.

Korowód (Pol.), **Khorovod** (Russ.) Ritual round dance, often performed near lakes and ponds, which symbolizes the womb that spins out life.

Kostrobonko Dying and reviving Ukrainian spring god.

Kudurru Babylonian stella.

Lasyrenn Young aspect of the Haitian triple goddess, represented as a siren and identified with the patron Saint of Cuba, Our Lady of Charity of El Cobre.

Loa Haitian god or goddess, analogous to the Brazilian **orixá** and the Cuban **oricha.**

La Llorona (Sp.) "The Crying One." Mythical Mexican figure representing a long-suffering mother who appears near rivers and creeks looking for her children she drowned out of desperation. The story of La Llorona has pre-Hispanic and colonial meanings superimposed.

Los tres grandes (Sp.) "The three great ones." Three famous Mexican muralists of the twentieth century: Diego Rivera, Clemente Orozco, and David Alfaro Siqueiros.

Lotería (Sp.) "Lottery." A game of European origin, very popular among the Mexican and Mexican American population.

Lowrider Car lowered to the ground that may display customized lacquer jobs, murals, and other flashy details. Meant to go "low and slow."

Lucumí Yoruba (in Cuba).

Magna Mater (Lat.) "Great Mother," a Mother Goddess archetype.

La Malinche Also called **Malinalli, Malintzin, Doña Marina**. Translator, advisor, and consort to the Spanish conqueror of Mexico, Hernán Cortés. She was offered to him as a slave by her own people.

Malinchismo (Sp.) An excessive love for the foreign, in Mexico. Comes from the **La Malinche** figure.

Mami Wata or **Mama Wata** Yoruban water goddess, often represented as a beautiful, white mermaid with long hair.

Mañanitas (Sp.) "Little mornings." Singing and playing music for a person's birthday, performed outside of his or her residence at sun break.

Mapou (Fr.) **Ceiba** or **iroko** tree. Sacred tree of the Haitian Voodoo.

Marzanna or **panna moru** (Pol.) "Death maiden," also called **Morena, Murena, Morana, Mara, Marzaniok, Śmiertka, Śmiercicha, Śmierć** ("Death"). Female figure, part of the **Topienie Marzanny** ritual.

Matachines Also called "Los soldados de la Virgen" (Sp.) or the "Virgin's Soldiers." Traditional dances for the Feast of the Virgin of Guadalupe each 12 December, performed by **mestizos** of Mexican origin, dressed as Aztec Indians. These dances are related to the Christians vs. infidels type of dances, such as **Moros y cristianos** (Sp.) "Moors and Cristians," popular in Spain and Latin America.

Mater Salvatoris (Lat.) "Mother of the Savior."

Matka Boska (Pol.) "Mother of God."

Matka Polka (Pol.) "Mother Pole."

Mayahuel "Powerful Flow" or "Lady Maguey." Aztec goddess.

Mesa Branca (Port.) "White Table." Brazilian Spiritist ceremony in honor of the spirits of deified ancestors, such as Jesus Christ, the **orixá** Oxalá, and the **caboclo** Cacique Pedra Branca (Port.) "Chief White Stone," all of them characterized by being warriors for peace and justice and by the color white.

Mestizo/a (Sp.) Mixed breed of Indian and Spaniard.

Mociuaquetzque Aztec women who died in childbirth, considered equal to brave warriors who perished in battle. Descended on earth as "Goddess Women," **Cihuateteo**.

Mokosh Finno-Slavic Great Mother Goddess figure. Goddess of marriage and spinning.

Moros y cristianos (Sp.) "Moors and Christians." Type of dances performed in Spain and Latin America that dramatize battles between infidels and Christians.

Mother Moist Earth or **Holy Earth**, among the Eastern and the Western Slavs, respectively. Also called goddess **Zhiva** (**Żywa**) "Alive" or **Zhivie** (**Żywie**) in Poland. Mother Goddess archetype, probably derived from such all-encompassing Great Mother figures as the Finno-Slavic **Mokosh** and the Slavic **Złota Baba**.

Movimiento Chicano, La Causa Chicana (Sp.) Mexican American movement for civil rights, cultural equity, and self-determination, started in California in the 1960s.

Nagô Name given in Brazil to the Yoruba tradition.

Nanã (**Nanan**) Yoruba-Brazilian goddess representing the old wise woman archetype, associated with muddy waters, which are transformed into earth. In Brazil, one of the trinity **Oxum–Iemanjá–Nanã**.

Naná Burukú Afro-Cuban male **oricha**, corresponding to the Afro-Brazilian **Nanã**.

New Spain (**Nueva España**) First viceroyalty established in the New World by the Spaniards in 1535 in the areas of today's Mexico, the states of California, Texas, New Mexico, Arizona, Utah, Nevada, and part of Colorado, Central America, part of the Caribbean (excluding Cuba, Santo Domingo, and Puerto Rico), and since 1565, the Philippines.

Nikopoi (Gr.) "Victorious God Birth-Giver." Cult born during the Byzantine Empire's struggles against foreign troops in the seventh and eighth centuries AD.

El Niño de Atocha A particular representation of Baby Jesus, in Cuba syncretized with **Elegguá**.

Non fecit talliter omni nationi (Lat.) "[God] Has Not Done the Like for Any Other Nation." Legend taken from Psalm 147 and attached to the image of the Mexican Virgin of Guadalupe in the eighteenth century.

Nopal (Sp. from Nah.) Prickly pear cactus. Part of the Aztec coat of arms.

Obá Afro-Brazilian female **orixá**.

Obatalá Creation god of universal love, peace, and justice, syncretized with Our Lady of Mercy in Cuba.

Obí Divination system that uses four pieces of coconut, practiced in **Santería**.

Oferenda (Port.) "Offering."

Ogão Initiated and "confirmed" man at an Afro-Brazilian **terreiro**. The **ogãos** are involved in different activities, usually external to the religion, such as performing sacrifices, making altars, and playing the ritual drums. They may also be financial contributors.

Ogum God of iron and war, syncretized with Saint Anthony in Brazil.

Old Europe Term coined by Lithuanian American archeologist Maria Gimbutas to describe a native European civilization dating from 7,000–3,500 BC and characterized by a matriarchal social organization.

Olmec culture Foundational Mesoamerican culture, dating from the preclassical period (1,500–400 BC), and centered in the Mexican Gulf coast. Some of its main ceremonial centers were La Venta and Tres Zapotes, near today's city of Veracruz.

Olodum or **Olodumaré** Yoruban abstract supreme God.

Olúo or **olúwo** Foremost chief of the **babalawo** community of Ifá diviners. Function disappeared in Brazil.

Omolú God of diseases and their cure, syncretized with Saint Lazarus in Brazil.

Opele (**oguele**) Chain, part of the **Ifá Divining Tray,** a **Santería** divination system.

Orixá (Brazil), **Oricha** (Cuba), or **Òrìṣà** (West Africa) God or goddess from the Yoruba culture, in Brazil and Cuba syncretized with a Catholic saint. In Brazil sometimes also called *anjo da guarda,* or guardian angel.

Ọ̀ṣun Yoruban water goddess, expression of female mystical power, beauty, motherhood, and divination.

Oxalá Afro-Brazilian creation god of universal love, peace, and justice, syncretized with Jesus Christ.

Oxum (Braz.) or **Ochún** (Cuba) Young, coquettish goddess of fresh waters, syncretized with the Virgin of Charity of El Cobre in Cuba. Her colors are yellow and gold.

Oyá or **Iansã** Afro-Brazilian female **orixá**, one of the **iyá-mi**.

Pachuco Type of Mexican American from the 1940s characterized by a particular dress, hair, and walking style. Part of the search for identity and protest of the Chicano.

Padê de Exú Ritual for the **orixá Exú** involving the placing of offerings and dancing at the center of the **barracão** or ritual space before a public ceremony, in order to prevent the negative forces of other **Exús** from entering.

Pano da costa (Port.) "Cloth from [the African] coast." Piece of cloth wrapped over ceremonial garments at **Candomblé** ceremonies.

Pastores (Sp.) "Shepherds." Popular performance of Spanish origin connected to traditional Christmas festivities.

Patakí Myth or narrative from Afro-Cuban and Afro-Brazilian traditions.

Patria (Sp.) "Homeland."

Pêjigã Male maker of the altar in Afro-Brazilian religions.

Peyote (Sp. from Nah.) Cactus with narcotic qualities, used for Indian ritual ceremonies.

Posadas (Sp.) "Lodging." Part of traditional Christmas festivities that re-creates the quest of Mary and Jesus looking for a place to stay in Bethlehem.

Potop (Pol.) "Deluge." Popular name given to the devastating Swedish invasion of Poland of 1655-60, called "Wojna północna" ("Northern War").

Prêto/a Velho/a (Port.) "Old Black Man/Woman." An ancestral African spirit in Afro-Brazilian religions.

Quechua South American Indian language spoken by millions of people.

Quetzal Sacred bird of the Aztecs.

Quetzalcoatl Aztec civilizing god, associated with vegetative renewal. Represented as a plumed serpent. From quetzalli (Nah.), "very green feather."

Quilombo (Braz.) or **Palenque** (Cuba) Self-liberation space of runaway Afro-Brazilian or Afro-Cuban slaves, respectively. In Brazil, the most famous is the Quilombo dos Palmares, which commemorated its three-hundred-year anniversary in the 1990s.

Quinceañera (Sp.) "The fifteen-year-old one." Sumptuous feast celebrating the fifteenth birthday and coming out of a girl.

Rasquachismo (Mex. Am.) "Esthetic of the poor," characterized by an excessive amalgamation of hybrid objects and often the reversal of their original meaning.

Reconquista (Sp.) Gradual "Reconquest" of Spain from the Moors during their domination from
  AD 711 till 1492.

Regla de Ocha or **Santería** Afro-Cuban syncretic religion composed of Yoruban (**Lucumí**) and
  Catholic elements, analogous to Brazilian **Candomblé**.

Regla de Palo, Palo Monte, Regla Conga, or **Mayombe** Afro-Cuban religion from the Congo
  tradition.

Retablo (Sp.) Painting representing a story or event, usually religious in nature.

Rusałka (Pol.) Most often appears as one of a group of Rusałki, in the Polish tradition. Other
  names given to such groups are **Topielice, Wodnice, Panny Wodne, Panny Morskie**, or
  Boginki. Believed to be a young maiden with long, flowing hair, running freely in the
  proximity of lakes and trees. Represents the untamed life-giving and life-taking forces of
  woman and nature. Sometimes perceived as a female demon. She is the young aspect of an
  original trinity of goddesses.

Santera (Sp.) or **iyalocha** Afro-Cuban priestess.

Santería or Regla de Ocha Afro-Cuban syncretic religion composed of Yoruban (**Lucumí**) and
  Catholic elements, analogous to Brazilian **Candomblé**.

Santero (Sp.) or **babalocha** Afro-Cuban priest.

Santocalli (Nah.) Aztec domestic chapel.

Solidarność (Pol.) "Solidarity" movement that started in the Gdańsk shipyards in 1980 and led to
  the collapse of the communist regime in Poland in 1989.

Stella Maris (Lat.) "Star of the Sea."

Stilla Maris (Lat.) "Drop of the Sea."

Subcomandante Marcos Leader of the Mexican Indian Chiapas uprising, started on 1 January
  1994 and continuing until this day.

Światowid/Świętowit Important pre-Christian Slavic god from the area of Poland.

Syncretism Cultural phenomenon in which two or more components form different cultural
  traditions enter into contact with each other, giving a product different from its components.
  Examples are the Afro-Brazilian and the Afro-Cuban religions, such as **Candomblé** and
  Santería (**Regla de Ocha**).

Tanit Carthaginian goddess from the fourth–third century BC, represented crowned, seated on
  her throne, and holding a dove at her navel.

Temazcalteci "Grandmother of the Bathhouse." Aztec goddess.

Tenochtitlan Capital of the Aztec Empire, constructed on the Texcoco Lake. Today's Mexico City.

Terreiro or **roça** (Port.) Literally, "terrain" or "thicket." A physical space where Afro-Brazilian
  religions are practiced, which symbolically re-creates a mythical African village community.

Teteo innan or **Toci** "Mother of the Gods" or "Our Grandmother." Aztec goddess.

Theonymphos (Gr.) "Wedded to God."

Theotocos (Gr.) "Mother of God." Official title given to the Virgin Mary at the Council of
  Ephesus in AD 431.

Tilma (Sp.) "Cloak."

Tlaloc Mesoamerican god of lightening, thunder, and rainwater.

Tlapialli Aztec lineage divinity or "idol."

Tlazolteotl Aztec "Goddess of Filth."

Tlazolteotl–Cihuapilli Aztec "Goddess of Filth"–"Fair Lady."

Tlazolteotl–Ixcuina Aztec "Goddess of Filth"–"Lady Cotton."

Toci "Our Grandmother." Aztec goddess.

Tonacaciuatl "Lady of Our Nutrition." Aztec goddess of the upper skies, also called **Citlalicue**.

Tonantzin "Our Mother." Aztec Mother Goddess, syncretized with the Virgin of Guadalupe.

Topienie Marzanny (Pol.) "Drowning of Marzanna." Traditional Polish ritual, probably connected to pre-Christian sacrificial spring rituals.

Umbanda The newest (twentieth-century) and most syncretic of Afro-Brazilian religions, which includes African **orixá** worship, Catholic, and Spiritist elements, among others. Practiced mainly in central Brazil.

Veladora (Sp.) from *velar*—"to keep vigil" or "to hold a wake." A large votive candle meant to burn for seven days for an intention or a cause.

Xangô (Braz.) or **Changó** (Cuba) Virile god of thunder and lightening, syncretized with Saint Jerome in Brazil and with Saint Barbara in Cuba.

Xochiquetzal "Flowery Quetzal Feather." Young Aztec goddess.

Yemoja or **Yemaja** Yoruban water goddess, avatar of **Mami Wata**.

Yggdrasil Scandinavian Tree of Life, Cosmic Tree, or World Tree.

Yoruba West African culture and language from the area of today's Nigeria and Benin, whose members were brought to Brazil (**Nagô**) and Cuba (**Lukumí**) as the last slave group, from the second half of the eighteenth through the nineteenth century. They greatly influenced local cultures, creating syncretic religions such as **Candomblé** and **Santería** (**Regla de Ocha**).

Złota Baba (Pol.) "Golden Woman." Slavic Mother Goddess figure.

Bibliography

Acosta-Belén, Edna, and Carlos E. Santiago. "Merging Borders: The Remapping of America." Darder and Torres 29–42.

"Adamah." *Adama: Hebrew Word Studies for Bible Study: Amos.* 11 Nov. 2004 <http://www.bible.gen.nz/amos/hebrew/alep/adama.htm>.

Afanasiev, A. H. "Bajka o żabie i bohatyrze." Trans. Ludwik Flaszen. *Bajki rosyjskie.* Cracow: Wydawnictwo Literackie, 1962. 127–39.

———. "Czarevna Liagushka." *Narodnyie Russkie skazki.* Vol. 2. Moscow: Gosudarstviennoie Izdatelstvo Hudozhestvennoi Literatury, 1957. 329–37.

———. "Vasilisa prekrasnaia." *Narodnyie Russkie skazki.* Vol. 1. Moscow: Gosudarstviennoie Izdatelstvo Hudozhestvennoi Literatury, 1957. 159–65.

Alcántara Arruda, Alda d'. Personal interview. Itaparica Island, Braz., 19 July 1996.

Alcántara Arruda, Celeste d' Personal interview. Salvador, Bahia, Braz., 23 July 1996.

Alcover, Joan. "La Balanguera." *Cap al Tard.* Barcelona: Gustau Gili, 1909. 3–5.

Aleksieiev, C.B. *Drevnie verovania vostochnikh Slovian.* Moscow: Institut Molodezhi (Katedra Istorii), 1996.

Alicja Łukasiak Baba. Warsaw: Centrum Sztuki Współczesnej Zamek Ujazdowski, 2003.

Alma Lopez, Los Angeles Visual and Public Artist. 18 and 19 May 2003 <http://home.earthlink.net/~almalopez/digital/lupesire.html>.

Álvarez, José Rogelio, ed. *Enciclopedia de México.* Vol 6. 1972. Mexico City: n. p., 1975.

Amado, Jorge. *Mar morto.* 69th ed. Rio de Janeiro and São Paulo: Record, 1995.

Anaya, Rudolfo. *Bless Me, Ultima.* 1972. Warner Bros., 1999.

Anaya, Rudolfo, and Francisco Lomelí, eds. *Aztlán: Essays on the Hispanic Homeland.* 1989. Albuquerque: U of New Mexico P, 1998.

Anzaldúa, Gloria. *Borderlands/La Frontera: The New Mestiza.* San Francisco: aunt lute, 1987.

———. "Chicana Artists: Exploring *Nepantla*, el Lugar de la Frontera." Darder and Torres 163–70.

———. "Coatlalopeuh: She Who Has Dominion over Serpents." Castillo, *Goddess of the Americas* 52–55.

Anzaldúa, Gloria, and Maya Christina Gonzalez. *Prietita and the Ghost Woman/Prietita y la Llorona.* San Francisco: Children's Books, 1995.

Arredondo, Gabriela, et al., eds. *Chicana Feminisms. Durham and London: Duke UP, 2003.*

Attawater, Donald. The Penguin Dictionary of Saints. 1965. Baltimore: Penguin, 1966.

Augras, Monique. "De Iyá Mi a Pomba Gira: Transformações e símbolos da libido." *Escritos sobre a religião dos orixás*. Ed. Carlos Eugênio Marcondes de Moura. São Paulo: Edicon, 1989. 14–33.

Averinciev, S. S. "Marija." *Mifologicheskii slovar'*. Ed. E. M. Mieletinskii. Moscow: Sovietskaia entsiklopedia, 1990. 338–40.

Azevêdo, Carlos Alberto. "Mitos e ritos nos grupos de culto afrobrasileiros." BA thesis. Universidade Federal de Pernambuco, Braz., 1971.

Baamonde, José María. *Cultos afrobrasileños*. Buenos Aires: Ediciones Paulinas, 1992.

Báez-Jorge, Félix. *La parentela de María*. Xalapa, Mexico: Universidad Veracruzana, 1994.

Bahiatursa. Sistema de informações turísticas: Relatório de informações gerais por cidade e tipo. Salvador, Bahia, Braz: Bahiatursa, 12 Jan. 1996.

Bania, Zbigniew, and Stanisław Kobielus. *Jasna Góra*. Warsaw: Instytut Wydawniczy Pax, 1983.

Barber, Elizabeth Wayland. *Women's Work: The First 20,000 Years*. New York and London: W. W. Norton, 1994.

Barnet, Miguel. *Afro-Cuban Religions*. 1995. Trans. Christine Renata Ayorinde. Princeton: Marcus Wiener, 2001.

Barnstone, Willis, ed. *The Other Bible*. New York: HarperCollins, 1984.

Barriga, María Cristina. "Malinalli, Marina, Malintzin, Doña Marina, y la Llorona: Una mujer y cinco mundos diferentes." *South Eastern Latin Americanist: Quarterly Review of the South Eastern Council of Latin American Studies* 37.4 (1994): 1–4.

Bartmiński, Jerzy, et al. *Kosmos*. Vol. 1 of *Słownik stereotypów i symboli ludowych*. Lublin, Pol.: Wydawnictwo Uniwersytetu Marii Curie-Skłodowskiej, 1999.

Bastide, Roger. *The African Religions of Brazil: Toward a Sociology of the Interpretation of Civilizations*. 1960. Trans. Helen Sebba. Baltimore: Johns Hopkins UP, 1978.

Bayley, Harold. *The Lost language of Symbolism*. Vols. 1 and 2. 1912. London: Bracken, 1996.

Begg, Ean. *The Cult of the Black Virgin*. 1985. London: Arkana Penguin, 1996.

Belán, Kyra. *The Virgin in Art*. New York: Barnes & Noble, 2005.

Benítez-Rojo, Antonio. *The Repeating Island: The Caribbean and the Postmodern Perspective*. 1992. Trans. James Maraniss. Durham and London: Duke UP, 1996.

Benz, Ernst. *The Eastern Orthodox Church*. 1957. Trans. R. Winston and C. Winston. Garden City, NY: Doubleday, 1963.

Berger, Peter. *The Sacred Canopy*. 1967. Garden City, NY: Anchor, 1969.

Bernotienė, Stasė, et. al. *Lietuvių Llaudies Menas (Lithuanian Folk Art)*. Vilnius: n.p., 1993.

Berry, Philippa, and Andrew Wernick, eds. *Shadow of Spirit: Postmodernism and Religion*. London and New York: Routledge, 1992.

Beyer, Peter. *Religion and Globalization*. London: SAGE, 1994.

La Biblia. Madrid: Ediciones Paulinas and Estrella: Verbo Divino, 1985.

Birnbaum, Lucia Chiavola. *Black Madonnas*. 1993. San Jose: toExcel, 2000.

———. *dark mother*. San Jose: Authors Choice, 2001.

———. *liberazione della donna feminism in Italy*. Middletown: Wesleyan UP, 1986.

Boff, Frei Clodovis. *Maria na cultura brasileira*. Petrópolis, Braz.: Vozes, 1995.

Bolívar Aróstegui, Natalia. *Los orichas en Cuba*. Havana: PM Ediciones, 1994.

———. Personal interview. Havana, 13 Nov. 1999.

Bolívar Aróstegui, Natalia, and Valentina Porras Potts. *Orisha Ayé: Unidad mítica del Caribe al Brasil*. Guadalajara, Sp.: Ediciones Pontón, S.A., 1996.

Borovskii, A. E. "O nazvanii velikoi bogini Slavian." *Drievnie Slaviane i Kievskaia Rus'*. Kiev: Naukova Dumka, 1989. 84–92.

Brading, D. A. *Mexican Phoenix*. Cambridge: Cambridge UP, 1991.

Bramly, Serge. *Macumba: The Teachings of Maria-José, Mother of the Gods*. 1975. Trans. St. Martin's Press. San Francisco: City Lights, 1994.

Brandstaetter, Roman. "Hymn de Czarnej Madonny." Rakoczy 157.

Briffault, Robert. *The Mothers*. Vol. 3. New York: Macmillan, 1927.

Brown, Karen Mc Carthy. *Mama Lola: A Vodou Priestess in Brooklyn*. Berkeley: U of California P, 1991.

———. "Olina and Erzulie: A Woman and a Goddess in Haitian Vodou." *Anima* 5 (1979): 110–17.

Brückner, Aleksander. *Mitologia polska*. Warsaw: Bibljoteka Polska, 1924.

Buey, Félix del, and Miguel Vallecillo. *Santa María de Regla*. N.p., [Sp.]: Grafibérica, 1987.

Burciaga, José Antonio. *Drink Cultura: Chicanismo*. Santa Barbara, CA: Joshua Odell Editions, 1993.

Cabrera, Lydia. *El Monte (Igbo—Finda; Ewe Orisha. Vititi Nfinda)*. 1983. Miami: Ediciones Universal, 1992.

———. *Yemayá y Ochún: Kariocha, iyalorichas y olorichas*. 1974. Introd. and bibliog. Rosario Hiriart. 2nd ed. New York: [Ediciones] CR, 1980.

Campbell, Joseph. *The Mythic Image*. Princeton: Princeton UP, 1974.

———. *Occidental Mythology: The Masks of God*. 1964. New York: Penguin, 1987.

Carneiro, Edison. *Candomblés da Bahia*. 8th ed. Rio de Janeiro: Civilização Brasileira, 1991.

———. "The Structure of African Cults in Bahia." *Journal of American Folklore* 53.210 (1940): 271–78.

Castellanos, Isabel. "A River of Many Turns: The Polysemy of Ochún in Afro-Cuban Tradition." Murphy and Sanford 34–45.

Castillo, Ana. "Extraordinary Woman." Castillo, *Goddess of the Americas* 72–78.

———, ed. *Goddess of the Americas La Diosa de las Américas: Writings on the Virgin of Guadalupe*. New York: Riverdead, 1996.

———. *So Far from God*. New York: Plume, 1994.

Castillo, Richard Grisfold del et al., eds. *Chicano Art Resistance and Affirmation, 1965–1985*. Los Angeles: U of California, Wright Art Gallery, 1990. "Ceiba." *fUSION Anomaly. Ceiba*. 6 Nov. 2004 <http://fusionanomaly.net/ceiba.html>.

Cervantes, Miguel de. *Los trabajos de Persiles y Sigismunda*. Ed. Florencio Sevilla Arroyo. Alicante, Sp.: Biblioteca Virtual Miguel de Cervantes, 2001. 6 July 2006 <http://www.cervantesvirtual. com>.

Chavasse, Ruth. "The Virgin Mary: Consoler, Protector, and Social Worker in Quattrocento Miracle Tales." *Women in Italian Renaissance Culture and Society*. Ed Letizia Penizza. Oxford: Legenda/European Humanities Research Center, University of Oxford, 2000. 138–64.

Chaveco, Raúl. Personal interview. Havana, 12 Nov. 1999.

Chávez-Silverman, Suzanne. "Gendered Bodies and Borders in Contemporary Chican@ Performance and Literature." Gaspar de Alba, *Velvet Barrios* 215–27.

Cisneros, Sandra. *Woman Hollering Creek and Other Stories.* New York: Vintage, 1991.

Cockcroft, Eva Sperling, and Holly Barnet-Sánchez, eds. *Signs from the Heart: California Chicano Murals.* Venice, CA: Social and Public Art Resource Center, 1990.

Costa, Fernando. *A prática do candomblé no Brasil.* Rio de Janeiro: Editora Renes, 1974.

Costa Lima, Vivaldo da. "A família-de-santo nos candomblés jeje-nagôs da Bahia: Um estudo de relações intra-grupais." MA thesis. Universidade Federal da Bahia, Braz., 1977.

———. "Organização do grupo de candomblé: Estratificação, senioridade e hierarquia." *Bandeira de Aairá.* São Paulo: Nobel, 1982.

Cros Sandoval, Mercedes. *La religión afro-cubana.* Madrid: Playor, 1975.

Cruz, Anne J., et al., eds. *Disciplines on the Line: Feminist Research on Spanish, Latin American, and U.S. Latina Women.* Newark, DE: Juan de la Cuesta, 2003.

Cuadriello, Jaime, comp. *Artes de México 29: Visiones de Guadalupe.* Santa Ana, CA: Bowers Museum of Cultural Art, n.d.

———. "Mirada apocalíptica: Visiones en Patmos Tenochtitlan, La Mujer Aguila." Cuadriello 10–23.

Cunningham, Lawrence. *Mother of God.* Photogr. Nicolas Sapieha. San Francisco: Harper & Row, 1982.

I Curso de noções básicas para ogan's e ekejí's. Salvador, Bahia, Braz.: Ilé Asé Orisan'lá J'Omin Terreiro São Bento, 1997.

Custodian. Personal interview. Virgen de Regla Sanctuary, Chipiona, Sp., 9 June 2004.

Czapliński, Konrad Kazmierz. *Sanktuaria w Polsce.* 1999. Katowice, Pol.: VIDEOGRAF II, 2001.

Czarnowski, Stefan. "Kultura religijna wiejskiego ludu polskiego." *Dzieła.* Vol. 1. Warsaw: Państwowe Wydawnictwo Naukowe, 1956. 88–107.

Częstochowa Poland. Warsaw: Polish Tourist Information Center, n.d.

DaMatta, Roberto. *A casa e a rua.* Rio de Janeiro: Editora Guanabara S.A., 1987.

D'Ancona, Mirella Levi. *The Iconography of the Immaculate Conception in the Middle Ages and Early Renaissance.* N.p.: College Art Association of America in conjunction with the Art Bulletin, 1957.

Darder, Antonia, and Rodolfo D. Torres, eds. *The Latino Studies Reader.* Malden, MA and Oxford, UK: Blackwell, 1998.

De La Torre, Miguel A. "Ochún: [N]either the [M]Other of All Cubans [N]or the Bleached Virgin." 11 Oct. 2003 <http://www.hope.edu/delatorre/articles/ochun.htm>.

Delgado Oquendo, René. Personal interview. Havana, 12 Nov. 1999.

Derwich, Marek, and Marek Cetwiński. *Herby, legendy i dawne mity.* Wrocław, Pol.: KAW, 1989.

Díaz del Castillo, Bernal. *Historia de la conquista de Nueva España.* 1632. Ed. Joaquín Ramírez Cabañas. 1955. Mexico: Porrúa, 1986.

Díaz Fabelo, Teodoro. *Lengua de santeros Güiné Gongorí.* Havana: n.p., 1956.

"Distaff." *Merriam-Webster OnLine.* 11 Feb. 2006. <http://www.m-w.com/cgi-bin/dictionary>.

Doroszewski, Witold, ed. *Słownik języka polskiego PAN.* Vol 1. Warsaw: Wiedza Powszechna, 1958.

D'Oxum, Dalva. *Mirongas magia e feitiço.* Rio de Janeiro: Pallas, 1991.

Drescher, Timothy W. *San Francisco Bay Area Murals: Communities Creating Their Muses, 1904–1997*. St. Paul: Pogo, 1998.

Drewal, Henry John, and Margaret Thompson Drewal. *Gẹlẹdẹ: Art and Female Power among the Yoruba*. Bloomington: Indiana UP, 1990.

Droogers, André, and Sidney M. Greenfield. "Recovering and Reconstructing Syncretism." Greenfield and Droogers 21–42.

Dunitz, Robin J., and James Prigoff. *California Murals*. Los Angeles: RJD Enterprises, 1998.

———. *Painting the Towns: Murals of California*. Los Angeles: RJD Enterprises, 1997.

Dunnington, Jacqueline Orsini. *Celebrating Guadalupe*. Photogr. Charles Mann. Tucson: Rio Nuevo, 2004.

———. *Guadalupe: Our Lady of New Mexico*. Santa Fe: Museum of New Mexico Press, 1999.

———. *Viva Guadalupe!* Photogr. Charles Mann. Santa Fe: Museum of New Mexico Press, 1997.

Durán, Fray Diego. *Book of the Gods and Rites and The Ancient Calendar*. Trans. and ed. Fernando Horcasitas and Doris Heyden. Foreword by Miguel León-Portilla. Norman: U of Oklahoma P, 1971.

Durant, Will. *The Story of Civilization, Part I: Our Oriental Heritage*. New York: Simon & Schuster, 1954.

Ecos desde un vientre de barro: Homenaje al señor Alfonso Castillo Orta y familia Castillo. San Antonio: Esperanza Peace and Justice Center, 2002.

Eisele, Wanda, and Krzysztof Renik. "Sanktuaria maryjne w Polsce." *Kult maryjny* 37–46.

Elbein dos Santos, Juana. "A percepção ideológica dos fenômenos religiosos: Sistema nagô no Brasil, negritude versus sincretismo." *Vozes* 7 (1977): 23–34.

———. *Os nàgô e a morte*. Petrópolis, Braz.: Vozes, 1975.

———. Personal interview. Salvador, Bahia, Braz., 5 Aug. 1996.

Eliade, Mircea. *Mity, sny i misteria*. 1989. Trans. Krzysztof Kocjan. Warsaw: Wydawnictwo KR, 1999.

El Vez. *Graciasland*. Music CD. Sympathy for the Record Industry, 1994.

Escalada, Xavier, SJ. *Enciclopedia guadalupana*. Vols. 1 and 4. Mexico City: n.p., 1995.

Fatunmbi, Awo Fá'lokun. *Oshun: Ifá and the Spirit of the River*. Plainview, NY: Original Publications, 1993.

Fernandes, Rubem César. "Aparecida, Our Queen, Lady, and Mother, Saravá!" *Social Science Information* 24.4 (1985): 799–819.

Ferretti, Sergio F. "Religious Syncretism in an Afro-Brazilian Cult House." Greenfield and Droogers 87–97.

———. *Repensando o sincretismo*. São Paulo: EDUSP, 1995.

Florescano, Enrique. *Memory, Myth, and Time in Mexico: From the Aztecs to Independence*. Trans. Albert G. Bork. Austin: U of Texas P, 1997.

———. *The Myth of Quetzalcoatl*. Trans. Lysa Hochroth, illustr. Raúl Velázquez. Baltimore: Johns Hopkins UP, 1999.

"Fox empezó la jornada en la Basílica." *Diario de Yucatán* 2 Dec 2000. 7 Feb 2003 <http://www.yucatan.com.mx/especiales/tomadeposesion/02120008.asp>.

Franco, Jean. *Critical Passions*. Ed. Mary Louise Pratt and Kathleen Newman. Durham and London: Duke UP, 1999.

Friedman, Jonathan. *Cultural Identity and Global Process*. London: SAGE, 1994.

Fry, Peter. *Para inglês ver*. Rio de Janeiro: Zahar Editores, 1982.

Galembo, Phillis. *Divine Inspiration: From Benin to Bahia*. Albuquerque: U of New Mexico P, 1993.

Galland, China. *Longing for Darkness, Tara and the Black Madonna: A Ten Year Journey*. New York: Viking Penguin, 1990.

García Canclini, Néstor. *Culturas híbridas: Estrategias para entrar y salir de la modernidad*. Mexico City: Grijalbo, 1990.

García Nieto, José. "A Nuestra Señora la Virgen María." *Gratia Plena* 39.

Gardner, Laurence. *Bloodline of the Holy Grail*. New York: Barnes & Noble, 2003.

Garibay K., Angel María. *Poesía nahuatl*. 3 vols. Mexico City: UNAM, 1964–68.

Gaspar de Alba, Alicia. *Chicano Art Inside/Outside the Master's House: Cultural Politics and the CARA Exhibition*. Austin: U of Texas P, 1998.

———. "Rights of Passage: From Cultural Schizophrenia to Border Consciousness in Cheech Martín's *Born in East L.A.*" Garpar de Alba, *Velvet Barrios* 199–213.

———, ed. *Velvet Barrios: Popular Culture & Chicana/o Sexualities*. New York: Palgrave/Macmillan, 2003.

Gasparini, Evel. *Il matriarcato slavo: Antropologia culturale dei protoslavi*. Florence: Sansoni, 1973.

"Gèneres: La poesia Modernista." *Universitat Oberta de Catalunya*. 11 Mar. 2003 <http://www.xtec. es/~lrius1/ alcover/contextbaix.htm>.

Georgian State Dance Company. Performance. Laurie Auditorium, Trinity U, San Antonio. 18 September 2002.

Giesler, Patrick V. "Selling 'Africa' in Brazil." Unpublished essay, 2000.

Gieysztor, Aleksander. *Mitologia Słowian*. Warsaw: Wydawnictwo Artystyczne i Filmowe, 1986.

Gillespie, Jeanne L. "La Malinche and the China Poblana: Gender, Identity, and Image from the Colonial Era to the Twenty-first Century." Unpublished essay, 2000.

Gimbutas, Marija. *The Goddesses and Gods of Old Europe*. 1974. Berkeley: U of California P, 1992.

———. "An Interview with Kell Kearns." *The Age of the Great Goddess*. Audiotapes 1 & 2. Boulder: Sounds True Recordings, 1992.

———. *The Language of the Goddess*. 1989. New York: HarperCollins, 1991.

———. *The Living Goddesses*. Berkeley: U of California P, 1999.

———. "Women and Culture in Goddess-Oriented Old Europe." Spretnak 22–31.

———. *The World of the Goddess*. Parts 1–2. Videocassette. Mystic Fire Video.

Giobellina Brumana, Fernando. *Las formas de los dioses: Categorías y clasificaciones en el candomblé*. Cádiz: Servicio de Publicaciones Universidad de Cádiz, 1994.

Gliński, Antoni J. "O królewnie zaklętej w żabę." Wortman 38–47.

Gloger, Zygmunt. *Rok polski w życiu, tradycji i pieśni*. Warsaw: Jan Fiszer, 1900.

Głosik, Jerzy. *Zanim nastali Słowianie*. Warsaw: Agencja Wydawniczo-Handlowa Halina & Jerzy Głosik, 2001.

"Goddesses of Africa." *Avatars of the Goddess*. 11 Nov. 2004 <http://www3.sympatico.ca/ chartreuse/AvatarsOfTheGoddess/Africa.htm>.

Goddess Tanit. Necropolis of Puig des Molins, Ibiza, Sp.

Goldman, Shifra. "The Iconography of Chicano Self-Determination: Race, Ethnicity, and Class." *Art Journal* 49.2 (1990): 167–73.

Gomes Arruda, Dílson. Personal interviews. Itaparica Island, Braz., 19 July 1996 and 20 July 1996.

Gómez-Peña, Guillermo. "The Two Guadalupes." Castillo, *Goddess of the Americas* 178–83.

González Dorado, Antonio. *De María conquistadora a María libertadora: Mariología popular latinoamericana.* Santander, Sp.: Sal Terrae, 1988.

Gratia Plena. Comisión diocesana del patrimonio histórico-artístico. Torreón de Lozoya, Segovia, Sp.: Caja de Ahorros y Monte de Piedad de Segovia, 1988.

Graves, Robert. *Mammon and the Black Goddess.* Garden City, NY: Doubleday, 1965.

Greenfield, Sidney M. "The Reinterpretation of Africa: Convergence and Syncretism in Brazilian Candomblé." Greenfield and Droogers 113–29.

Greenfield, Sidney M., and André Droogers, eds. *Reinventing Religions.* Lanham: Rowman & Littlefield, 2001.

Grisfold del Castillo, Richard et al., eds. *Chicano Art Resistance and Affirmation, 1965–1985.* Los Angeles: U of California, Wright Art Gallery, 1990.

Gruzinski, Serge. *La guerra de las imágenes: De Cristóbal Colón a "Blade Runner" (1492–2019).* 1994. Mexico City: Fondo de Cultura Económica, 1995.

"Guadalupe, Virgen de." *Enciclopedia de México.* 1972. Comp. José Rogelio Álvarez. Vol. 6. Mexico City: n.p., 1975. 4–15.

Guevara, María. Personal interview. Warsaw, 11 July 2000.

Gurría Lacroix, Jorge. "La conquista de México." *Historia de México.* Vol. 4. Comp. Miguel León-Portilla. Mexico City and Barcelona: Salvat, 1974. 17–40.

Gustafson, Fred. *The Black Madonna.* Boston: Sigo, 1991.

———, ed. *Moonlit Path: Reflections on the Dark Feminine.* Berwick, ME: Nicolas-Hays, 2003.

Harrington, Patricia. "Mother of Death, Mother of Rebirth: The Mexican Virgin of Guadalupe." *Journal of the American Academy of Religion.* 56.1: 25–50.

"Heaven, Digital Billboard at Galeria de la Raza, Bryant & 24th Street San Francisco." *Alma Lopez, Los Angeles Visual and Public Artist.* 20 and 21 May 2003 <http://home.earthlink. net/~almalopez /murals/heaven2/heaven2.html>.

Heelas, Paul, ed. *Religion, Modernity, and Postmodernity.* Oxford, UK and Malden, MA: Blackwell, 1998.

Henning, Christoph, and Hans Oberländer. *Voodoo: Secret Power in Africa.* Cologne: Taschen, 1996.

Hernandez, Yasmin. "Yemaya y Ochun." *Artwork: Yemaya y Ochun.* 5 Sept. 2003 <http://www. yasminhernandez.com/yemayaochun.html>.

Herrera-Sobek, María. *The Mexican Corrido.* Bloomington: Indiana UP, 1990.

"Historia de la Virgen de Remedios de la Villa de Abades." *Historia Virgen de los Remedios.* 17 Sept. 2003 <http://www.abadescity.com>.

Hubbs, Joanna. *Mother Russia: The Feminine Myth in Russian Culture.* 1988. Bloomongton: Indiana UP, 1993.

Huynen, Jacques. *El enigma de las vírgenes negras.* Trans. R. M. Bassols. 1972. Barcelona: Plaza & Janes S.A., 1977.

"The Indigenous Languages of Mexico." *The Indigenous Languages of Mexico: Indigenous Groups*. 24 Feb. 2003 <http://www.elbalero.gob.mx/kids/about/html/indigenous/lenguas.html>.

"Institut Joan Alcover." *Govern de Les Illes Balears*. 12 Mar. 2003 <http://www.iesjalcover.com/ Historia/Nom.html>.

Ivanov, V., and Toporov, V. "Baba-Yaga." *Mifologicheskii slovar'*. Ed. E. M. Mieletinskii. Moscow: Sovietskaia Entsiklopedia, 1990. 85–86.

———. "K rekonstruktsii Mokoshi kak zhenskovo personazha v slavianskoi versii osnovnogo mifa." *Semantika i struktura 7*. Ed. R. Tsibian Nguka. Moscow: n.p., 1983. 175–97.

Iwashita, Pedro. *Maria e Iemanjá: Análise de um sincretismo*. São Paulo: Edições Paulinas, 1991.

Iyá-mi agbá: Mito e metamorfose das mães nagô. Dir. Juana Elbein dos Santos. Videocassette. Sociedade de Estudos da Cultura Negra no Brasil SECNEB.

Jacher-Tyszkowa, Aleksandra. *Matka Boska Częstochowska w polskiej sztuce ludowej i popularnej*. Cracow: Muzeum Etnograficzne w Krakowie, 1982.

Janus, Elżbieta, and Anna Renata Mazerowa, eds. *Semiotyka kultury*. Warsaw: Państwowy Instytut Wydawniczy, 1977.

Joseph Campbell and the Power of Myth. Program Five, "Love and the Goddess." Videocassette. Apostrophe Productions, 1988.

Jung, Carl. G., and L. M von Franz, eds. *Man and His Symbols*. 1964. Garden City, NY: Doubleday, 1972.

Kinsley, David. *The Goddesses' Mirror: Visions of the Divine from East and West*. Albany: State U of New York P, 1989.

Kopaliński, Władysław. *Słownik symboli*. Warsaw: Wiedza Powszechna, 1990.

Kuczyńska-Iracka, Anna. *Malarstwo ludowe kręgu częstochowskiego*. Ed. Władysława Jaworska et al. Studia z historii sztuki 28. Wrocław, Warsaw, Cracow, and Gdańsk: Ossolineum, 1978.

Kult maryjny. Pochitanie Bozhei Materi. Warsaw: Novum; Moscow: Izdatelskii Otdel Moskovskovo Patriarkhata, 1989.

Kunz, O. Konstancjusz, ed. *Cuda i łaski zdziałane za przyczyną Jasnogórskiej Matki Bożej*. Jasna Góra, Częstochowa, Pol.: Paulinianum, 1994.

Kunzle, David. *The Murals of Revolutionary Nicaragua, 1979–1992*. Berkeley, Los Angeles, and London: U of California P, 1995.

Lafaye, Jacques. *Quetzalcóatl and Guadalupe: The Formation of Mexican National Consciousness, 1531–1813*. 1974. Trans. Benjamin Keen. Chicago and London: U of Chicago P, 1976.

Landes, Ruth. "A Cult Matriarchate and Male Homosexuality." *Journal of Abnormal and Social Psychology* 3 (1940): 386–97.

———. *The City of Women*. 1947. Albuquerque: U of New Mexico P, 1994.

"*Las Four* by Alma Lopez." *Alma Lopez, Los Angeles Visual and Public Artist*. 19 May 2003 <http:// home.earthlink.net/~almalopez&murals/estrada/four.html>.

"Latina in the Land of Hollywood, 1999." *Alma Lopez, Los Angeles Visual and Public Artist*. 19 May 2003 <http:home.earthlink.net/~almalopez/digital/graphics/books/latinahwd.html>.

Latorre, Guisela. "Gender, Muralism, and the Politics of Identity: Chicana Muralism and Indigenist Æsthetics." *Disciplines on the Line: Feminist Research on Spanish, Latin American, and U.S. Latina Women*. Ed. Anne J. Cruz et al. Newark, DE: Juan de la Cuesta, 2003.

Laval, Babatunde. "New Light on Gelede." *African Arts* 11.2 (1978): 65–70, 94.

Lazarev, V. N. *Novogrodian Icon-Painting.* Moscow: Iskusstvo, 1976.

Leal, Luis. "In Search of Aztlán." *Aztlán.* 1989. Ed. Rudolfo Anaya and Francisco Lomeli. Trans. Gladys Leal. Albuquerque: U of New Mexico P, 1991.

Lee, Morgan. "Controversy Heads to Museum: Regents to Hear Opinions Wednesday about Collage." *Journal North*, 2 Apr. 2001: 1, 3.

Leon-Portilla, Miguel. *La filosofía nahuatl estudiada en sus fuentes.* Mexico City: Universidad Nacional Autónoma de México, Instituto de Historia: Seminario de Cultura Nahuatl, 1959.

Lesko, Barbara S. *The Great Goddesses of Egypt.* Norman: U of Oklahoma P, 1999.

Leszczyński, Zbigniew. "Pagan Gods of the Slavs." Typescript. [Warsaw]: Cardinal Stefan Wyszyński University, 1996.

Lippard, Lucy. *Mixed Blessings.* New York: Pantheon, 1990.

Loddy, Raul. *O povo do santo.* Rio de Janeiro: Pallas, 1995.

Lurker, Manfred. *Leksykon bóstw i demonów.* Warsaw: Bellona, 1999.

Luz, Marco Aurelio. *Agadá: Dinâmica da civilização africano-brasileira.* Salvador, Braz.: Centro Editorial e Didático da UFBa Sociedade de Estudos da Cultura Negra no Brasil-SECNEB, 1995.

Łowmiański, Henryk. *Religia Słowian i jej upadek w VI–XII.* Warsaw: PWN, 1979.

Łukasiak, Alicja. *Baba.* Exhibit. Galeria Laboratorium, Warsaw, 28 June–3 Aug. 2003.

———. "Baba." *Warszawa i kultura.* July–Aug. 2003: 55.

The Madonna. Videocassette. Vision Video, n.d.

Mãe Stella. Interview with Ana Maria Guerreiro, Carlota Gottschall, and Neilto Barreto. "Mãe Stella: Sacerdotisa e guardiã do candomblé na Bahia." *Analise & dados* 3 (1994): 42–46.

The Magic Ring: Russian Folktales from Alexander Afanasiev's Collection. 1985. Illustr. Alexander Kurkin. Moscow: Raduga, 2001.

Malinowski, Bronisław. Introduction. *Cuban Counterpoint: Tobacco and Sugar.* By Fernando Ortiz. Trans. Harriet de Onís. New York: Alfred A. Knopf, 1947. ix–xvi.

Maliński, Ks. Mieczysław. *Polska ikona.* Częstochowa, Pol.: Edycja Świętego Pawła, 1994.

"Mallorca un país enmig de la mar: Els símbols." *Consell de Mallorca.* 12 Mar. 2003 <http://www. gubia.conselldemallorca.net.pais/ sim_04_ca.html>.

Marín Arcones, Daniel. "Kudurrus." 10 Nov. 2003 <http:www.geocities.com/aratos_es/kudurru. html>.

"Mary, The Bride of God, Part 2: Church Teaching." 23 Sept. 2003 <http://home.nyc.rr.com/ mysticalrose/bride2.html>.

Marzal, Manuel, et al. *The Indian Face of God in Latin America.* Trans. Penelope R. Hall. Maryknoll, NY: Orbis, 1966.

Matka Boża Częstochowska w naszych dziejach. Warsaw: Wydział Nauki Katolickiej Kurii Metropolitarnej Warszawskiej, 1982.

Matory, James Lorand. "Homens montados: Homossexualidade e simbolismo da possessão nas religiões afro-brasileiras." *Escravidão e invenção da liberdade: Estudos sobre o negro no Brasil.* Ed. João José Reis. São Paulo: Brasiliense, 1988. 215–31.

Mayan Uprising in Chiapas. Video, Prod. PBS, n.d.

Maza, Francisco de la. *El gaudalupanismo mexicano*. 1953. Mexico City: Fondo de Cultura Económica, 1981.

McBride-Limaye, Ann. "Metamorphoses of la Malinche and Mexican Cultural Identity." *Comparative Civilizations Review* 19 (1988): 1–28.

McIntyre, Kellen. "An Introduction to the Art and Architecture of Viceregal Mexico." Lecture. U of Texas at San Antonio, 18 Sept. 2003.

McKinney-Johnson, Eloise. "Egypt's Isis: The Original Black Madonna." *Journal of African Civilizations*. 6.1 (1984): 64–71.

Megenney, William W. "The Fate of Some Sub-Saharan Deities in Afro-Latin American Cult Groups." Paper prepared for delivery at the Latin American Studies Association, Miami, 16–18 Mar. 2000.

Mesa-Bains, Amalia. "*Domesticana*: The Sensibility of Chicana *Rasquachismo*." Arredondo et al. 298–315.

Métraux, Alfred. *Voodoo in Haiti*. 1959. Trans. Hugo Charteris, Introd. Sidney W. Mintz. New York: Schocken, 1972.

Mickiewicz, Adam. *Pan Tadeusz*. Warsaw: Prószyński i S-ka, n.d.

Miller, Ivor L. "Religious Symbolism in Cuban Political Performance." *The Drama Review* 44.2 (2000): 30–55.

Miłosz, Oskar. "Królowa węży." *Baśnie i legendy litewskie*. Olsztyn, Pol.: Pojezierze, 1986. 91–98.

Mistewicz, Eryk. "Śmierć w powietrzu." *Wprost* 21 Aug. 1994: 25–26.

Morales, Aurora Levins, and Rosario Morales. *Getting Home Alive*. Ithaca, NY: Firebrand, 1986.

Moreira Neves, Dom Lucas, Archbishop Primate of Brazil. Personal interview. Salvador, Bahia, Braz. 10 Aug. 1996.

Moszyński, K. *Kultura ludowa Słowian*. Vol 2. Warsaw: KiW, 1967.

Motta, Roberto. "Ethnicity, Purity, the Market, and Syncretism in Afro-Brazilian Cults." Greenfield and Droogers 71–85.

———. "Sociologists Managing Religion: The Formation of Afro-Brazilian Theology." *MOST Journal on Multicultural Societies* 1.2 (1999). 10 Nov. 2003 <http://www.unesco.org./most/vl1n2mte.htm>.

"Mural # 10: End Barrio Warfare." *Murals*. 18 May 2003 <http://www.sananto.orgmural_10.html>.

"Mural # 18: Nicho / Mural para la Virgen de Guadalupe." *Murals*. 18 May 2003 <http://www.sananto.org/mural_18.html>.

Murphy, Joseph, and Mei-Mei Sanford, eds. *Ọ̀ṣun across the Waters: A Yoruba Goddess in Africa and the Americas*. Bloomington: Indiana UP, 2001.

Murray, Alexander S. *Classical Mythology Super Review*. Piscataway: Research & Education Association, 2002.

The Nag Hammadi Library in English. Trans. Members of the Coptic Gnostic Library Project of the Institute for Antiquity and Christianity. New York: Harper & Row, 1977.

Naib, Ivan the. "About Dvořák." 2002. *Rusalka's Voice*. 6 Nov. 2004 <http://www.rusalkasvoice.com/about/dv/>.

"Narration Text for 'The Tree of Life.'" *Ethnoscope*. 6 Nov. 2004 <http://www.docfilm.com/mexfilms/tol/Tolpoem.htm>.

Nebel, Richard. *Santa María Tonantzin Virgen de Guadalupe*. 1995. Trans. Carlos Warnholtz Bustillos. Mexico City: Fondo de Cultura Económica, 1996.

Nebrija, Antonio de. *Gramática de la lengua castellana (Salamanca, 1492): Muestra de la istoria de las antiguedades de España, reglas de orthographia en la lengua castellana*. Ed. Ig. González-Llubera. London and New York: H. Milford and Oxford UP, 1926.

Nervo, Amado. *Los cien mejores poemas de Amado Nervo*. Ed. Antonio Castro Leal. Mexico City: Aguilar, 1969.

———. *Poesías completas*. Madrid: Biblioteca Nueva, 1935.

Neumann, Erich. *The Great Mother*. 1955. Trans. Ralph Manheim. Princeton: Princeton UP, 1991.

The New American Bible. 1970. Trans. Members of the Catholic Biblical Association of America. Wichita, KS: NAB Catholic Bible Publishers, 1972–73.

Newman, Lucia. "La fe cubana en la Virgen de la Caridad." *CNN en español*. 10 Sept. 2003 <http://cnnenespanol.com/especial/papa/dia.quatro/cuba.caridad/index.html>.

Nikitin, W. "Kult Matki Bożej a literatura rosyjska." *Kult maryjny* 101–12.

Noguez, Xavier. *Documentos guadalupanos*. 1993. Mexico City: Fondo de Cultura Económica, 1995.

"Nuestra Señora de la Caridad del Cobre." *La Religión* 19 Sept. 2000. 15 Sept. 2003 <http://www.padrecelestial.com/principal/caridad_del_cobre.htm>.

"Nuestra Señora de la Caridad del Cobre." *Virgen de la Caridad*. 15 Sept. 2003 <http://www.celam.org/sitios/ce_cuba/Virgen/Virgen.htm>.

"Nueva imagen submarina." *UNIVISION.com*. 2 Feb. 2003. <http://www.univision.com>.

Nuevo Mundo. Dir. Gabriel Retes and Nicolás Echeverría Cabeza de Vaca. Mexico City, 1975.

O'Carroll, Michael. "Spouse of God." *Theotokos: A Theological Encyclopedia of the Blessed Virgin Mary*. Wilmington, DE: Glazier, 1982. 333.

Ochała, F. "Strażniczko granic." 1995. Rakoczy 277.

Ochs, Carol. *Behind the Sex of God*. Boston: Beacon, 1977.

O'Gorman, Edmundo. *Destierro de sombras: Luz en el origen de la imagen y culto de Nuestra Señora de Guadalupe del Tepeyac*. Mexico City: Universidad Nacional Autónoma de México, 1991.

Ogrodowska, Barbara. *Święta polskie: Tradycja i obyczaj*. Warsaw: ALFA, 2000.

Olbryś, Danuta. Personal interview. Warsaw, 22 June 2004.

Oleksik, Klemens. "Czarownica znad Bełdan." Wortman 163–68.

Oleszkiewicz, Eligiusz. Personal interviews. Warsaw and Vilnius, 1997–2005.

Oleszkiewicz, Małgorzata. "El ciclo de la muerte de Atahualpa: De la fiesta popular a la representación teatral." *Allpanchis* 39 (1992): 185–220.

———. "Color, género y poder: La figura femenina en las religiones de Europa y de Afrolatinoamérica." *Epifanías de la etnicidad: Estudios antropológicos sobre vírgenes y santos en América Latina*. Bogotá: Corporación Colombiana de Investigaciones Humanísticas HUMANIZAR, 2002. 85–94.

———. "Los cultos marianos nacionales en América Latina: Guadalupe/Tonantzin y Aparecida/Iemanjá." *Revista Iberoamericana* 182–82 (1998): 241–52.

———. "La danza de la pluma y el sincretismo cultural en México." *Revista de crítica literaria latinoamericana* 46 (1997): 105–14.

———. "Fluidez y transformación: Religión, arte y género en las fronteras de Norte y Sudamérica." *Revista brasileira de literatura comparada* 5 (2000): 113–24.

———. "Hybridity and Appropriation: The Subversion of Images in the Mexican American Southwest." *XXV International Congress of the Latin American Studies Association (LASA).* CD-ROM. Las Vegas, Nevada, 2004.

———. "Ilê Asé Orisanlá J'Omin: Syncretism or Orthodoxy?" *Proceedings of the Brazilian Studies Association (BRASA), Fourth Conference, 1997.* Albuquerque: Brazilian Studies Association, 1998.

———. "Mother of God and Mother Earth: Religion, Gender, and Transformation in East-Central Europe." *Hawaii International Conference on Arts and Humanities Conference Proceedings, January 13–15, 2003.* CD-ROM. Honolulu, 2003.

———. "El papel de la mujer en el Candomblé." *Religion in Latin America in the Twenty-first Century.* Austin: Benson Latin American Collection, U of Texas, 1999. 193–200.

———. *Teatro popular peruano: Del precolombino al siglo XX.* Warsaw: Warsaw U and Austrian Institute for Latin America, 1995.

Olimón Nolasco, Manuel. Interview. *Gazeta Wyborcza.* 27–28 July 2002: 22.

Omari, Michelle Smith. *From the Inside to the Outside: The Art and Ritual of Bahian Candomblé.* UCLA Monograph Series 24. Los Angeles: Museum of Cultural History, 1984.

Orgelbrand, S. *Encyklopedia powszechna.* Vols. 2 and 18. Warsaw: n.p., 1860.

Ortiz, Fernando, "Los factores humanos de la cubanidad." 1939. *Estudios etnosociológicos.* Comp. Isaac Barreal Fernández. Havana: Editorial de Ciencias Sociales, 1991. 10–30.

Ortiz Echaniz, Silvia. "El guadalupanismo en la frontera de México." Unpublished essay, 2000.

"'Our Lady' by Alma Lopez ©1999." *Our Lady, Digital Print by Alma Lopez, Los Angeles Visual and Public Artist.* 19 May 2003 <http://www.almalopez.net>.

"Our Parent above, and His Son, the one with pierced hands, and Holy Spirit." *Our Parent Above.* 19 May 2003 <http://www.udayton.edu/mary/gallery/trinity.html>.

Pagels, Elaine. *The Gnostic Gospels.* 1979. New York: Vintage, 1989.

Palacios, Isidro Juan. *Apariciones de la Virgen: Leyenda y realidad del misterio mariano.* Madrid: Ediciones Temas de Hoy, 1994.

Palmer, Gabrielle, and Donna Pierce. *The Spirit of Transformation in Spanish Colonial Art.* Albuquerque: Santa Barbara Museum of Art in Cooperation with the U of New Mexico P, 1992.

Paprocki, Henryk. "Mariologia—wspólne źródło prawosławia i katolicyzmu." *Kult maryjny* 9–16.

Pascual Blázquez, José Luis. "En busca de los orígenes." *En busca de los orígenes por José Luis Pascual Blázquez.* 21 Sept. 2003 <http://cura.online.fr/xx/19pascua.html>.

Passos, Dílson Júnior. "A formação do sincretismo religioso no Brasil." *Vozes* 82 (1988): 57–78.

Paz, Octavio. *El laberinto de la soledad.* 1959. Mexico City: Fondo de Cultura Económica, 1976.

Perkowska, Ewa. *Złota Baba.* Typescript, n.d. Jacek Dobrowolski collection, Warsaw.

"Permanent Collection: Sub-Saharan African Art: Shrine Figure, 'Mami Wata.'" *Emory University.* 20 Nov. 2004 <http://carlos.emory.edu/COLLECTION/AFRICA/africa02.html>.

Perroud, Pedro Clemente, and Juan María Chouvenc. *Diccionario castellano kechwa kechwa castellano.* Lima: Seminario San Alfonso, Padres Redentoristas, 1970.

Peterson, Jeanette Favrot. "Creating the Virgin of Guadalupe: The Cloth, the Artist, and Sources in Sixteenth-Century New Spain." *Americas* 61.4 (2005): 571–610.

———. "The Virgin of Guadalupe: Symbol of Conquest or Liberation?" *Art Journal* 51 (1992): 39–47.

Pinkola Estés, Clarissa. *Women Who Run with the Wolves*. 1992. New York: Ballantine, 1995.

Podgórzec, Zbigniew. "Kult obrazów Maryi w Polsce." *Kult maryjny* 25–36.

Ponce Campos, Xavier. *La Virgen de Guadalupe y la diosa Tonántzin*. Mexico City: n.p., 1970.

Poole, Stafford. *Our Lady of Guadalupe*. 1995. Tucson: U of Arizona P, 1997.

Prasał, Aneta. *Mały słownik ikon maryjnych*. Warsaw: Ośrodek Dokumentacji Zabytków, 1996.

Preston, J., ed. *Mother Worship*. Chapel Hill: U of North Carolina P, 1982.

"Przeor Jasnej Góry przeciwko '*Wprost*.'" *Życie Warszawy* 22 Aug. 1994: 1.

El pueblo mexicano que camina. Dir. Juan Francisco Urrusti. Videocassette. Mexico City: Instituto Nacional Indigenista, 1996.

Pykała, Bolesława, and Czesław Krakowiak, comps. *Niepokalana: Kult Matki Bożej na ziemiach polskich w XIX wieku*. Lublin, Pol.: Redakcja Wydawnictw KUL, 1988.

Quispel, Gilles. *The Secret Book of Revelation*. New York: McGraw-Hill, 1979.

Rakoczy, Eustachy. *Jasnogórska Hetmanka*. Warsaw: Dom Wydawniczy Bellona, 1998.

Ramos Salles, Nívio. *Rituais negros & caboclos*. 3rd ed. Rio de Janeiro: Pallas, 1991.

Randall, Margaret. "Guadalupe, Subversive Virgin." Castillo, *Goddess of the Americas* 113–23.

Redd, Danita. "Black Madonnas of Europe: Diffusion of the African Isis." *African Presence in Early Europe*. 1985. Ed. Ivan Van Sertima. New Brunswick and London: Transaction, 1996. 108–33.

"Regla de Ocha." *CaribeInside.com*. 5 Sept. 2003 <htpp://religions.caribeinside.com/showreligion. do?code007>.

La Reina de las Américas: Works of Art from the Museum of the Basílica de Guadalupe. Chicago: Mexican Fine Arts Center Museum, 1996.

Ribera CMF, P. Luis. *Misal diario*. Illustr. Soler G. Barcelona: Editorial Regina, SA, 1954.

Ripalta, P. Jerónimo. *Catecismo de la doctrina cristiana*. Madrid: Librería Escolar Hijos de Antonio Pérez, 1949.

Rivero, Padre Jordi. "Historia de la Virgen de la Caridad." *Virgen de la Caridad del Cobre*. 10 Sept. 2003 <http://www.corazones.org/maria/america/cuba_caridad_cobre.htm>.

Rodriguez, Jeanette. *Our Lady of Guadalupe: Faith and Empowerment among Mexican-American Women*. Austin: U of Texas P, 1994.

Rodríguez Prampolini, Ida, org. *A través de la frontera*. Mexico City: Centro de Estudios Económicos y Sociales del Tercer Mundo, A.C. Instituto de Investigaciones Estéticas U.N.A.M., 1983.

Rueda Esquibél, Catriona. "Velvet Malinche: Fantasies of 'the' Aztec Princess in the Chicana/o Sexual Imagination." Gaspar de Alba, *Velvet Barrios* 293–307.

Ruether, Rosemary Radford. "No Church Conspiracy against Mary Magdalene." *National Catholic Reporter*, 9 Feb. 2001. Findarticles.com. 23 Sept. 2003 <http://www.findarticles.com/cf_0/ m1141/15_37170926901/print.jhtml>.

Sáenz de Tejada. "Raza y género en la narrativa femenina afro-brasileña." *Revista de crítica literaria latinoamericana* 46 (1992): 269–85.

Sahagún, Fray Bernardino de. *Florentine Codex: General History of the Things of New Spain.* Trans. Charles E. Dibble and Arthur J. O. Anderson. Santa Fe, NM: School for American Research; Salt Lake City: University of Utah, bk. 1, 1950; bk. 2, 1951 (2nd ed. 1981); bks. 4 and 5, 1957 (2nd ed. 1979); bk. 6, 1969 (2nd ed. 1976).

———. *Historia general de las cosas de Nueva España.* 4 vols. Mexico City: Editorial Pedro Robredo, 1938.

———. *Historia general de las cosas de Nueva España.* 4 vols. 1938. Ed. Angel María Garibay K. Mexico City: Porrúa, 1956.

Saldívar, José David. *Border Matters: Remapping American Cultural Studies.* Berkeley: U of California P, 1997.

Saldívar, Ramón. *Chicano Narrative: The Dialectics of Difference.* Madison: U of Wisconsin P, 1990.

Samelson, William. Personal interview. San Antonio, 8 Nov. 2002.

San Antonio Mural Tour. San Anto Cultural Arts. 7 Nov. 2003.

Sandoval, Denise Michelle. "Cruising through Low Rider Culture: Chicana/o Identity in the Marketing of *Low Rider Magazine.*" Gaspar de Alba, *Velvet Barrios* 179–96.

Santana Braga, Julio. "El Candomblé de Caboclo y sus relaciones con la cultura indígena." Trans. José Jorge de Carvalho. *Cuadernos afro-americanos* 1 (1975): 117–24.

"Santuario Virgen de Regla." *Chipiona.net :: Tu punto de encuentro.* 5 Sept. 2003 <http://turismo.chipiona.net>.

Sarlo, Beatriz. *Escenas de la vida posmoderna.* Buenos Aires: Ariel, 1994.

Schiller, Gertrud. *Iconography of Christian Art.* 1966. Trans. Janet Seligman. Greenwich, CT: New York Graphic Society, 1971.

Segato, Rita Laura. *Santos e daimones.* Brasília: Editora UnB, 1995.

Seljan, Zora A.O. *Iemanjá mãe dos orixás.* São Paulo: Editora Afro-Brasileira, 1973.

"Semana Santa en Málaga: Real Muy Ilustre y Venerable Hermandad y Cofradía de Nazarenos de Nuestro Padre Jesús de la Puente del Cedrón y María Santísima de la Paloma." *Semana Santa en Málaga.* 17 Oct. 2003 <http://wwwangelfire.com/ma/pinchauva/foto10.html>.

Serra, Ordep. *Águas do rei.* Petrópolis: Vozes, 1995.

Siemionov, S. P. *Mokosh: Publichnaia propovied bogochelovechestva.* St. Petersburg: Assotsiatsia "Istok," 1991.

Silva Lima, Antônio Lúcio da, comp. *Rezando com Nossa Senhora Aparecida.* São Paulo: Paulus, 1991.

Siqueira, Maria de Lourdes. "Iyámi, iyá agbás: Dinámica da espiritualidade feminina em templos afro-baianos." *Estudos feministas* 3 (1995): 436–45.

Słupecki, Leszek Paweł. "Problem istnienia pogańskiego ośrodka kultowego na Łyścu." *Klasztor na Świętym Krzyżu w polskiej kulturze narodowej.* Ed. Daniel Olszewski and Ryszard Gryza. Kielce, Pol.: KTN 2000. 17–29.

Smykowska, Elżbieta. "Maryjne teksty liturgiczno-poetyckie." *Kult maryjny* 47–52.

Sójka, Ks. Krzysztof. *Modlitwy za ojczyznę.* Cracow: n.p., 1994.

Soustelle, Jaques. *Pensamiento cosmológico de los antiguos mexicanos.* Paris: Librería Hermann y Cia. Editores, 1959.

Spotkanie Świętych Obrazów The Meeting of the Sacred Images. Phoenix: Guadalupe Institute, 1991.

Spretnak, Charlene, ed. *The Politics of Women's Spirituality: Essays on the Rise of Spiritual Power within the Feminist Movement.* Garden City, NY: Anchor /Doubleday, 1982.

Staal, Jeannette Parvati. *Women, Food, Sex, and Survival in Candomblé: An Interpretive Analysis of an African-Brazilian Religion in Bahia, Brazil.* Diss. U of California, Los Angeles, 1992. Ann Arbor: UMI, 1992. 9301561.

Starbird, Margaret. *The Woman with the Alabaster Jar.* Rochester: Bear, 1993.

Stomma, Ludwik. *Antropologia kultury wsi polskiej XIX w.* Warsaw: Instytut Wydawniczy Pax, 1986.

Suhr, Elmer G. *Venus de Milo the Spinner.* New York: Exposition, 1958.

Sullivan, Thelma D. "Tlazolteotl–Ixcuina: The Great Spinner and Weaver." *The Art and Iconography of Late Post-Classic Central Mexico.* Ed. Elizabeth Hill Boone. Org. Elizabeth P. Benson. Washington, DC: Oaks Trustees for Harvard U, 1982.

Szafrański, Włodzimierz. *Pradzieje religii na ziemiach polskich.* Cracow: Ossolineum, 1987.

Szyjewski, Andrzej. "Problem bóstwa żeńskiego." Unpublished essay, n.d. Author's collection. Cracow.

Śnieżyńska-Stolot, Ewa. "Geneza, styl i historia obrazu Matki Boskiej Częstochowskiej." *Folia Historiae Artium* 9 (1973): 5–43.

Taylor, William B. "The Virgin of Guadalupe in New Spain: An Inquiry into the Social History of Marian Devotion. *American Ethnologist* 14 (Feb. 1987): 9–33.

Terreiro de São Bento, twenty members. Personal interviews. Itaparica Island, Braz., 19 and 20 July 1996; Salvador, Bahia, Braz., 1 Aug. 1996.

Tlapoyawa, Kurly. "The Myth of La Virgen de Guadalupe." 2000, 24 Feb. 2003 <http://www.mexica.org/Lavirgin.html>.

Torre Villar, Ernesto de la, and Ramiro Navarro de Anda, comps. and eds. *Testimonios históricos guadalupanos.* Mexico City: Fondo de Cultura Económica, 1982.

Tweed, Thomas A. *Our Lady of the Exile: Diasporic Religion at a Cuban Catholic Shrine in Miami.* Oxford: Oxford UP, 1997.

Tyszkiewicz, Jan. "O schyłkowym pogaństwie na ziemaiach polskich." *Kwartalnik Historyczny* 3 (1966): 549–61. Warsaw: Instytut Historii PAN.

Urbańczyk, Stanisław. *Religia pogańskich Słowian.* Cracow: Wydawnictwo Studium Słowiańskiego Uniwersytetu Jagiellońskiego "Ossolineum," 1947.

Uspienski, Borys A. *Kult Świętego Mikołaja na Rusi.* Lublin, Pol.: TZN KUL, 1985.

Valeriano Ribeiro, Father Osman. Personal interview. Igreja da Conceição, Salvador, Bahia, Braz., 30 July 1996.

Vargas Ugarte, Rubén. *Historia del culto de María en Iberoamérica y de sus imágenes y santuarios más celebrados.* Vol. 1. Madrid: n.p., 1956.

Vásquez y Sanchez, Ramón. Personal interview. San Antonio, 4 Feb. 2000.

———. Telephone interview. 7 Feb. 2000.

Velásquez, Gloria L. *I Used to be a Superwoman.* Santa Monica: Santa Monica College P, 1994.

Velázquez Oliverez, Roberto. *La Virgen de Guadalupe: Reina del trabajo.* Mexico City: Obra Nacional de la Buena Prensa, 1981.

Vélez-Ibáñez, Carlos G. *Border Visions: Mexican Cultures of the Southwest United States.* Tucson: U of Arizona P, 1996.

Verger, Pierre. "Esplendor e decadência do culto de Iyàmi Osòròngà: 'Minha Mãe a feiticeira' entre os iorubas." *Artigos, Tomo I.* São Paulo: Corrupio, 1992. 5–91.

———. "Syncrétisme." *Recherche, pédagogie et culture* 63–64 (1983): 41–45.

Verger, Pierre Fatumbi. *Orixás: Deuses iorubás na África e no Novo Mundo.* São Paulo: Corrupio, 1981.

Villanueva, Alma Luz. *Weeping Woman: La Llorona and Other Stories.* Tempe: Bilingual, 1994.

"Virgen de la Caridad Patrona de Cuba." *Documentos de la Iglesia Cubana—Virgen de la Caridad.* 15 Sept. 2003 <http://www.exilio.com/iglesia/caridad/caridad>.

La Virgen del Tepeyac. Dir. Kinan Valdez. Performance. Teatro Campesino. Mission San Juan Bautista, CA., 9 Oct. 2000.

"La Virgen de Regla. Fiesta: 8 de septiembre." *Virgen de Regla.* 5 Sept. 2003 <http://216.109.117.135/search/cache?p+virgen+de+regla&ei=UTF-8&n=20&fl=0&url=IRQI . . . >.

Wachlmayr, Alois. *Das Christgeburtsbild der früchen Sakralkunst.* Munich: Otto Wilhelm Barth Verlag GMBH, 1939.

Walker, Barbara G. *The Woman's Dictionary of Symbols and Sacred Objects.* New York: HarperCollins, 1988.

———. *The Woman's Encyclopedia of Myths and Secrets.* New York: HarperCollins, 1983.

Walker, Sheila. "Candomblé: A Spiritual Microcosm of Africa." *Black Art: An International Quarterly* 5 (1984): 10–22.

———. "Everyday and Esoteric Reality in the Afro-Brazilian Candomblé." *History of Religions* 30 (1990): 103–28.

Warner, Marina. *Alone of All Her Sex.* New York: Alfred A. Knopf, 1976.

"Where Does the Name Guadalupe Come From?" *The Aztec Virgin.* Sausalito, CA: Trans-Hyperborean Institute of Science, 2000. 3 Mar. 2003 <http://www.aztecvirgin.com/guadalupe. html>.

Whittick, Arnold. *Symbols, Signs, and Their Meaning and Uses in Design.* 1960. 2nd ed. Newton, MA: Charles T. Branford, 1971.

Wilkinson, Richard H. *Symbol and Magic in Egyptian Art.* London: Thames & Hudson, 1994.

Wolf, Eric R. "The Virgin of Guadalupe: A Mexican National Symbol." *Journal of American Folklore* 71 (1958): 34–39. JSTOR. 2 Dec. 2004 <http://www.org/search>.

Wolkstein, Diane, and Samuel Noah Kramer. *Inanna, Queen of Heaven and Earth: Her Stories and Hymns from Sumer.* New York: Harper & Row, 1983.

Woortmann, Klaas. *A família das mulheres.* Rio de Janeiro: tempo Brasileiro, 1987.

Wortman, Stefania, comp. *U złotego źródła baśnie polskie.* 1968. Warsaw: Nasza Księgarnia, 1996.

Wprost. Cover. 21 Aug. 1994.

Ybarra-Fausto, Tomás. "Notes from Loisaida: A Foreword." Gaspar de Alba, *Velvet Barrios* xv–xxviii.

Yúdice, George. "Culture as Resource." Lecture. U of Texas at San Antonio, 23 Apr. 2004.

Zabkar, Louis V. *Hymns to Isis in Her Temple at Philae*. Hannover and London: UP of New England (for Brandeis UP), 1988.

Zahoor, A. *Names of Arabic Origin in Spain, Portugal and the Americas*. 1992, 1997. 15 Mar. 2003 <http:cyberistan.org/islamic/places2.html>.

Zakrzewski, Andrzej J. *W kręgu kultu maryjnego: Jasna Góra w kulturye staropolskiej*. Częstochowa, Pol.: WSP, 1995.

Zerón-Medina, Fausto. *Felicidad de México*. Mexico City: Editorial Clío, 1995.

Zguta, Russell. "The Ordeal by Water (Swimming of Witches) in the East Slavic World." *Slavic Review* 36.2 (1977): 221–30.

Zowczak, Magdalena. *Biblia ludowa: Interpretacje wątków biblijnych w kulturze ludowej*. Wrocław, Pol.: Fundacja Na Rzecz Nauki Polskiej, 2000.

Ceremonies Cited

Candomblé. Terreiro Gantois. Salvador, Bahia, Braz., 28 July 1996.

Candomblé. Xangô Ceremony. Terreiro Axé Opó Afonjá. Salvador, Bahia, Braz., 29 June 1996.

Candomblé de Caboclo. Terreiro of Mãe Aída. Salvador, Bahia, Braz., 31 July 1996.

Catholic Mass. Sant'Anna Church. Salvador, Bahia, Braz., 28 July 1996.

Confirmação das Ekédes de Oxaguian [initiation]. Terreiro de São Bento. Itaparica Island, Braz., 20 July 1996.

Del Villar, Giovana. Quinceañera. San Martín de Porres Church. San Antonio, 20 Dec. 2003.

Mãe Alda. Divination. Salvador, Bahia, Braz., 1 Aug. 1996.

Matachines. Danza Guadalupana de Pablo Olivarez, Sr., San Antonio, 12 Dec. 2005.

Matachines. San Fernando Cathedral. San Antonio, 12 Dec. 1998.

Mesa Branca. House of Mãe Alda. Salvador, Bahia, Braz., 1 Aug. 1996.

Index

Note: Italic page numbers refer to figures and plates.

Abakuá, 121
abebe (*agbebe*), 109
abião, 96
Abiodun, Rowland, 97
Adam: Jesus Christ as "New Adam," 109; and Mother Earth, 34
Adelita, soldier in Mexican Revolution, 152
Aegean region, 22
African female deities: manifestations of, 2, 161, 182n1. *See also specific deities*
African slave trade, 82, 177n1
Aganjú, 108
As Águas de Oxalá (the Waters of Oxalá), 87–88, 87
Agustín, Saint, 181n55
ajiaco, 81–82
alabê (drummer), 97
Albania, 65
Alcántara Arruda, Alda d,' 96, 111, 116, 117, 178nn15, 17
Alcántara Arruda, Celeste d,' 178n17
Alcántara Arruda, Marcia d,' 178n17
Alcover, Joan, 172n32
aldeias de caboclos, 111, 114, 116
Aldrich, Ania: Baba Yaga and her hut, 13; caduceus, 66
Alfonso XI (king of Spain), 54
Altamirano, Ignacio Manuel, 48, 59–60
Anaya, Rudolfo, 140, 158
anjo da guarda (guardian angel), 91
Anne, Saint, 32, 106, 114–15
Anthony, Saint, 84
Anzaldúa, Gloria, 140, 146, 158
Aphrodite, 34, 67
Aquino, Marcos Cipac de, 53, 55, 174n9
archeological findings, 14, 20, 170n11
arte de paño, 43, 45, 138, 144, 146, 154
Artemis, 35, 170n18
Ashtoreth, 36
Asia Minor, and cult of Mother Goddess, 35, 67
assimilation, resistance to, 141

Astarte, 36, 67
atabaques (ritual drums), 94, 95
Athene, 29
Atropos, 29
axé (life force), 95, 96, 164; as *terreiro* or spiritual community, 91, 178n10
axôgún (performer of sacrifices), 93, 97
Aztec: and Mexican American Southwest, 144, 145, 146, 147, 148, 150, 152, 155, 156, 159; and Mexican national identity, 67, 69, 70; and snake figures, 65, 176n33; and Virgin of Guadalupe, 56, 57–58
Aztec coat of arms, 61, 70
Aztec lineage idols (*tlapialli*), 71
Aztec Mother Goddesses: and birth of sun-son god, 108; Coatlicue, 13, 169n1; and spinning, 29, 30; and Virgin of Guadalupe, 2, 103. *See also* Tonantzin (Our Mother)
Aztlán, 9, 144, 147, 156, 159

baba: as derogative name of old woman, 170n8; and feast of Zielone Świątki, 25; and Tree of Life, 72, 73
Baba (Łukasiak), 28, 171n26
Baba (Żywa) as center of flowering Tree of Life, Poland, 27, 28
babalawos (fathers of the secrets), 100, 121, 167
babalorixás (priests), 91, 99–100
Baba Yaga: "good" and "bad" qualities of, 23; illustration of, 13; and presence of Virgin Mary, 11, 19; and Rusałka, 26; and Slavic folktales, 16, 19, 23, 24, 28, 169n1, 170n15; and spinning, 23, 26, 29; transformation powers of, 23, 26; as triune goddess of birth, death, and regeneration, 16, 19, 23–24, 26; wooden representation of, 20
Babenberg, 28
Babia Góra, 28
Babiec, 28
Babie Łono, 28
Babi Jar, 28

Babylonia, 65, 108

"La Balanguera" (The Spinner), 30–31, 172n32

Balts, 22, 65

Bantu linguistic family, 82

Barbara, Saint, 86

Barnet, Michael, 82

Baroque style, 7, *8*, 9, 70, 87

barracão, 111, *112*, *113*, 114, 179n38

barroco de la pobreza, 181n4. *See also* esthetic of the poor

Basques, 22

Batista, Fulgencio, 121

Benedict XIV (pope), 60

Benítez-Rojo, Antonio, 80, 86, 88, 162

Berger, Peter, 162

Biblical Tree, 77

bicha, 100

bird figures: and Baba Yaga, *13*, 23; dove, 67, 121, *122*, 179n34; in Mexican imagery, 65; and Neolithic goddess figure, 20, *21*, 67, 170n12; and Tree of Life, 72. *See also* eagle; eagle feathers

Bird of Fire, 65

Birnbaum, Lucia Chiavola, 182n1

Black Madonna: black associated with Wisdom, 23; and borderlands, 9, 161; and Christianization process, 1, 2; commodification of, 162, 164–67, *165*, *166*; contemporary uses and transformations of, 3, 6, 9; evolution as cross-cultural symbol, 167; and national identity, 1; prehistoric origins of, 14, *15*, 16, 18–23; sacred colors of, 24, 170n16; and social justice, 50, 167; as successor of Holy Earth, 47; transformation and adaptation of, 9, 162; trinity of, 24; as ubiquitous symbol in Catholicism, 161. *See also* Our Lady of Częstochowa; Virgin of Guadalupe

Black Madonna of Częstochowa. *See* Our Lady of Częstochowa

Black Madonna of Czestochowa Shrine and Grottos, Eureka, Missouri, 3, *4*

Black Madonna with the Polish coat of arms, *44*

Blanco Ruiz, Pilar, 4

Boff, Frei Clodovis, 120

Boguroditsa (God Birth-Giver), 35–36, 41

"Bogurodzica Dziewica" (God Birth-Giver Virgin), 41

Bolívar Aróstegui, Natalia, 180n51

Bomfim Catholic Basilica, 87

Bonet, Maria del Mar, 172n32

borderlands: butterfly as metaphor for resilience in, 156; and Chicano identity, 146; and levels of resignification, 142; and manifestations of Black Madonna, 9, 161; meaning of, 181n1; and syncretism, 124, 141, 161; Virgin Mary as keeper of, 39, 40; and Virgin of Guadalupe, 160

bori, 95, 178n11

Borutini, Lorenzo, 54–55

botánicas, 4, 118–119, *136*, *163*

bóveda de aguas or *bóveda espiritual* (Spiritist altar), 100, *101*, 118

Boże zbaw Polskę (God Save Poland), *44*

Brandstaetter, Roman, "Hymn do Czarnej Madonny" (Hymn to the Black Madonna), 39

Brazil: and African slave trade, 82, 177n1; Brazilian paradox, 165; and commodification of Black Madonna, 162, 164; and fluidity and flexibility of society, 89, 161; and manifestations of Black Madonna, 9, 161; matrilineal culture of, 99, 100; Our Lady Aparecida as patroness of, 83, 103, 119–20; representation of icons, 64–65, 79; syncretism of Afro-Indo-European worship in, 1, 2–3, 7, 9, 83–88, 89, 107, 115–16, 117, *118*, 124; and theatricality, 71; trinities of goddesses in, 16; types of Afro-Indo-European religions in, 88–97; Virgin of the Immaculate Conception as patroness of, 106–7, 119. *See also* Candomblé religion; Iemanjá

Brazilian *terreiros*: and Candomblé religion, 91, 95–97, 99, 114; ceremonies of, 4, 91; marketing of, 162, 164; and Oxum, *84*, *85*; as spiritual families, 97, *98*, 178n17; spiritual leader of, 95–96, 99; syncretism in, 111; and veneration of *ceiba* trees, 76, *77*; and white dress, *118*; woman-focused organization of, 2–3, 96–97, *98*, 99. *See also* Ilê Asé Orisanlá J'Omin (*Terreiro* de São Bento)

Brześć Kujawski, 170n11

Burciaga, José Antonio, *The Last Supper of the Chicano Heroes*, *149*, *150*, 182nn8, 9

Bustamante, Francisco de, 53, 56

Byzantine Empire, 42

Caboclo (Candomblé de Caboclo), 99, 105, 117–18

caboclos (Indian spirits), 111, 116, 118, 180n45

Cabrera, Lydia, 88, 179n34

caduceus, 65, 66

calavera (skeleton), 150

calendar art, 144, 182n10

California vineyard workers, 141, 148, 181n3. *See also* United Farm Workers Union

calunga, 109

canastilleros, 101, *102*, 118, 179n23, 180n51

Candlemas Virgin, 105

candomberos, 6, 169n3

Candomblé de Caboclo ceremonies, 117–18

Candomblé religion: and Brazilian *terreiros*, 91, 95–97, 99, 114; and Catholic symbols, 9, 83, 86, 114, 115, 116, 165; ceremonies of, 4, *8*, 9, 117, 164, 180n46; and divination, 95, 100, 111, 117–18, 164, 178n14; and Iemanjá, 4, *8*, 16, 85, 87, 105, 107; and Iemanjá/Virgin Mary phenomenon, 84; initiation ceremony of, *92*, 95; and Irmandade de Boa Morte, 87; and matriarchal beliefs, 83; and Mesa Branca ceremony, 116–118; as purely African religion, 89, 111, 114, 164, 167, 177–78n9; re-Africanization movement, 164–65; and survival, 123, 124; and tourism, 164; and trinity of goddesses, 24; and Yoruba culture, 88, 89, 91, 123, 177–78n9

Cantinflas, Mario Moreno, 152

Capoeira, 83, 177n2

Cardenas, Michael Isaac, *Water Lady*, *157*, 158

Caribbean: Black Madonna in, 9; syncretism of Afro-Indo-European worship in, 2, 4, 161, 162. *See also* Cuba; Haiti

Caribbean Americans, 6

Carlos V (Spanish emperor), 177n1

Carneiro, Edison, 97

Casa Branca *terreiro*, 89, *90*, 97, 99

Casa de Iemanjá (House of Iemanjá), 106–7, *106*, *107*, *134*

Castellanos, Isabel, 88

Castillo, Ana, 158

Castillo family, 76

Castillo Orta, Alfonso, 76

Castro, Fidel, 120, 121, *122*, 123

Catholicism: Black Madonna as ubiquitous symbol in, 161; Catholic symbols and Candomblé religion, 9, 83, 86, 114, 115, 116, 165; and hierodules, 173n50; and images of Black Madonna, 166–67; and manifestations

of Virgin Mary, 177n6; and Marian holidays, 37; New World central altarpieces, 180n51; Poland and Mexico compared, 50; and power of images, 70, 71–72; and role of family altar, 50, 158–59; slaves disguising religious practices with Catholic symbols, 82–83; and snake figures, 65; and syncretic contact, 1; virginity stressed by, 35

Catimbó, 88–89

La Causa Chicana, 157

ceiba (*yaxche*) tree, 30, 72, 76, *77*

Ceres, 34

Cervantes, Miguel de, 67

Chalchutlicue (The One with a Skirt of Green Stones), 56, *57*

Changó, *85*, 86

Chaveco, Raúl, 180n49

Chávez, César, 142, *142*, 144, 148, 152, 181n3

Chávez, Milton, *137*

Chicana lesbians: and Kahlo, 157; and Virgin of Guadalupe, 3, 150, 156, 159, 176n28, 182n18

Chicano identity: as border identity, 146; and mural art, 148; and Virgin of Guadalupe, 142, *147*, *151*, 152, *152*, 154–56, 158–59

Chicano/mexicano culture, 141, 144

La China Poblana: costume of, *63*; as icon, 49; and Mexican cultural identity, 2, 62, 64–65; in San Antonio, Texas, *128*, 169n4

la chingada, 62

Cholo, 144

Chopin, Fryderyk, 34

Christianization process: and Black Madonna, 1, 2; in east-central Europe, 19, 25, 28–29; in New Spain, 2, 182n16; in Old Europe, 2; in Russia, 28; superimposition of Christian over pagan beliefs, 16, 18, 19, 31–32, 35, 37, 50, 52, 53, 67, 70, 71–72, 172n33; Virgin of Guadalupe, 2

Christmas trees, 72

Church of Sant' Anna (Saint Anne), 106, *106*, 115

Cihuateteo, 175–76n27

circular objects, magical powers of, 171n21

Cisneros, Sandra, 158

Citlali, La Xicana Super Hero (vasquez), 11, *13*, 156

Citlalicue, *57*

Ciuacoatl (Snake Woman): and eagle feathers, 58, 175n20, 176n40; and Mesoamerican Indian beliefs, 52, 53; and Tepeyac hill, 53, 174n6; and Virgin of Guadalupe, 103; weaving stick of, 30; weeping associated with, 176n27

Clavijero, Francisco Javier, 52

Clement XI (pope), 42

Cleusa (mãe), 115

Clotho, 29

Coahuiltec Indians, 159, 182n17

Coatlicue: as Aztec Mother Goddess representing death, 13, 169n1; and birth of sun-son god, 108; and immaculate conception, 56; and presence of Virgin Mary, 11

Colón, Cristóbal (Columbus), 54, 105–6

Columba, Saint, 67, 176n36

Congo-Angola region, 82

contas (sacred necklaces), 91, 91

Cortés, Hernán: banner of Virgin of the Immaculate Conception, 54–55, 56, 57, 131, 174n13; and La Malinche, 62, 157; and Our Lady of Charity of El Cobre, 180–81n55

Cosmic Tree, 72. See also Tree of Life

Costa Lima, Vivaldo da, 100

Council of Ephesus, 35

Council of Lima (1552), 53

countercultures, 141

Coyolxauhqui, 152

Cracow, Poland, 25

Creoles: and image of ajiaco, 82; and Virgin of Guadalupe, 49, 58–60

Cristeros Rebellion (1927–29), 60

cross: road crosses, 32, 33, 75, 75; and syncretism, 72, 75, 75; transformation and superimposition of, 2, 32, 71; as Tree of Life, 76; as world axis, 72, 75

crucifixes: and Chicano/mexicano culture, 144; in Ilê Asé Orisanlá J'Omin terreiro, 111, 113, 114, 114

Los Cuatros Grandes (Loza), 152

Cuba: and African female deities, 2; African slave trade in, 82, 177n1; divination as male domain, 100; icons of, 79; and Our Lady of Charity of El Cobre, 120–21, 161; and Spiritism, 100–101; syncretism in, 4, 81–84, 86, 121, 123, 124, 161, 167; and Virgin of Regla, 103, 103, 104, 123. See also Santería

Cybele, 34, 35

Czarownica. See Baba Yaga

"Czarownica znad Bełdan" (The Witch from Bełdany), 26

Częstochowa, Poland, 18

Częstochowa, Texas, 3, 5

DaMatta, Roberto, 80, 91

Damballah-wèdo, 65, 66

dance: and Candomblé religion, 95; Capoeira disguised as, 83, 177n2; Matachines dances, 8, 9, 128, 169n4; round dance, 25, 29; and voodoo ceremonies, 104

Danza de la conquista, 54

Danza de la pluma, 54

Danza Guadalupana de Pablo Olivarez, Sr., 128, 169n4

De La Torre, Miguel A., 100

Demeter, 34, 35

derroche, 7, 70

Descourtilz, M. E., 72

Diana, 14, 15, 35

Diego Cuauhtlatonzin, Juan, 53, 56, 60, 61

distaff, meaning of, 172n31

divination: and Candomblé religion, 95, 100, 111, 117–18, 164, 178n14; and Santería, 100, 118, 178n22

Długosz, Jan, 41

domestic chapels (santocalli), 71

Doña Marina. See La Malinche

dove, 67, 121, 122, 179n34

dragons, 65, 67, 70

Drewal, Henry John, 97

Drewal, Margaret Thompson, 97

Duron, Armando, 148

dvoievierie (two faiths), 37

Dvořák, Antonin, Rusalka, 171n23

eagle: and Aztlán, 159; and Our Lady of Częstochowa, 62; and Tree of Life, 72; and United Farm Workers Union, 142, 144; Virgin of Guadalupe associated with, 56, 57, 58, 59, 61, 62, 70. See also bird figures

eagle feathers: and Ciuacoatl, 58, 175n20, 176n40; and Toci, 176n40

east-central Europe: Black Madonna in, 9, 161; Christianization process in, 19, 25, 28–29; Great Mother Goddess in, 1; migrations and invasions of, 18; and Old European civilization, 20; preservation of ancient customs and beliefs, 22–23. See also Poland; Slavic folktales

ébomin, 96

Ecclesia, 108

eguns, 111, 114, 114, 118, 121, 180n50

Eileithyia, 29

ékédes, 92, 95, 96, 97
Elbein dos Santos, Juana, 97
Elegguá, 121, *122*, 123
El Santo Niño de Atocha, 121, *122*, 123
El Vez, 140
Emboabas War (1708–9), 120
End Barrio Warfare (mural), San Antonio, Texas, 148, *148*
environmentalist issues, and Our Lady of Częstochowa, 2, 47, *47*, 173n56
Ephesus, 35
esthetic of the poor, 144. See also *barroco de la pobreza*
Estrada Courts, Los Angeles, California, 150, 182n12
evangelizing theater, 70–71
Eve, 65, 109
Ewa, 99
Extremadura region, Spain, 54, 174n12
La Extremeña. *See* Virgin of Guadalupe of Extremadura (Villuercas or Cáceres) Spain
Exú, *136*
ex-votos, 50, *51*
Ezili Dantò: attributes of, 110–11; original images of, 124; and Our Lady of Częstochowa, 2, 103, *104*, 109–10, *110*; trinity of, 103, 109
Ezili Freda, 103, 109, 110, 111

fairy tales, witches in, 29–30
família-de-santo (spiritual family), 97, *98*, 178n17. *See also* Costa Lima, Vivaldo da
Feast of the Blessed Virgin Mary, Queen of Heaven (Velázquez), 67, *68*
Fernandes, Rubem, 119–20
Ferretti, Sergio, 83, 115
festas (ceremonies), 91
Figueiredo, Maria Júlia, 97
filha-de-santo (*iaô*), 95, 96, 97, 99, 178n13
Florencia, Francisco de, 60, 182n16
Florentine Codex, 176n27
Florescano, Enrique, 174n7
Foligno, Lattanzio da, 55
Fon (Jeje), 88
Fox, Vicente, 60–61
France, 109
Franco, Jean, 167
francophone society, 2
Frank, Hans, 42, 175n23
Freya, 29, 34

Fridays, female deities associated with, 28–29
frog-bride, 24, 170n18
Fry, Peter, 178n21

Gaia, 34
Gaik Zielony (Little Green Grove), 25
Gałczyńska, Wanda, *Stabat Mater*, 43, *45*
Gantois *terreiro*, 89, *90*, 99, 115, 116
Gardner, Laurence, 23
Gaspar de Alba, Alicia, 146, 156, 158
Geledé feminine society, 97, 99, 109
Gęlędę festivals, 97
gender roles: in Cuba, 100; feminine gender of earth, 32; fluidity of, in Candomblé religion, 99, 100
Gentileiro, 111, 116
George, Saint, 115
Georgian State Dance Company, and triangular necklaces and earrings, 170n13
Germany, and snake figures, 65
Gimbutas, Marija, 28, 170n10, 176n34
Giuliani, John, 176n39
global market, 162
goat, sacrifice of, 93, 94, 95
God Birth-Giver (Boguroditsa), 35–36, 41, 42
Goddess of the Cave, 75–76
Gomes Arruda, Dílson, 178n17
González, Elián, 123
Gonzalez, Maya Christina, 158
graffiti, *151*, 152
Greater Mexico, 9, 181n1. See also Mexican American Southwest
Great Mother Goddess figure: and Baba Yaga, 23, 24; and bird figures, 67; and Mokosh, 28; prehistoric origins of, 14, *15*, 16, 18–23; and snake figures, 65; and syncretism, 1; and Virgin of Guadalupe, 50. See also Mother Earth; Mother Moist Earth; Tree Goddess
Greek region, 22, 65, 176n33
Greenfield, Sidney, 89
Grunwald battle against Teutonic Order (1410), 42
Gruzinski, Serge, 70, 71
Guadalupe Defending Xicano Rights (Hernandez), *153*, 154
Guadalupe-Hidalgo Treaty (1848), 146
Guevara, Ernesto "Che," 150
Guevara, María, 174n13
Gwizd-Pogwizd, 32

hair, magical powers of, 171n21

Haiti: icons of, 79; and Mami Wata, 177n3; and Our Lady of Częstochowa/Ezili Dantò, 2, 103, *104*, 109–10, *110*; syncretism in, 124; and Tree of Life, 72

Heaven (Lopez), 150

Hecate, and frog, 170n18

Henriques, Alfonso, 105

Hera, and frog, 170n18

Hernandez, Ester: *Guadalupe Defending Xicano Rights*, *153*, 154; Virgin Mary in paintings of, 11, 170n9

Hetman Coat, 43, *46*, 47

Hidalgo y Costilla, Miguel, 60

hierodules, 173n50

Hieros Gamos (Holy Matrimony), 108

hispanophone society, 2

Hitler, Adolf, 42

Hodegetria ("Indicator of the Way"), 18, 41, *125*

Holda, 29

Holy Earth: Black Madonna as successor of, 47; characteristics of, 26, 28; pre-Slavic matriarchal worship of, 2

The Holy Family (Zurbarán), 16

Holy Matrimony (Hieros Gamos), 108

Holy Spirit, and Virgin Mary, 67, 70

Hołyszowa, Paulina, 10

Holy Trinity: and bird figures, 67; in Mexican art, 67, *68*, 176n39; pagan triunes replaced with, 32; as patriarchal adaptation of three-in-one theme, 103; in Polish art, 67, *68*, 176n39; triangle as symbol of, 21, *22*; and Virgin Mary as Bride of Christ, 108; Virgin Mary as part of, 14, 16

The Holy Trinity, *Misal Diario*, Spain, 21, *22*

homen, 100

homosexuals, as *babalorixás*, 99–100

Horus, 14, *15*, 36, 108

Hoyos, Juan de, 121

Hoyos, Rodrigo de, 121

Hubbs, Joanna, 28

Huerta, Dolores, 142, 150

Huitzilopochtli, 56, 108

Huixtocihuatl (Goddess of Salt), 30

Huynen, Jacques, 170n16

hybridity: coexistence with homogeneity, 162; as creative and enriching, 167; and Ilê Asé Orisanlá J'Omin, 111, 118; and individuals' identity and strength, 124; in Latin America, 123, 161, 162; and manifestations of Black Madonna, 9; and Mexican American Southwest, 144, 159, 162; of popular devotion in Mexico, 7; in postmodern global space, 1; and Virgin of Guadalupe, 53, 141, 160

"Hymn do Czarnej Madonny" (Hymn to the Black Madonna) (Brandstaetter), 39

iabás, 97, 99, 109

iaô (*filha-de-santo*), 95, 96, 97, 99, 178n13

Iara, 83, 103

Iemanjá: attire of, *107*, 108–9, *133*; and Candomblé religion, 4, *8*, 16, 85, 87, 105, 107; and death, 109; feast day of, 107; and Mami Wata, 83, 103; as manifestation of Black Madonna, 9, 161; as mermaid, *134*; and mirror, 109, *134*; original images of, 124; and Our Lady Aparecida, 2, 9, 120, 161; and power of iyá-mi, 97; as Queen of the Seas figure, 83, 105, 106–7; role of, 103, 105; statues of, *107*, *133*; trinity of, 16, 24, 103, 109; and Umbanda, 105, 108–9, 120; Virgin Mary linked to, 83–84, 101, 107; and Virgin of the Immaculate Conception, 2, 103, 105, 108, 111, 114, 124. *See also* Yemayá

Iemanjismo, 108, 124

Ifá, 95, 100, 111, 178n14

Ilê Asé Iyá Nassô Oká (Casa Branca do Engenho Velho da Federação), 89, *90*, 97, 99

Ilê Asé Opô Afonjá, 89, 99, 164

Ilê Asé Opô Aganjú, 99

Ilê Asé Orisanlá J'Omin (*Terreiro* de São Bento): as Águas de Oxalá procession, *87*; and Alcántara Arruda, 96, 178nn15, 17; and *atabaques*, 94; *barracão*, 111, *112*, *113*, 114, 179n38; blood family structure of, 178n17; ceremonies of, *8*, 85, *86*, 92, 116–17, *118*, 164, 180n46; crucifixes in, 111, *113*, 114, *114*; entrance to, *112*; fieldwork on, 99, 111, 177n8; and goat sacrifice, 93; house of Oxalá, 116, *116*; and Itaparica Island, 111, *115*; members of the *família-de-santo*, 98; and sacred dishes, 93, 98; setting of, 111; and syncretic altar, 118, *118*

Ilê Iyá Omí Asé Iyá Massê (Sociedad São Jorge do Gantois), 89, *90*, 99, 115, 116

Imagen de la Virgen de Guadalupe con san Miguel y san Gabriel y la visión de san Juan en Patmos Tenochtitlan, 59

images: of Black Madonna, 166–67; evolution

of, 124; of Our Lady Aparecida, 123; and
    syncretism, 70–72; triangular images of
    Virgin Mary, 21, 22, *130*
Immaculata Tota Pulcra, 107, 109
immigrant workers, and Virgin of Guadalupe,
    141, 144
Inanna, 14, 36
Iraq war demonstrations, 141
Irmandade da Boa Morte (Sisterhood of the
    Good Death), 86–87, *87*
iroko (*ceiba*) tree, 30, 72, 76, *77*
Ishtar, 34, 35, 36, 173n50
Isis: and birth of sun-son god, 108; and creative
    principle, 36; cult of Mother Goddess, 35, 47;
    as direct predecessor of Virgin Mary, 14; and
    frog, 170n18; with Horus, 14, *15*; and Mother
    Earth, 34; and spinning, 29
Itaparica Island, 111, *115*
Ixchel, 29
ixiptla ("idols"), 71
Ixtacihuátl, *145*, *146*, 150, 152
iyá bassê, 96, 178n16
iyá kêkêrê, 96
iyalorixá or *mãe-de-santo* (priestess), 91, *92*,
    95–96, 99, 100, 111, *113*, 167, 178nn12, 15
iyá-mi/ìyámì (our mothers or my mother), 97,
    99

James, Saint, 54
Jan Kazimierz (king of Poland), 42
jarabe tapatío, 64
Jasna Góra, Poland, Pauline monastery of, 18, *18*,
    32, 41, 166
Jasnogórska Hetmanka, 40. See also Hetman Coat
Jędza. See Baba Yaga
Jeje (Fon), 88
Jerome, Saint, Xangô linked to, 84
Jesus Christ: Cacique Pedra Branca linked to,
    117; as "New Adam," 109; as Nosso Senhor do
    Bomfim, 87; Oxalá linked to, 84, 107–8, 114,
    116, *116*, 117; represented on cross, 75; wounds
    of, 40
João IV (king of Portugal), 106
Jôgo de búzios, 91, 95, 111
Jôgo de Odú, 111
John, Saint, 58–59
John Paul II (pope), 34, 40, 41, 60, 119, 120, 174n11
Juana Inés de la Cruz, Sor, 152
justice: and Our Lady of Częstochowa, 2, 42, 47;

and Virgin Mary, Mother of God, 11, 47. *See
    also* social justice

Kahlo, Frida: and Chicana lesbians, 157; and
    Virgin of Guadalupe, *138*, 144, 146, *147*
kamienne baby (stone babas), 28, 171n25
Kardec, Allan, 89, 118
khorovod (round dance) Russ., 29
Kluiev, Nikolai, 10
Koré, 35
korowody (round dances) Pol., 25, 29
Kostrobonko, 25
Krusza Zamkowa, 170n11
kudurrus (stelae), 108
Kujawy region, Poland, 170n11
Kupalnocka, 25
Kupało, 25
Kurpie region, Poland, *21*, *68*, 170n12

labyrinth, cross penetrating, 75
Lachesis, 29
Lafaye, Jacques, 55–56, 58
lake, as symbol, 26
Landes, Ruth, 99, 178n21
Lara, Gregorio José de, *Visión de san Juan en
    Patmos Tenochtitlan*, 59, 70
The Last Supper of the Chicano Heroes
    (Burciaga), *149*, 150, 182nn8, 9
Lasyrenn, as part of trinity, 103, 109
Latina in the Land of Hollywood (Valdivia),
    155–56
Latin America: Afro-Latin American culture,
    124, 181n57; Afro-Latin American religions,
    88; and cult of Guadalupanismo, 79;
    hybridity in, 123, 161, 162; syncretism in, 1, 81,
    82–88, 111; Virgin Mary in, 101. *See also specific
    countries*
A Lavagem do Bomfim (the Washing of
    Bomfim), 87
Lazarev, V. N., 35
Lazarus, Saint, 84, 114
The Legacy of César Chávez (Vasquez), 142, *142*,
    144
Lienzo de Tlaxcala, 62, 175n26
life-creating female body, symbols related to, 20
linden tree, 72, *74*
Lithuania: Our Lady of Ostra Brama, 6, *7*; road
    crosses of, 75, *75*; and snake figures, 65, *66*
La Llorona, 62, 156, 157, 158, 175–76n27

Lloyd, P. C., 99

Lopez, Alma: *Las Four*, 150, 152; *Heaven*, 150; *Lupe & Sirena* series, 156, 182n14; *Our Lady*, 155

López, Yolanda M.: *Margaret F. Stewart: Our Lady of Guadalupe*, 154–55, *154*; *Portrait of the Artist as the Virgin of Guadalupe*, *139*, 154; *Victoria F. Franco: Our Lady of Guadalupe*, 154–55, *154*; *The Walking Guadalupe*, *153*, 154; works of, 154, 170n9

lowrider cars, *137*, *143*, 144, 148

Loza, Ernesto de la, *Los Cuatros Grandes*, 152

Lucia, Saint, 118

Lucian of Samosata, 171n21

Lupe & Sirena series (Lopez), 156, 182n14

lusophone society, 2

Łada, 32, 172n35

Łukasiak, Alicja, *Baba*, 28, 171n26

Łysa Góra (Bold Mountain), 32

Łysiec, 32

Machado, Gerardo, 121

Macumba, 89

Madonna del Soccorso, 55

Mãe Bebé, 99

mãe-de-santo. See *iyalorixá* or *mãe-de-santo* (priestess)

mãe pequena, 96

Magna Mater, 109

Malinalli. *See* La Malinche

La Malinche, 2, 49, 62, 156–58

malinchismo, 62

Malinowski, Bronisław, 82

Malintzin. *See* La Malinche

Mallorca, 30–31, 172n32

Mami Wata: colors of, 83; in Haiti, 177n3; and Iemanjá, 83, 103; as white mermaid, 83

mapou (*ceiba*) tree, 30, 72, 76, *77*

Marcos (Subcomandante), 148

Margaret F. Stewart: Our Lady of Guadalupe (López), 154–55, *154*

María Dolorosa del Monte Calvario, 110

Maria-José, Mother of the Gods, 1, 80

Marzal, Manuel, 83, 116

Marzaniok, 25

Marzanna, 25, 171n20

Master of Erfurt, *Virgin Mary with a Distaff*, 31, 171n30

Matachines dances, San Antonio, Texas, *8*, *9*, *128*, 169n4

Mater Salvatoris, and Our Lady of Częstochowa/Ezili Dantò, 2, *104*, 109, 110

Matka Boska (Mother of God), 35

Matka Boska Częstochowa, 9

Matka Polka/Polska, 39, 173n51

Matko uwięzionych i internowanych módl się za nami (Mother of the Interned and the Imprisoned, Pray for Us), 45

matriarchal beliefs: and Candomblé religion, 83; Madonna as symbol of, 1; in Old Europe, 2, 20, 22; pre-Slavic matriarchal worship, 2, 14, 52; and triple goddess, 103

matrilineal culture: of Brazil, 99, 100; of Old Europe, 20, 22; of Slavic women, 29, 171n28

Mayahuel (Powerful Flow, Lady Maguey), 57

Mayan cotton tree (*yaxche*), 30, 72, 76, *77*

Mayan lunar calendar, 14

Mayan sun, 108

Mayan Tree of Life, 76

Maza, Francisco de la, 55

McBride-Limaye, Ann, 175–76n27

Mediterranean region, 22

Melanzio, Francesco, 55

Menchú, Rigoberta, 152

Mendiola, Lisa, *148*

Mendiola, Sonny, *148*

Mercado, San Antonio, Texas, *147*

Mesa-Bains, Amalia, 158

Mesa Branca ceremony, 116–18

Mesoamerican Indians, 52, 53, 65, 162, 170n12

Mesopotamia, 176n33

Mestizo Head, 144

mestizo identity, 62, 141

Métraux, Alfred, 72

Mexica. *See* Aztec

Mexican American Southwest: and Aztec, 144, *145*, *146*, *147*, 148, 150, 152, 155, 156, 159; Black Madonna traditions in, 9; and creation of oppositional spaces, 144; and hybridity, 144, 159, 162; and identity, 146; and mural art, 71, 142, *142*, *143*, 144, *146*, 147–48, *148*, *149*, 150, *151*, 152, 176–77n42; syncretism in, 159, 182n17; Virgin of Guadalupe in, 3, 141, 142, *143*, 144, *147*, *151*, 152, 154–56, *154*, 158

Mexican clay tree, *78*

Mexican independence, 2, 60, 146

Mexican Indians, 71, 76–77

Mexican Revolution: and Adelita, 152; and division between church and state, 61; and mural art, 71, 146–48; and Virgin of Guadalupe, 2, 60

Mexico: Catholicism in, 50; as chosen land, 59; and commodification of Virgin of Guadalupe, 165, *165*, 166–67; and cult of Guadalupanismo, 79; and manifestations of Black Madonna, 9, 161; and Mexican symbology, 70; Mother's Day in, 62; Poland compared to, 49–50, 52; and power of images, 71; superimposition of Christian over pagan beliefs, 50, 52; syncretic religious practices in, 4, 6, 7, 49, 159; syncretized tradition of Tree of Life, 76; trinities of goddesses in, 16; Virgin Mary as central deity in popular art, 67, 176n39. *See also* Virgin of Guadalupe

Mexico-Tenochtitlan—"The Wall That Talks" (Quetzalcoatl Mural Project), 147–48

Miami, Florida, 121, 123

Michael, Archangel, 65, 67, 69, 70

Milking Madonna, 14, *16*

Miller, Ivor L., 121

mirror, and Iemanjá, 109, *134*

Mociuaquetzque, 30, 79, 175–76n27

Moera (Greek goddess), 29

Mokosh (goddess): Black Madonna as successor to, 47; and Mother Moist Earth, 19, 28; and names of villages, 32, *33*; and Paraskeva Piatnitsa, 28, 29; pre-Slavic matriarchal worship of, 2

Mokrzesz, Poland, 32, *33*

Montevideo, Uruguay, 6

Moreira Neves, Lucas, 115

Morelos, José María, 60

Moreno, Juan, 121

mortar and pestle, 23

Mother Earth: Baba Yaga compared to, 23; cult of, 34–38, 47; Great Mother Goddess identified with, 14; in Slavic folktales, 26, 28–38; stones as bones of, 28; traditions linking women to, 29; and triune goddess of birth, death, and regeneration, 32–34, 47; Virgin Mary as, 39; Virgin of Guadalupe as, 158

Mother Earth, Poland, *15*

Mother Moist Earth: characteristics of, 26, 28, 47; and Mokosh, 19, 28; pre-Slavic matriarchal worship of, 2, 14; and Russia, 14, 34, 36; trinity of, 16, 24

Mother of God of Święta Lipka, 72, *74*

Mother of God of the Berries, 37

Mother of God of the Herbs, 37–38, *38*

Mother of God of the Opening, 37, 38

Mother of God of the Sowing, 37, 38

Mother's Day, in Mexico, 62

Motta, Roberto, 88, 123, 164, 165

Movimiento Chicano, 144

mural art: and esthetic of the poor, 144; and Mexican American Southwest, 71, 142, *142*, *143*, 144, *146*, 147–48, *148*, *149*, 150, *151*, 152, 176–77n42; and Mexican Revolution, 71, 146–48; and Virgin of Guadalupe, 147, *149*, 150, 152

Murillo, Bartolomé Esteban, 106; *Virgin of the Immaculate Conception of El Escorial*, 129

Nahua, 71, 76

Nahuatl language, 56, 175n17

Nanā: and Candomblé religion, *8*, 16; as part of trinity of goddesses, 16, 24, 103, 109; and power of *iyá-mi*, 97; and presence of Virgin Mary, 11; and Saint Anne, 114–15; as Yoruba goddess representing old wise woman, 169n1

Naná (Naná Burukú), 24, 103, 179n26

Napoleon Bonaparte, 42, 109

national identity: and Aztec, 67, 69, 70; and Black Madonna, 1; and Matachines groups, 169n4; and Mexican symbology, 70; Our Lady Aparecida as symbol of, 119–20; Our Lady of Charity of El Cobre as symbol of, 120–21, 123; Our Lady of Częstochowa as symbol of, 2, 42, 47, 49, 50, 62, 119; and Rusałka, 171n23; Virgin of Guadalupe as symbol of, 2, 49, 50, 58, 59, 60–62, 79, 119

Native American art, and Tree of Life, 72, *73*

Native American Church, 182n17

Near East, 22

Nebrija, Antonio de, 54

Necropolis Puig des Molins, Ibiza, Spain, 67

Neith, 29

Neolithic goddess figure: and bird figures, 20, *21*, 67, 179n34; origins of, 11; regenerative symbols of, 20; triads of, 103, 110; triangular stone representing goddess, 21

Neolithic period, 3, 75

nepantla, 141

Nervo, Amado, 64

Netet, 29

Neumann, Erich, 23

New Orleans, Louisiana: and commodification of Black Madonna, 162; voodoo altars, 66, 110, *110*

New Spain: Christianization process in, 2, 182n16; and Mexico as chosen land, 59; and popular medieval Catholic traditions, 7; and search for identity, 79; and Virgin of Guadalupe, 53

New World: central altarpieces, 180n51; syncretic contact in, 1

Nican Mopohua (Valeriano), 173n5, 174n7

Nicaragua, 71, 141

Nicho/Mural para la Virgen de Guadalupe, San Antonio, Texas, *149*, 150

Noc Świętojańska, 25

northern Europe, 22

Nossa Senhora Aparecida/Iemanjá, 9. *See also* Our Lady Aparecida

Nossa Senhora da Conceição da Praia (Our Lady of Immaculate Conception of the Beach), *105*, 106

Nosso Senhor do Bomfim (Our Lord of the Good End), Jesus Christ as, 87

Nuestra Señora de Guadalupe de México, Patrona de la Nueva España, 61

Nuestra Señora de la Caridad del Cobre. *See* Our Lady of Charity of El Cobre

Nuestra Señora de la Caridad y los Remedios, and Our Lady of Charity of El Cobre, 180n55

Obá, 179n34

Obatalá, as Our Lady of Mercy, 86, 121, 179n34

Ochs, Carol, 103, 109, 178n19

Ochún: and Our Lady of Charity of El Cobre, 2, 88, 103, 109, 123, *135*, 161; and Our Lady of Mercy, 179n34; paths of, 88, 177n6; and ritual fan, 109; trinity of, 24, 103

ogãos, 86, 95, 97

O'Gorman, Edmundo, 55

Ogum, 84

"O królewnie zaklętej w żabę" (About a Princess Bewitched into a Frog), 24

Old Europe: geographical area of, 20, 169n1; Indo-European tribes' invasion of, 18–19, 20, 22; matriarchal worship in, 2, 20, 22; trinity of goddesses in, 24

old women: in matrilineal society, 20; as powerful women, 19; in Russian folktales, 24; and Saint Anna, 32, 114; and Yoruba beliefs, 97. *See also* Baba Yaga

Oleszkiewicz, Eligiusz, 6, 176n34; caduceus, *66*

Olimón Nolasco, Manuel, 60

Olmec culture, 76

Olodumaré, 180n41

olúwo, 100

Omolú: African character of attire, 177n5; Saint Lazarus linked to, 84, 114; in trance, *86*

opele (*oguele*) chain, 178n22

Orgelbrand, S., 25, 171n24

oriaté, 100

orichas: and *canastilleros*, 180n51; dove as ritual bird of, 179n34; fluidity and adaptability of, 88; saints linked with, 86

òrìṣà worship, 1, 83, 84, 87, 89

orixás: drums used to call, 95; and European Baroque-inspired clothes, 8, 87; feminine *orixás*, 97, 99; and *festas*, 91; fluidity and adaptability of, 88; and Iemanjá, 107, 108; and *pano da costa*, 87, 177n5; possession by, 100; saints identified with, 14, 86, 114; trinity of, 109

Orozco, Clemente, 71, 147

Ortega, Jerry, 148

Orthodox Church, 34, 35

Ortiz, Fernando, 81–82

Orungán, 108

Òṣun, 83

Othin, 72

Our Lady Aparecida: and African female deities, 2; as Catholic patroness of Brazil, 83, 103, 119–20; and Iemanjá, 2, 9, 120, 161; images of, 123; miracles of, 119; Our Lady of Częstochowa compared to, 119–20; as Queen of Brazil, 119; role of, 120; and syncretism, 161; and triangle as symbol, 21, 22

Our Lady of Charity of El Cobre: legend of, 120, 121, 123; and Nuestra Señora de la Caridad y los Remedios, 180n55; and Ochún, 2, 88, 103, 109, 123, *135*, 161; as symbol of national identity, 120–21, 123

Our Lady of Częstochowa: commodification of, 166, *166*; and ex-votos, 50, *51*; and Ezili Dantò, 2, 103, *104*, 109–10, *110*; grotto in San Antonio, 3, *5*; as manifestation of Black Madonna, 2, 161; military cult of, 42; miracles of, 18, 41–42; Our Lady Aparecida compared to, 119–20; and patriotism, 39–43, 47, 62; pervasive presence of, 3; procession for, *127*; as Queen of Poland, 40, 42; as Queen of the World, 42;

role of, 2, 4; as symbol of national identity, 2, 42, 47, 49, 50, 62, 119; and syncretism, 18; Virgin of Guadalupe compared to, 2, 4, 49–50, 52, 175n23; wearing gas mask, 47, *47*, 173n56; wounded image of, 39–40, 110

Our Lady of Częstochowa, dressed and crowned, Jasna Góra, Poland, *12*

Our Lady of Częstochowa, Jasna Góra, Poland, icon, *18*, *41*, *49*, *125*

Our Lady of Częstochowa Wearing a Hetman Coat, 40, 43, 46, 47

Our Lady of Guadalupe Veladora (Treviño), *149*, *150*

Our Lady of Loretto, 53

Our Lady of Mercy, 86, 121, 179n34

Our Lady of Milk, 14

Our Lady of Ostra Brama, 6, *7*

Our Lady of Sailors, 105

Oxalá: As Águas de Oxalá (the Waters of Oxalá), 87–88, *87*; house of Oxalá, 116, *116*; and Iemanjá, 107; Jesus Christ linked to, 84, 107–8, 114, 116, *116*, 117; in trance, *85*

Oxossi, *8*, 115

Oxum: feast day of, 107; house of, *85*; and Mami Wata, 83; as mermaid, *84*, *134*; and mirror, 109; as part of trinity of goddesses, 16, 24, 103, 109; and power of *iyá-mi*, 97; and Virgin Mary, 84; and Virgin of the Immaculate Conception, 103

Oyá, 99, 179n34

Pachucos, *143*, *144*, *148*

padê, 95, 99, 178n11

Pajelança, 89

Paleolithic female figurines, 11, 14, 21, 67

Panna Maria, Texas, 3, *5*

Panno Święta co Jasnej bronisz Częstochowy, 1939–1945 (Holy Virgin, Thou Who Defend the Bright Częstochowa, 1939–1945), *43*

pano da costa, 87, 177n5

Paraskeva Piatnitsa, saint, 28, 29

Parcae, 29

pataki, 76

patriarchal society: and aspects of goddess of life, death, and regeneration, 19; and Indo-European invasion of Old Europe, 22; and La Llorona, 156; and three-in-one theme, 103

Patriarch of Constantinople, 29

patriotism: and Our Lady Aparecida, 119–20;

and Our Lady of Charity of El Cobre, 120–21, 123; and Our Lady of Częstochowa, 39–43, 47, 62; and Virgin of Guadalupe, 61, 64, *77*

Paz, Octavio, 62

peace movement, 3

pectorals from eighteenth century with Our Lady of Częstochowa, *44*

Pedra Branca, Cacique (Chief White Stone), 116, *117*

pêjigã (maker of the altar), 97

Percht, 29

Peru: and *barroco de la probreza*, 181n4; procession of Virgin of El Carmen, 7, *7*; syncretism of Afro-Indo-European worship in, 7

pilgrimages: to Our Lady of Częstochowa, 41; Poland and Mexico compared, 50; to Virgin of Guadalupe Basilica in Mexico City, 50, *51*, 52, 60

Pious XI (pope), 119

"Poem about a Beautiful Queen," 35–36

Pogoda, 32

Poland: Catholicism in, 50; and commodification of Our Lady of Częstochowa, 166–67; display of icons in, 6, *127*; effects of World War II on, 6; and manifestations of Black Madonna, 3, 9, 49; Mexico compared to, 49–50, 52; and Mother of God figure, 36–43, *38*, 47; petrified images of, 124; representation of icons, 65; rituals and customs of, 25–26, 28, 29, 37–38; superimposition of Christian over pagan beliefs, 31–32, 50, 52; Swedish invasion of, 18; Virgin Mary as central deity in popular art, 67, *68*, 176n39. *See also* Our Lady of Częstochowa

Polish Black Madonna. *See* Our Lady of Częstochowa

Polish language, feminine gender of earth, mountains, and rivers, 32

Pomba Gira, *136*

Popocatépetl, *145*, *146*, *150*

Portrait of the Artist as the Virgin of Guadalupe (López), *139*, 154

Portugal, 105, 124

Portuguese language, 117

Poświst, 31

Potop (Deluge), 18, 41

powerful woman: and ancient roots of

contemporary Slavic women, 29, 171n28;
and Indo-European invasion of Old Europe,
22; Madonna as embodiment of, 16, 19; and
Virgin of Guadalupe, 156, 159
pre-Aztec, 2, 29, 30, 75, 103
pre-Columbian motifs, 144, 145, 146
pre-Slavic matriarchal worship, 2, 14, 52
Protection of the Virgin, 37, 38
Prythiwi, 34
public art, 146, 148, 181n6. See also mural art
Puerto Rico, 4

Quetzalcoatl, 21, 65, 75, 146, 148, 152, 159
Quetzalcoatl Mural Project, 147
quinceañera rituals, 144

Rasquachismo, 144, 158–159, 182n15
re-Africanization, 89, 177–78n9
Regla de Ocha. See Santería
Regla de Palo altars, 101, 101, 179n23
La Reina de los Mares (the Queen of the Seas),
174n11
religious practices, Madonna as symbol of, 1
resistance, and manifestations of Black
Madonna, 9
Revelation, Book of, 36, 56–59, 65, 67, 70
Ribera i Argomanis, Josefus de, Verdadero retrato
de santa María Virgen de Guadalupe, 61, 132
rituals and customs: ancient ways of life
preserved in, 25; and barracão, 111, 112,
179n38; and Candomblé religion, 91, 95–96;
and Golden Baba, 28; lack of syncretism
in, 83; and Paraskeva Piatnitsa, 28, 29; and
rural ritual calendar, 37; and spinning, 29–31,
172n32; and summer solstice, 25–26; of
Yoruba culture, 87–88, 87
Rivera, Diego, 71, 106, 147
road crosses, 32, 33, 75, 75
Rodrigues, Nina, 86
Rodríguez, Ildefonso, 180n55
Rodriguez, Isis, 11
Rodriguez, Mary Agnes, 149
Roman Empire, 22
Ross, Fred, 142
rural populations, 19
Rusałka: as female demon, 171n22; as Slavic folk
figure, 17, 26, 171n23; and spinning, 26, 29;
transformative powers of, 26; trinity of, 16,
24, 26

Rusalka (Dvorák), 171n23
Russia: Christianization process in, 28; and
dvoievierie (two faiths), 37; and God Birth-
Giver, 35–36, 42; and Golden Baba, 28; and
Mother Moist Earth, 14, 34, 36; and snake
figures, 65
Russian folktales, 24
Russian language, feminine gender of earth,
mountains, and rivers, 32

sacred dishes, 91, 93, 95, 98
Sacred Heart symbol, 144
Sahagún, Bernardino de, 48, 52, 53
Saint Linden (Święta Lipka), Poland, 72, 74
San Antonio, Texas: grotto dedicated to Our
Lady of Częstochowa in, 3, 5; Matachines
dances, 8, 9, 128, 169n4; Mercado, 147; mural
art in, 148, 148, 149, 150; and Virgin of
Guadalupe, 8, 9
Sánchez, Miguel, 58–59
Sandinistas, 71, 141
San José, Francisco de, 55
San Juan, Catarina de, 64
San Miguel Arcángel con estandarte guadalupano
(Saint Michael Archangel with the
Guadalupan Banner), 67, 69, 70
Santería: and ceiba tree, 76; and Cuban
government, 101; divination in, 100, 118,
178n22; and gender identity, 100; and
González, 123; offerings to Elegguá, 122; and
syncretism, 118; and trinity of goddesses, 24;
and white dove, 121, 122
santocalli (domestic chapels), 71
Santoyo, Felipe, 59
Sardinia, 21–22
serpents. See snake figures
Siqueiros, David Alfaro, 71, 147
La Sirena (The Siren), 155
slaves and slavery: and African slave trade, 82,
177n1; and Afro-Latin American culture, 124,
181n57; and Ezili Dantò, 110; and hiding/
disguising of religious practices, 82–83, 164;
and Iemanjá, 107; and matrifocal social
structure, 99
Slavic folktales: and Baba Yaga, 16, 19, 23, 24, 28,
169n1, 170n15; and Black Madonna, 6; hidden
meanings in, 25; Mother Earth in, 26, 28–38;
and snake figures, 65
Słupecki, Leszek Paweł, 172n35

snake figures: and Aztec, 65, 176n33; caduceus, 65, 66; and Mother of God of the Opening, 38; mythological associations of, 65, 67; and Neolithic goddess figure, 20; and Quetzal-coatl, 21; Quetzalcoatl, 21, 65, 75, 146, 148, 152, 159; on structures, 170n12; and Tree of Life, 72, 77, 78; and Virgin Mary, Mother of God, 65, 70; and Virgin of Guadalupe, 154, 154, 155

Sobótka, 25

Sobótki ceremonies (witches' Sabbaths), 32, 172n37

Social and Public Art Resource Center (SPARC), 148

social justice: and Black Madonna, 50, 167; and Our Lady of Częstochowa, 43, 62; and Virgin of Guadalupe, 141, 156

Los soldados de la Virgen (the Virgin's Soldiers), 9

Solidarity movement, and Our Lady of Częstochowa, 2, 40, 43, 45

South Asia, 22

Soviet Union, 6

Soy el Corazón (Vásquez y Sanchez), 157, 158

Spanish colonization, 2, 14, 162

Spanish Conquest: and African slave trade, 82; and Catholic influence in Mexico, 50; and Cortés's banner of the Virgin Mary, 54; and cross as Tree of Life, 76; and La Llorona, 157; and La Malinche, 62; and Reconquista, 54; Sánchez on, 58–59; and syncretism, 146; trans-formation of ancient religious symbols, 2

spinners and spinning: and Aztec Mother Goddesses, 29, 30; and Baba Yaga, 23, 26, 29; and Cihuateteo, 175–176n27; and distaff, 30, 172n31; and Mokosh, 29; and Paraskeva Piatnitsa, 28, 29; and rituals and customs, 29–31, 172n32; and Vasilisa the Fair, 24; and Virgin Mary, Mother of God, 29, 30–31, 31, 171n29

Spiritism, 89, 100–101, 117, 118–19

Stabat Mater (Gałczyńska), 43, 45

stella maris (sea star), 105, 179n29

stilla maris (drop of the sea), 179n29

"Strażniczko granic" (Guardian of Borders), 39, 40

Sultão das Matas, 111, 116

summer solstice, 25–26

sun, 22, 108

Swedish Deluge of Poland, 18, 41

Święta Anna, Poland, iron road crosses of, 32, 33

Święty Krzyż (Holy Cross), Poland, 31–32

Świst, 31

syncretism: of Afro-Indo-European worship in Brazil, 1, 2–3, 7, 9, 83–88, 89, 107, 115–16, 117, 118, 124; of Afro-Indo-European worship in Peru, 7; and borderlands, 124, 141, 161; and botánicas, 118–19; and cross as symbol, 72, 75, 75; in Cuba, 4, 81–84, 86, 121, 123, 124, 161, 167; and dynamic cultural contact, 16; and east-central Europe, 19; and Iemanjismo, 108; in Latin America, 1, 81, 82–88, 111; and manifestations of Black Madonna, 9, 81; in Mexican American Southwest, 159, 182n17; and power of images, 70–72; and Spanish Conquest, 146; and transformation of sacred symbols, 1, 124, 141; and Tree of Life as symbol, 72; and Virgin Mary, Mother of God, 16, 18, 19; and Virgin of Guadalupe, 49, 159–160

Tabares Orneles, Janie, 149

Tambor de Mina, 88

Tanit (goddess), 67, 68

tattoos, 144, 145, 152, 154, 165

Teatro Campesino, 142

Temazcalteci (Grandmother of the Bathhouse), 30, 57

Tepeyac hill, 52, 53, 55, 58, 59, 60

Terreiro de São Bento. See Ilê Asé Orisanlá J'Omin (Terreiro de São Bento)

Teteo-innan (Mother of the Gods), 30, 52, 70, 176n40

Theonymphos (Wedded to God), 108

Theotocos (Mother of God), 35

The Thunder, Perfect Mind, 36

Tlalli yiollo (Heart of the Earth), 52, 176n40

Tlaloc, 75

tlapialli (Aztec lineage idols), 71, 158

Tlapoyawa, Kurly, 55

Tlazolteotl (Goddess of Filth), 56

Tlazolteotl–Cihuapilli (Goddess of Filth–Fair Lady), 57

Tlazolteotl–Ixcuina (Goddess of Filth–Lady Cotton), 29, 30, 57, 175n19

Toci (Our Grandmother), 16, 24, 30, 52, 176n40

Todorov, Tzvetan, 62

Tonacaciuatl, 57

Tonantzin (Our Mother): and Tepeyac hill, 52, 53,

174n6; trinity of, 16, 24; Virgin of Guadalupe syncretized with, 52, 53, 103, 150, 161

Tonantzin–Ciuacoatl (Our Mother–Snake Woman), 52, 53, 58

Topienie Marzanny (Drowning of Marzanna), 25, 171n20

Torquemada, Juan de, 52

Touré, Sékou, 121

tourism, 162, 164

Tradicion Cultura (mural), 143

Tragedia de la muerte de Atahuallpa, 54

transculturation: as exchange between cultures, 82; and manifestations of Black Madonna, 9; and Mexican American Southwest, 144; and re-Africanization movement, 165

tree: as axis of world, 72; linden tree, 72, 74; as symbol, 26; transformation and superimposition of, 2. *See also* Tree of Life

Tree Goddess, 27, 72, 73, 74

Tree of Knowledge, 72

Tree of Life: associations of, 75; in Nahuatl poetry, 76; and Neolithic goddess figure, 20; origin of, 72; in Polish folklore imagery, 27, 28, 170n12; in Polish popular art, 72, 73; and snake figures, 72, 77, 78; syncretized tradition of, 76

Treviño, Jesse, *Our Lady of Guadalupe Veladora*, 149, 150

triangle: as regenerative symbol of goddess, 20, 21–22, 170n13; as symbol of Holy Trinity, 21, 22; and Virgin of Guadalupe (Villuercas or Cáceres), 54

Ukraine, 21–22, 25, 28

Umbanda: as Afro-Indo-European religion in Brazil, 88, 89, 118, 177n7; and Iemanjá, 105, 108–9, 120; and trinity of goddesses, 24

"Under Your Protection," 41

United Farm Workers Union, 3, 142, 144, 148

Urth, 29

Valdez, Luis, 142

Valdivia, Angharad N., *Latina in the Land of Hollywood*, 155–56

Valeriano, Antonio, *Nican Mopohua*, 173n5, 174n7

"Vasilisa prekrasnaia" (Vasilisa the Fair), 24, 170n15

vasquez, deborah kuetzpalin, *Citlali, La Xicana Super Hero*, 11, 13, 156

Vasquez, Emigdio, *The Legacy of César Chávez*, 142, 142, 144

Vásquez y Sanchez, Ramón: and Native American Church, 182n17; *Soy el Corazón*, 157, 158

Vega, Lazo de la, 58

Velázquez, Diego, 106; *Feast of the Blessed Virgin Mary, Queen of Heaven*, 67, 68

velvet paintings, 144, 145, 182n10

Venus, 29, 34

Venus Columba, 67

Vénus of Laussel, 14, 15

Verdadero retrato de santa María Virgen de Guadalupe (Ribera i Argomanis), 61, 132

Verger, Pierre, 115, 116, 180n43

Victoria, Guadalupe, 60

Victoria F. Franco: Our Lady of Guadalupe (López), 154–55, 154

Viking structures, and snake figures, 170n12

Villa, Augustine, 148

Villa, Pancho, 152

Villanueva, Alma, 158

Villar, Giovana del, 180n42

La Virgen de la Paloma (Virgin of the Dove), 67

La Virgen de los Mareantes (Virgin of the Sailors), 55, 105

Virgen de los Remedios, 60, 181n55

virgin, 38, 109, 173n50

Virgin Earth-Moon, 108

Virgin La Candelaria, 7

Virgin Mary, Mother of God: apparitions of, 72; and bird figures, 67; as Bride of Christ, 108; and Cortés, 54; and cult of Mother Earth, 34–38, 47; dark skin tones of, 20; and Holy Spirit, 67; Iemanjá linked to, 83–84, 101, 107; Isis as direct predecessor of, 14; in Latin America, 101; manifestations of, 177n6; and Mokosh, 19; officially sanctioned qualities of, 19; and *orixás*, 107; and Paraskeva Piatnitsa, 29; and patriotism, 39–43, 47, 62; in Poland, 36–43, 47; in popular art of Mexico, 67, 176n39; in popular art of Poland, 67, 68, 176n39; as Queen of Heaven and Earth, 36; representations of, 11, 16, 129; role of, 11, 16, 19, 36, 37, 39, 109; seas associated with, 54, 174n11; and snake figures, 65, 70; and spinning, 29, 30–31, 31, 171n29; and syncretism, 16, 18, 19; as

Tree Goddess, 27, 72, *73*, *74*; triangular images of, 21, 22, *130*; trinities of, 14, 16

Virgin Mary with a Distaff (Master of Erfurt), *31*, 171n30

virgin/mother/crone trinity, 16, 24, 26, 103, 109

Virgin of El Carmen, Paucartambo, Peru, 7, *7*

Virgin of Guadalupe: in advertising, *152*, 154, 166; apparitions of, 52, 53–54, 58–59, 70, 174n9, 175n21; attire of, 56, 175n17; Basilica of, 4, 52, 60, *165*, 174n11; cactus associated with, 58, 61; and Chicano identity, 142, *147*, *151*, 152, *152*, 154–56, 158–59; commodification of, *152*, 154, 165–67, *165*; Cortés's banner compared to, 54–55, 56, 57, *131*, 174n13; cult of, 58; in Czestochowa, Texas, 5; derivation of name, 56; devotional objects for sale, *165*; eagle associated with, 56, 57, 58, 59, 61, 62, 70; feast day of, 56, 60; as Great Mother, 50; history of image, 54–56; and *ixiptla*, 71; and Kahlo, *138*, 144, 146, *147*; and La China Poblana, 64; and La Malinche, 62; and layers of meaning, 79; legend of, 53, 60, 174n7; and lowrider cars, *137*, *152*; as manifestation of Black Madonna, 9; on Mexican American *arte de paño*, 43, *45*, *138*, 144, 146, 154; in Mexican American Southwest, 3, 141, 142, *143*, 144, *147*, *147*, *151*, *152*, 154–56, *154*, 158; Mexicanization of, 61–62, *61*; and Michael, Archangel, 65, 67, 69, 70; miracles of, 53; and mural art, *147*, *149*, 150, 152; naturalization of, 58–62; original images of, 124; Our Lady of Częstochowa compared to, 2, 4, 49–50, 52, 175n23; and patriotism, 61, 64, 77; as protectress against inundations, 60; role of, 3, 4, 43, 50, 59, 79, 141–42, 156, 158–59; as symbol of national identity, 2, 49, 50, 58, 59, 60–62, 79, 119; syncretic blending of Aztec goddesses and Catholicism, 2; syncretic blending of Spanish and Indian cultures, 49, 50, 52–53, 56, 59–60, 79, 159–60; Tonantzin syncretized with, 52, 53, 103, 150, 161; Virgin of the Immaculate Conception compared to, 54

Virgin of Guadalupe, Basilica of Guadalupe, Mexico City, 49, *126*

Virgin of Guadalupe of Extremadura (Villuercas or Cáceres) Spain, 14, 54, 55, *130*, 175n16

Virgin of Regla, Chipiona, Spain, 21, 22, 123, 181n55

Virgin of Regla, Cuba, 103, *103*, *104*, 123

Virgin of the Assumption, 105, 107, 179n27

Virgin of the Glory, 105

Virgin of the Immaculate Conception: and African female deities, 2; Cortés's banner of, 54–55, 56, 57, *131*, 174n13; feast day of, 97, 107, 175n16; and Iemanjá, 2, 103, 105, 108, 111, 114, 124; as patroness of Brazil, 106–7, 119; and Portugal, 124; and Woman of the Apocalypse, 56–57, 107; and Yemoja, 83, 124

Virgin of the Immaculate Conception of El Escorial (Murillo), *129*

Virgin of Montserrat, Catalonia, Spain, 14, *16*

Virtuous Mexican Woman, archetype of, 64

Visión de san Juan en Patmos Tenochtitlan (Lara), 59, 70

Vives, Amadeu, 172n32

Voodoo, 65, 66, *104*, 110, *110*

Wałęsa, Lech, 40

Walker, Barbara, 67, 72

The Walking Guadalupe (López), *153*

War of Reformation, 60

warrior culture, 18–19

Warsaw, Poland, 6, 25, 42, 166

Water Lady (Cardenas), *157*, 158

western Europe, 22

white dove, 121, *122*

Wianki (Wreaths), 25–26

Wiedźma, 19, 23, 170n6. *See also* Baba Yaga

Wilno (Vilnius), Lithuania, and Our Lady of Ostra Brama, 6, *7*

Wisdom (Sophia), 23

Wolf, Eric R., 50

Woman of the Apocalypse, 56–59, 107

women: in Old Europe, 19, 22; in pagan Europe, 170n7; role of spiritual leadership, 159; woman-focused organization of Brazilian *terreiros*, 2–3, 96–97, *98*, 99; Yoruba culture, 97, 99, 100. *See also* old women; powerful woman

World Tree, 72

Wyszyński, Stefan, 40

Xangô, 84, 86, 88, 164

Xochiquetzal (Flowery Quetzal Feather), 16, 24, 57

yaxche (*ceiba*) tree, 30, 72, 76, *77*

Ybarra-Frausto, Tomás, 144

Yemayá: original images of, 124; sacrificial bird

of, 179n34; trinity of, 24, 103; and Virgin of
Regla, 103, 123. *See also* Iemanjá
Yemoja, 83, 124
Yggdrasil (Cosmic Tree), 72
Yoruba culture: and Africanization of Catholic
saints, 87, 89, 114, 180n41; and Candomblé
religion, 88, 89, 91, 123, 177–78n9; in Cuba,
82; Mother Goddess of, 105; and old women,
97; rituals of, 87–88, *87*; and syncretism
of Yemoja and Virgin of Immaculate
Conception, 83; and Virgin Mary, 101;
and women as priests, 100; and women's
economic independence, 99
Yoruba region, and African slave trade, 82

Zapata, Emiliano, 144, 147, 152
Zapatistas, 141, 148
Zhiva (Żywa), 28, 29
Zhivie (Żywie), 28
Zielone Świątki, 25
Złota Baba (Golden Woman), 28, 32, 171n24
Zumárraga, Juan de, 53
Zurbarán, Francisco, 106; *The Holy Family*, 16
Zygmunt Stary (king of Poland), 42
Żywa (Baba) as center of flowering Tree of Life,
Poland, *27*
Żywa (Zhiva), 28, 29
Żywie (Zhivie), 28